CAMBRIDGE Professional English

English 365

Teacher's Book 2

Bob Dignen   Steve Flinders   Simon Sweeney
Matt Smelt-Webb

CAMBRIDGE
UNIVERSITY PRESS

PUBLISHED BY THE PRESS SYNDICATE OF THE UNIVERSITY OF CAMBRIDGE
The Pitt Building, Trumpington Street, Cambridge, United Kingdom

CAMBRIDGE UNIVERSITY PRESS
The Edinburgh Building, Cambridge CB2 2RU, UK
40 West 20th Street, New York, NY 10011–4211, USA
477 Williamstown Road, Port Melbourne, VIC 3207, Australia
Ruiz de Alarcón 13, 28014 Madrid, Spain
Dock House, The Waterfront, Cape Town 8001, South Africa

http://www.cambridge.org
http://www.cambridge.org/elt/english365

First published 2004

Printed in the United Kingdom at the University Press, Cambridge

Typeface Swift *System* QuarkXpress® [HMCL]

A catalogue record for this book is available from the British Library

ISBN 0 521 75368 6 Teacher's Book 2
ISBN 0 521 75367 8 Student's Book 2
ISBN 0 521 75369 4 Personal Study Book 2 with Audio CD
ISBN 0 521 75370 8 Student's Book 2 Audio Cassette Set
ISBN 0 521 75371 6 Student's Book 2 Audio CD Set

Thanks and acknowledgements

The authors would like to thank:
- Will Capel and Sally Searby of Cambridge University Press for their unflinching support from start to finish;
- Alison Silver for her eagle eye for detail, for her good sense and good cheer throughout the editorial and proofreading process;
- Sue Nicholas for the picture research and Ruth Carim for proofreading;
- James Richardson for producing the recordings at The Soundhouse Ltd, London;
- Hart McLeod for the design and page make-up;
- Sue Evans; Lorenza, Mathieu, Jérôme and Michael Flinders; Lyn, Jude, Ruth and Neil Sweeney; Catherine Jarvis for their continuing patience;
- colleagues and friends at York Associates, the School of Management, Community and Communication at York St John College and the EFL Unit, University of York for their tolerance of authorial distraction;
- and Chris Capper of Cambridge University Press for his immeasurable contribution to the project. It is above all his huge efforts which have made this book possible.

The authors and publishers would like to thank:
- Iyad Takrouri (Syngenta), Ablaziz Esseid (Total), Joanna Baker (Edinburgh International Festival), Judy Irigoin, Gerry Kregor (York St John College), Javier Alvarez (Henkel), Zac Goldsmith (The Ecologist), Elaine Williams, Henry de Montebello (Russell Reynolds Associates), Chris Wait, Harald Petersson (Statoil), Gwenaëlle Puntous (Alstom Power Centrales), Christophe Lehy and Bernard Gaudiez (HP), Susanna Longley, Vanessa Chen (Sherwood Taipei Hotel), Nicholas Bate (Strategic Edge Ltd), Richard Scase (University of Kent), Sylvia Heinzen (Bombardier Flexjet Europe), Clare Abbott, Anna Teevan, Ron Ragsdale, Jenny Cutler (Image Counts), Anke Schweikart (Lafarge Zement), Arnauld Schwalm (Douwe Egberts), Lesley Downer, Janie O'Connor (Events Promotions Casting), Tony Weston (the Vegan Society) for their help with the interviews;
- John Davidson of BCD, Paris, for providing the introduction to Henry de Montebello;
- the interviewees for their photographs; Joanna Baker – photographer Douglas Robertson;
- Tim Banks, Gareth Davies, Helena Sharman, George Tomaszewski and Julian Wheatley for reviewing the material in its early stages.

The authors and publishers would like to thank the following for permission to use copyright material. Every effort has been made by the publishers to gain permission for all copyright material used. In the cases where this has not been possible, copyright holders are encouraged to contact the publishers.

Information and texts
p. 18 Syngenta © 2004, all rights reserved, www.syngenta.com; p. 24 Edinburgh International Festival, www.eif.co.uk; p. 30 The Ecologist, www.theecologist.org; p. 41 Eden Project, www.edenproject.com; p. 45 Wal*Mart Stores Inc., USA © 2004.

Better learning activities
- Falcon Press, Malaysia and York Associates, York, England for permission to use ideas in Better learning activities 3, 7 and 8 which were first developed in *How to Learn Languages for International Business* by Steve Flinders (Down to Business Minimax second series, Falcon Press 2000);
- James R. Chamberlain, Director, Language Centre, Bonn-Rhein-Sieg University of Applied Sciences, Sankt Augustin, Germany – a good source of ideas on learner training and intercultural communication; some of his materials are available from the website of the Berlin-Brandenburg English Language Teachers' Association at www.eltabb.com;
- Sylvie Donna and Cambridge University Press for permission to borrow ideas from her book *Teach Business English* (Cambridge University Press 2000, pp. 56–7) for Better learning activity 2;
- Mary-Ann Christison for ideas in Better learning activity 4 from 'Applying Multiple Intelligence Theory', *English Teaching Forum*, Vol. 36, No. 4, p. 8.

Illustrations on page 127 by Louise Wallace.

Contents

Student's Book Contents

1 Introduction to *English365* Book 2

Welcome

Who is *English365* for?
This course is for working adults who want English for their working and personal lives. Students using Book 2:
- are at a lower-intermediate to intermediate level
- will have studied English in the past but need a new extensive course to refresh, practise and consolidate what they know as well as to learn new language
- need a supportive environment to build speaking skills by activating known language and by learning new language and communication skills.

How long is the course?
This book provides at least 60 hours of classroom teaching. The Student's Book contains:
- 30 units which each provide 90 minutes of classroom teaching material per lesson (45 hours)
- two revision units with up to 60 minutes of extra classroom or self-study exercises to work on (2 hours).

The Teacher's Book provides an extra classroom activity linked to each unit, plus ten activities to develop students' learning strategies. Each activity takes at least 15 minutes to complete and some of them can occupy 30 minutes or more (10–20 hours).

What does *English365* give to the learner?
The course aims to provide:
- a balance between English for work, travel and leisure
- a balance between grammar, vocabulary, pronunciation and professional communication skills (at this level: writing emails, telephoning, presentations and communicating in meetings)
- a balance between the skills of speaking, listening, reading and writing
- clear and relevant learning aims in every unit
- stimulating content and activities to motivate adult learners
- sensitive support to students who have problems achieving the transition from passive to active use of English
- a strong emphasis on recycling and consolidation
- motivation to students to achieve a useful balance between classroom and self-study.

What about levels?
We have provided references to the Council of Europe Common European Framework levels as this can provide a useful point of reference for teachers gauging the three levels of *English365*. However, please note that these are not meant as exact comparisons due to the different purpose and nature of these coursebooks.

English365 Book 1 aims to take post-elementary students (students who have reached the end of Common European Framework level A2 approximately) up to lower-intermediate level (approximating to Common European Framework level B1).

English365 Book 2 aims to take low-intermediate learners to intermediate level (approximately through level B1 to the beginning of level B2). So by the time they complete *English365* Book 2, and with sufficient exam preparation, students should be ready to sit the Cambridge Examinations Preliminary Business English Certificate (BEC Preliminary).

English365 Book 3 aims to take intermediate level learners to the beginning of upper-intermediate level (progressing part of the way through level B2).

How is it different?
1 **Authenticity** Much of the material is based on authentic interviews with real working people, many of them doing similar jobs and with similar personal and professional concerns as the people likely to be studying the book. Each unit focuses in part on a professional individual who provides the context for the subject matter. The original interviews have been converted into simplified texts for reading or rerecorded to make listening comprehension easier, but the reading and listening texts still retain the original flavour which we believe will be motivating and involving for your students.
2 **Organisation** The units are divided into three types (see Organisation of the Student's Book on page 9). We think that working through cycles of three units provides the right balance between learners' dual need for variety and for a sense of security.
3 **Vocabulary** The book has an ambitious lexical syllabus: we believe students can learn vocabulary successfully if exposed to it in the right way and that vocabulary is an important key to better understanding, better communication, progress and motivation.
4 **Grammar** The book's approach to grammar is based less on traditional PPP (Presentation – Practice – Production) and more on TTT (Teach – Test – Teach). We think that the majority of adult students at this level have been subjected to the grammar features of our syllabus through PPP already; they do need to revise and extend their existing knowledge but they don't want to be bored going through traditional presentations all over again.
5 **Self-study**
   - The Teacher's notes for each unit offer suggestions to pass on to students about how they can consolidate their classroom learning.

- The Personal Study Book with Audio CD provides students with 15 to 30 minutes' worth of self-study material per unit and up to 15 minutes of listening material (recyclable) for each unit with a listening component.
6 **Learner training** Additional activities in the Teacher's Book, as well as the Teacher's notes to the units in the Student's Book, encourage teachers and learners to focus on the learning process itself.

Course components

There are six components for this level:
1 Student's Book
2 Classroom Audio Cassettes/CDs
3 Personal Study Book
4 Personal Study CD
5 Teacher's Book
6 website.

The **Student's Book** contains:
- an introduction to the student
- 30 classroom units plus two revision units
- file cards for pair and groupwork exercises
- a grammar reference section
- a tapescript of the Classroom Audio Cassettes/CDs
- the answer key to the exercises.

The **Classroom Audio Cassettes/CDs** contain:
- all the tracks relating to listening work in the Student's Book.

The **Teacher's Book** provides:
- an introduction to the course and how to work with it
- detailed notes on the units in the Student's Book
- 30 extra photocopiable classroom activities, each one linked to a unit in the Student's Book, supported by Teacher's notes
- 10 extra photocopiable activities for better learning, designed to improve the effectiveness of students' learning, also supported by Teacher's notes.

The **Personal Study Book** contains:
- Language for language learning – two alphabetical lists of the grammatical and other terms used in the Student's Book together with definitions taken from the *Cambridge Learner's Dictionary*
- one page of self-study exercises per unit of the Student's Book for additional practice
- the answer key to the exercises
- a tapescript of the contents of the Personal Study CD.

The **Personal Study CD** contains:
- self-study listening exercises. These encourage students to practise talking about their job and personal life, welcoming visitors, telephoning and communicating in meetings. They are designed to support and consolidate the work in the Student's Book.
- the listening material relating to pronunciation work in the Student's Book (type 1 units)
- the social English dialogues in the Student's Book (type 3 units).

The **website** provides:
- information about the course
- information about the authors
- extra resources for students and teachers, including 30 tests for students to monitor their progress
- links to organisations referred to in the Background briefings in the Teacher's Book.

See www.cambridge.org/elt/english365.

Organisation of the Student's Book

The Student's Book has 30 units plus two revision units. The 30 units are clustered into ten groups of three, over which a full range of language items and communication elements are presented and practised. Whilst the units are designed to be delivered sequentially, their flexibility is such that they may be dealt with out of sequence if a specific need or occasion arises.

Each type of unit is designed as follows. All units contain a section called 'It's time to talk' which provides opportunities for transfer and freer practice of the main learning points. See page 15 for teaching approaches to each type of unit.

Type 1 units (Units 1, 4, 7, 10, 13, 16, 19, 22, 25 and 28)
Type 1 units present and practise:
- Listening on a work-related theme
- Grammar
- Pronunciation
- Speaking.

Rationale
Type 1 units present and practise a grammar point, introduced first through the medium of a listening exercise. The theme is work-related and the listening text also permits the passive presentation of useful vocabulary. The grammar point is then formally presented and practised and there is also extrapolation to presentation and practice of a discrete pronunciation point. The unit finishes with a supported but freer speaking practice activity which enables students to gain fluency and confidence with the grammar, whilst expressing their ideas on relevant work-related topics.

Type 2 units (Units 2, 5, 8, 11, 14, 17, 20, 23, 26 and 29)
Type 2 units present and practise:
- Reading on a work-related theme
- Work-related vocabulary
- Speaking
- Professional communication skills.

Rationale
Every second unit in the cluster presents professional vocabulary through the medium of a reading text on a work-related theme. Students develop reading skills like skimming and scanning and also have the opportunity (in 'What do you think?') to briefly discuss the issues raised in the text. There is explicit presentation and practice of vocabulary followed by a short fluency activity designed to enable students to use the vocabulary in freer and realistic exchanges. The unit finishes with a focus on professional

communication, with presentation and practice of key phrases and skills. These are often introduced by means of a short listening text. The professional communication skills targeted in *English365* Book 2 are:

- telephoning
- writing emails
- presentations
- communicating in meetings.

Type 3 units (Units 3, 6, 9, 12, 15, 18, 21, 24, 27 and 30)
Type 3 units present and practise:

- Social phrases
- Listening on a general theme
- General vocabulary
- Speaking.

Rationale
Every third unit in the cluster begins with a focus on social English. Students listen to a series of short dialogues presenting language for a range of everyday situations. The listening is followed by practice exercises. The second part of each unit focuses on the presentation and practice of general vocabulary, introduced via a listening exercise. The unit finishes with a speaking activity designed to practise the vocabulary and to foster fluency and confidence when speaking about general topics.

Revision units

There are two revision units in the Student's Book, one following Unit 15 and the other after Unit 30. These contain exercises summarising the work covered thus far. They can be used in a variety of ways, including:

- to test students' knowledge
- as supplementary classroom material
- as supplementary self-study material.

Students who have finished *English365* **Book 1**

Some or all of your students may have completed Book 1. If so, it is worth pointing out that Book 2 is organised along the same lines. Many of the early units revise and recycle language that appeared in Book 1, so remind them of the importance of revision and consolidation, and explain that while looking at items of vocabulary that they may have seen before, you are going to focus on the students' accurate and active use of these words. Tell them that recognising and understanding a word is one step along the road to learning it, but that the ultimate aim is to use the word accurately in appropriate situations.

Starting up the course

This section suggests different approaches to starting up a new course with *English365*. The first lesson of a new course is obviously important and can be handled in many different ways. Your aim should be not just to teach the language of Unit 1 but to create a positive attitude towards learning English in general in the mind of each student and to create a good group dynamic which will help this learning to take place. You want students to leave the lesson believing that this course is going to be:

- comprehensible
- coherent
- useful and
- enjoyable – or even fun!

Think about how you can achieve these goals. You should choose the way that you and (as far as you can anticipate) your students feel most comfortable with. You may know everyone in your group very well or you may never have met them. They may know each other, they may not. However, you should know something about them so, as you prepare, think about the best way to start up. Once you have told them what you plan to do in this lesson, there are many possibilities. You can't take up all of the suggestions which follow but doing one or two for five to ten minutes at the start of the lesson may help to tailor the book to your style and the style of your group.

Talk to your students

Tell them that you are going to talk to them for a few minutes so that all they have to do is relax and listen. Speaking fairly slowly and clearly, and using simple language, introduce yourself and tell your students a few things about yourself. You might introduce yourself to each student in turn. Talking to students at the beginning of a course in language they can understand can help them relax and attune their ears to the sounds and meanings of English. Remember that they will be nervous too – some of them very much so. If you know the group, clearly it won't be necessary to introduce yourself, but there may be newcomers as it is the start of the course and so it is important to make them feel welcome and comfortable with their new classmates. You could get students to ask you questions about yourself. Give them time to prepare some questions, perhaps in pairs – this will also give you some initial indication of their level of English. You will find that they will respond to you better if they can see you are open and willing to talk about yourself.

Tell them how you work

You may also wish to talk about how you like to work, what your objectives are, and about creating a winning team, the members of which will work together to achieve individual and group objectives. Working together will give better results for everyone.

Talk about the book

Give students the chance to look through their copies of *English365* Book 2 – to see how long each unit is, how many units there are, to find the grammar reference, etc. at the back of the book, and so on. You may want to ask questions to guide them, e.g. *Where is the grammar reference?* Even if students have completed *English365* Book 1 and so will be familiar with the structure of the course, getting students to look through Book 2 is worthwhile. The book is a prime learning tool for them. It's important for them to be able to find their way around and have an idea of its organisational principles. In particular, point out, or remind them of the colour coding for the three different types of unit and explain briefly what these are. Tell them too about the other components, and show them in particular a copy of the Personal Study Book and accompanying CD.

Do a needs analysis

Unless you have already had the chance to do so with the students themselves, do a needs analysis of the expectations and objectives of the group or of the learning backgrounds of the learners either at the beginning of this lesson or later on. If the group is continuing from *English365* Book 1, it is still a good idea to review their expectations and objectives as these can change over time. And, of course, you may have new students joining the group. You can use any or all of the first three Better learning activities to support this (see page 118). Unless you have received detailed briefing on your students, you will need to find out about their expectations and objectives during the first few lessons.

Do the admin

You may have administrative business to get out of the way: registers to take, attendance sheets to get signed, etc. Decide when in the lesson you want to do this.

Define principles

Get students to agree to a set of class rules for the course. For example:
- We will help each other to speak better English.
- We will not speak our own language in the classroom.

Check metalanguage

Metalanguage or classroom language (the language you or the book use to give instructions, talk about language, etc.) can be a problem and you may want to introduce or check some words in English which are important to successful classroom communication and management at this stage. You can do this progressively or you can use the Language for language learning section in the Personal Study Book.

Break the ice

Use your own ice-breaking technique for starting up with a new group of lower-intermediate learners. The main content of the unit will then consolidate what you have already done. You may want to do this in the Warm up (see page 14).

If you don't have a favourite ice-breaking activity, try the following, when (some of) the students know each other, but you don't know them:

Take one student in turn (who must remain silent) and ask the others what they know about him or her. At the end of each round of the class, you can summarise the information and the student can say if each detail is true or not. Suggest sentences like:
- Maria works for Coca-Cola.
- Pierre has worked in England.
- Ali has two children.
- Francesco has a new job in marketing.

Dive in

You may prefer to go straight into the unit: it is about working life and they will hear an interesting person talking about his work.

And remember

Don't try all of these suggestions for starting up. Choose the one or two which you feel are most appropriate to your teaching style and to the group, as far as you can tell.

2 Introduction to the Teacher's Book

Getting ready

The language of the Teacher's notes

The 30 sets of notes in the next section are intended to provide you with ideas and support if you need them. They are not prescriptive. They are designed to enhance, not cramp your own teaching style. The imperative style (as in 'Ask', 'Check', 'Tell', etc.) is therefore only to keep the notes short and simple, not to tell you how best to do something. The less imperative style 'You could also . . .', 'You may like to . . .' signals additional ideas not directly found in the Student's Book.

Talking to students

While most students at this level will be able to understand you, there may be some variation in their profiles. Some students may not have studied English for some time; some may have continued on from another course. It is worth repeating that when we speak to our students, we should remember to:

- speak slowly and clearly
- use vocabulary and structures (most of which) they can understand
- as far as possible, use intonation and pronunciation patterns which replicate speech at normal speed. So, for example, try to keep unstressed words and syllables unstressed even when you are speaking more slowly than usual.

It's your responsibility to make sure students understand what you say. You can help them maximise the usefulness of what language they already possess.

From passive to active

Teachers disagree about whether students should be thrown in at the deep end at the beginning of a lesson or a course by being asked to produce language straightaway, or whether they should be allowed time to get used to the language and build confidence before having big demands made on them. Both schools of thought are right – about different students. The design of these units tries to take both possibilities into account. More confident students are given opportunities to talk from the Warm up right at the start. On the other hand, more hesitant students can focus on the objectives at this stage without having to say very much. Some students may have a relatively good knowledge of English and it is important to stress that though some of the vocabulary and grammar work, especially, might have been covered before, you want to activate that language and get them to use it accurately.

Classroom language

Most students will understand the metalanguage in the book and the instructions you give them, but it is worth checking the main terms quickly. A list of words to check appears in the early units of the Teacher's notes, but this dwindles away to zero as you progress through the book and repeatedly use the same terms. A complete list of all the terms also appears in the Personal Study Book. Some students may know most if not all of these words but it is important to be sensitive to the possibility that some will not.

Classroom resources

The range of resources and equipment available to teachers ranges from the rudimentary, or worse, to the very sophisticated. If equipment is not so good, remember that in any case your best resources are your students and yourself.

Dictionaries

Students are recommended to buy a good learner's dictionary. For Book 1 we recommend the *Cambridge Essential English Dictionary* and for Books 2 and 3 the *Cambridge Learner's Dictionary*. See also www.dictionary.cambridge.org for online dictionaries. Dictionaries are not essential in the classroom but they are helpful, and students will benefit from access to them both for classroom work and for self-study. If students don't have their own dictionaries, it helps to have one or two available for them in class. At this level, students should be using an English–English dictionary rather than relying on a bilingual one.

The whiteboard

The Teacher's notes often recommend you to use the whiteboard to build up sets of vocabulary and collocations during a lesson both to develop students' vocabulary and also because it's good for students' morale when they can see how many words they can recognise and use.

The electronic whiteboard

One of the supreme advantages of these is that you can transfer what you have written on the board directly into a digital file on a computer instead of copying down everything you wrote up at the end of a lesson.

The overhead projector

OHPs are especially useful for pairs or small groups reporting back work in writing after an activity. They can write directly onto a transparency and then show other students the results. If you write your feedback – for example for a pairwork activity – on a transparency, you can also project it straightaway to the whole group.

Computers

Computers are especially useful for writing in the classroom. Whether you have time to provide individual correction for all your students' work outside class time is another issue!

Doing written exercises and checking answers

Written exercises can be approached in a number of different ways and you should try to vary what you ask students to do. Be attentive to their mood and level of concentration. They may welcome the opportunity to do two or three exercises alone in order to assimilate input thus far in the lesson and take a rest from the requirements of active language manipulation and production. In this case, give them time to do one or more exercises on their own (although don't always wait for the last student to finish before moving on). Then check the answers by going round the class. However, you don't always have to say immediately whether the answer given is correct or not. Write a suggestion up on the board and ask the others to reach agreement on whether it is right or not; or ask students to lead this part of the lesson; or ask students to work in pairs. In other words, exercises and checking can be carried out more or less passively or quite actively, depending on your and their mood and needs.

Pair and groupwork

Introduction

Pairwork is an opportunity not just for practice but also for students to develop support for each other and, potentially, for them to learn from each other in terms of language competence and learning style. Ensure that students work with different partners from lesson to lesson and within lessons.

Timing

Timing is important in pair and groupwork activities, especially more open ones as in 'It's time to talk' sections. Decide how much time you want to spend on the activity. In many cases, ten minutes is plenty. If you remember that feedback will also take at least five minutes and students performing for their colleagues another five, you can see that without careful time management, too much of the lesson will be taken up in this way.

Procedure

A basic procedure for pairwork is as follows.

1. Present the activity and read through the relevant input to check understanding. Pre-teach difficult vocabulary and provide any grammatical or other models which you would like students to use.
2. Choose pairs. If you have an odd number, work with the odd person yourself, or make a group of three.
3. If there is a preparation phase before the activity, decide whether to put some or all of the Student As and Bs together in separate groups or whether preparation should be done alone; or ask students to decide.
4. During the activity itself, walk round and monitor the activity. Make notes of good and not so good language. You can write good language on the board even while the activity is still going on. You may also like to make notes directly onto a transparency to save time later.
5. You may wish students to reverse roles later. Watch the time so that both get an equal chance in both roles.
6. After the activity itself, students usually report back. The form of this will depend on the nature of the activity.

You may want to summarise the findings on a problem or question for the class as a whole (or ask students to do so) – this is sometimes referred to in the Teacher's notes as doing a survey. For example, how many of them live in the town and how many in the country, how many travel by bus to work, how many by train, and by car, etc. If students were set to solve a problem, find out which solution was preferred and why. This may lead to more general discussion, so be conscious of the time available.

7. You may often invite selected pairs to perform the same activity in front of the others; or you may invite a new pair to do so. Encourage others to provide constructive criticism of these performances.
8. As the first stage in the debriefing, ask students what language or communication difficulties they had.
9. You will then provide feedback on the activity as a whole (see the section on feedback on page 14). Be conscious of the balance between feedback on the language and communication aspects of the activity.
10. Summarise the main points you want students to take away with them. Encourage them to write them down or make some other effort to retain them.
11. Ask students to assess the usefulness of the activity – in other words, for their feedback.

Serial pairwork

The non-alcoholic cocktail party is a variation on basic pairwork except that students talk to two or three others in turn during the activity. You should certainly encourage students to get up and walk around for this: getting students up and about now and again is good for their energy levels and good for kinaesthetic learners – ones who like moving about, touching and handling things, and physical activity. They will need to have pen and paper – usually a photocopy of the activity – to note down the answers to their questions. Timing is again important here because you may need to tell them when partners should swap from asking to answering questions, and when students should swap partners each time. So keep a check on your watch, and be strict.

Telephone pairwork

For pairwork on the telephone, you can suggest that students sit back-to-back, if you don't have telephone equipment for them. Some students may be surprised at this and perhaps resistant to the idea of sitting back-to-back, so it is a good idea to explain the rationale, which is that on the telephone the speakers do not get non-verbal help and need to rely only on their listening skills, and so it is more realistic if they don't look at each other.

Groupwork

The Student's Book and Teacher's notes generally refer to pairwork, but you can vary things by putting students into groups of three or four. You can also put students into pairs and nominate one or two others as observers. One can provide feedback to the group, the other can provide language feedback to the pair after they have finished. Before the lesson, think about how you are going to divide the class up into groups. It is probably better for you to organise this as it will save time.

File cards

If a lesson involves using the file cards at the back of the Student's Book, you should read the roles in advance so that you have a clear idea of what students will be required to do. They will often need time to prepare questions for their partner. Either there is specific guidance on what questions to ask or they can prepare questions on the basis of the information on their own file cards. Once again, you could decide to put all the As together in one group and all the Bs in another at this stage.

Feedback and correction

In addition to all of the above:

- Be selective. Identify the main points you want to make.
- Be positive. Give feedback on good language as well as the not so good.
- Be constructive. Praise students for their efforts before suggesting ways of doing it better.
- Get them to be constructive with each other. This is part of building a team which will help all its members to achieve more. Create an environment of mutual support.

Self-study, consolidating learning and making progress

Students are more likely to make progress if you build lots of recycling into the course and encourage them to work on their English outside the classroom. There are a variety of suggestions about how to achieve this in this book. In sum, we recommend you to:

1 revise the previous lesson of the same type at the start of every class
2 clearly state lesson objectives and remind students of these at the end of every lesson
3 make regular use of the Extra classroom activities (see pages 79 and 85) and Better learning activities (see pages 115 and 118).

We recommend you encourage students to:

1 reread the unit in the Student's Book which they have just done with you
2 do self-study exercises for the equivalent unit in the Personal Study Book and, where applicable, to use the Personal Study Audio CD
3 do follow-up activities suggested in the Teacher's notes for each unit
4 start and maintain vocabulary notebooks
5 keep learner diaries (in English or in their own language).

Teacher's diary

The Teacher's diary at the back of this book aims to help you in your own professional development. We suggest that you make multiple photocopies of it and put the copies in a separate file. The page is self-explanatory. It is designed – realistically we hope for busy teachers – for you to spend three minutes completing one sheet for every lesson. By getting into the habit of doing this and reflecting on what you do, we hope it will encourage you to experiment, develop and communicate with other teachers about the issues which interest and involve you.

Creating a dynamic group

Last, but perhaps most importantly, aim to help create a lively, energised group of learners, a group which is ready to:
- take risks with language
- ask questions when someone doesn't understand
- get up and walk round to refocus when concentration dips
- offer support and positive criticism to all its members
- openly discuss language without fear of losing face
- take the initiative to lead the class.

Common elements

This section offers guidance on how to handle the lesson stages which are common to every unit.

Why are we doing this?

Always make clear what the objectives of each lesson are. At the start of every lesson:
- explain which type of unit you are working on today
- then tell students the objectives of this lesson (see On the agenda)
- identify the main points and write up key words on the board or OHP (see Teacher's notes for each unit)
- leave them there through the lesson so that students have a clear idea of the basic structure of the lesson and also of where they are at any particular stage. Thinking about what you are doing and where you are going helps consolidate learning.

Warm up

As the name suggests, this is intended as a quick way into the unit, to help you and the students focus on the main objectives and to get them used to speaking the language. No matter what their level, students need time to warm up and an introduction to the content of the lesson. The Warm up is intended to be a short activity involving looking at the picture of the unit personality, answering or briefly discussing one or two questions, doing a simple matching exercise, etc. Do not let the Warm up go on for too long. There will be opportunities to discuss related questions in a more open-ended way later in the lesson.

It's time to talk

This is the open practice section of each unit, designed to consolidate the learning which you are aiming for learners to achieve within a relevant and useful context: a transfer from closed to open and from a generic to a more specific contextualisation, although this varies from unit to unit. See also notes on pair and groupwork above.

Remember

Check this section quickly with the whole class. Then ask: 'What did we do today?' If necessary, remind students of the objectives of this lesson (by referring to your key lesson structure words on the board or On the agenda).

Follow up

For you: use the Extra (photocopiable) classroom activity in this book which corresponds to the unit you are teaching.
For students: encourage students to consolidate their

learning by doing regular homework and self-study between lessons. This will make all the difference to the amount of progress many of them make. Standard ways to do this are:

1 to reread the unit in the Student's Book
2 to read the corresponding unit in the Personal Study Book and do the exercises.

See the Teacher's notes for each unit for other suggestions.

Background briefings

In the Teacher's Book, some units have extra information about the company or event covered (e.g. Syngenta in Unit 1 and the Edinburgh Festival in Unit 3). These are intended as a brief introduction for teachers who are perhaps unfamiliar with the subjects. If you or your students want more information, you can go to their websites via the *English365* website: www.cambridge.org/elt/english365.

Timing

The timings suggested in the following sections are based on a 90-minute lesson. They are intended to provide broad guidance only. Your timings will obviously depend enormously on the specific lesson, the kind of class you have and the kind of teacher you are. Give students time limits. They usually respond well to this and it can help to create a lively and pacy class. Be flexible. Don't allow too much planning to get between you and the students. Over-rigidity can stop you listening to your students and can destroy real communication.

Teaching type 1 units

Unit structure and timing

The structure of type 1 units, together with suggested approximate timings, is:

What did we do last time?	5 minutes
On the agenda: Why are we doing this?	5 minutes
Warm up	5 minutes
Listen to this	10 minutes
What do you think?	5 minutes
Check your grammar	10 minutes
Do it yourself	10 minutes
Sounds good	15 minutes
It's time to talk	20 minutes
Remember → What did we do today?	5 minutes
→ Follow up	

Listen to this

Logistics

Always make sure that you are ready to switch on your cassette or CD in the right place before the lesson starts.

Introducing listening

Introduce each track by saying in broad terms what students are going to hear and why. Make sure students have read the rubrics and that they understand what they have to do. As an alternative to students reading the rubrics, you could explain the activity yourself to provide variety.

Listening for gist

The instruction in the Teacher's notes is always simply to 'Play track 1.1'. It is for you to decide whether to play the track or part of the track more than once or not. However, playing any track more than three or four times altogether is likely to lead to boredom, so avoid any temptation to do so. Tell students that very often it's best to listen for the main message and not to worry about not understanding every word. In real life, there are rarely more than one or two chances.

Listening tasks

Specific suggestions are made in the Student's Book or the Teacher's notes for individual units, but you can also ask them:

- if they can predict part of a track from what they know about it before they listen
- if they can reproduce parts of a track after they have listened to it
- to listen for examples of particular words or types of word or grammar examples.

Tapescripts

You can encourage students to make use of the tapescripts at the back of the Student's Book for reading at the same time as they listen; and for doing grammar and vocabulary searches of texts they have already heard.

Check your grammar

The syllabus

- The grammar points taught in the type 1 units have been identified as being those of most use to working people. The grammar syllabus is selective rather than comprehensive in order to achieve a good balance between this and the other components of the syllabus – work-related and general vocabulary, communication skills, and so on.
- For information about particular grammar points and how to handle them in class, we strongly recommend *Grammar for English Language Teachers* by Martin Parrott (Cambridge University Press 2000).

Activating passive knowledge

For any given grammar point, you can ask students some basic questions to check the extent of their knowledge. They may have notions of the point in question and the listening will have jogged their memory. Otherwise, you can vary your approach from lesson to lesson. For example:

- first present the information given in a grammar section, then practise the points by filling the gaps; or
- ask students to elicit rules from the listening extract they have heard or from the tapescript of the listening, and then do the gap-filling exercise; or
- ask students to do the gap-filling exercise and then to formulate rules alone or in pairs or as a whole class.

Grammar reference

Always refer them to the Grammar reference section. Make sure students know where it is, and, if appropriate, go through it with them.

Sounds good

Tell students each time that this is the pronunciation part of the lesson. Pronunciation is important but it can also be fun and can appeal to a different kind of learner, some of whom may be less confident about other areas of language. Find out which students have a good ear and the ones who are good mimics, and exploit their talents in presentation and feedback.

Teaching type 2 units

Unit structure and timing

The structure of type 2 units, together with suggested approximate timings, is:

What did we do last time?	5 minutes
On the agenda: Why are we doing this?	5 minutes
Warm up	5 minutes
Read on	15 minutes
What do you think?	5 minutes
The words you need	10 minutes
It's time to talk	15 minutes
Communicating at work	25 minutes
Remember → What did we do today?	5 minutes
→ Follow up	

Read on

The Read on sections of these units are designed to develop students' ability to skim, scan and read for gist. Tasks vary from unit to unit, for example sometimes the reading asks students to match headings with paragraphs, which involves reading for gist, and then to answer some comprehension questions.

Procedure

A standard procedure for this section is as follows. There are further suggestions in each set of Teacher's notes.

1

1 Read the rubric and the questions.
2 Ask the students to skim the paragraphs before they answer the questions. Give them 20 or 30 seconds (more in the early units and less in the later ones).
3 When they have finished, check their answers and ask them how they proceeded: which key words did they spot in the text which helped them to do the task?

2

1 Read the rubric and the questions.
2 Ask them to read the paragraphs in more detail and do the exercise.
3 Check their answers.
4 Ask them to do a vocabulary search based on the theme of the text or the main vocabulary area of the unit, or to do a grammar-based search, for example to find adjectives or verbs of a certain kind.

Reading in other contexts in the Student's Book

More generally, the instruction 'Read' in the Teacher's notes for any unit can be handled in various ways:

- students can read silently
- individual students can take turns reading aloud

- you can read aloud to them
- students can read to each other in pairs.

If there is no specific suggestion, do different things at different times; and ask the students what they want to do.

The words you need

Suggestions are provided in each set of Teacher's notes.

Communicating at work

Suggestions are provided in each set of Teacher's notes.

Teaching type 3 units

Unit structure and timing

The structure of type 3 units, together with suggested approximate timings, is:

What did we do last time?	5 minutes
On the agenda: Why are we doing this?	5 minutes
Warm up	5 minutes
Social English dialogues	15 minutes
Have a go	10 minutes
Listen to this	10 minutes
What do you think?	5 minutes
The words you need	10 minutes
It's time to talk	20 minutes
Remember → What did we do today?	5 minutes
→ Follow up	

Social English dialogues

The objective of these dialogues is to equip students with useful survival English with real takeaway value, and, although the format is the same in every type 3 unit, you can handle them in different ways from lesson to lesson.

The standard procedure (also given in the Teacher's notes to Unit 3) is as follows.

- Ask students what they can see in each of the four pictures accompanying the dialogues.
- Ask students to fill the gaps with phrases from the list, working alone or in pairs.
- Play the appropriate track so that students can listen and check their answers.
- Check the answers with the group. Do some vocabulary checking questions, if appropriate.
- Ask students to read the dialogues in pairs, reversing roles if you have time.
- Ask selected pairs to perform for the class and give feedback on their performances.

This formula can of course be varied. For example, you can:

- ask students to listen to the appropriate track as they fill the gaps in the dialogues
- cover the list on the page and fill the gaps as they listen
- cover the list and predict the words which will fit the gaps and then check by looking at the list
- cover the list and predict the words which will fit the gaps and then check by listening to the track.

Use the standard procedure in the first one or two units (Units 3 and 6) and then vary the formula thereafter.

Have a go

This section leads straight on from the previous one and provides opportunities for less controlled practice of the social English dialogues. Once again you can adopt a standard procedure as follows.

1 Ask them to cover the dialogues.
2 Get students, working in pairs, to replicate the situation in each of the four dialogues. Stress that they are not expected to remember the exact words of the original dialogues but that they should try to produce appropriate language each time.
3 Ask selected pairs to perform for the class and give feedback on their performances.

The main variation on this procedure could be to ask students to think of and practise another dialogue relating to the same theme. They can then perform for other students, who have to identify the situation.

How you approach this part of the lesson will depend on the students in your particular class. Stronger students may be happy to go straight into freer practice. Others may appreciate more help, for example if you build a dialogue on the board.

One option would be to elicit a model dialogue, perhaps using symbols or pictures, for each situation. Drill the students to encourage good pronunciation, focusing on rhythm and sentence stress. Allow them time to practise the dialogue before giving them the chance to make up their own. You could choose when to write it on the board. As a variation, you could rub out key words, leaving only the first letters. This will encourage students to commit key words and phrases to memory and so help with freer reproduction in the later activity.

Potentially, there is a lot of new language to assimilate in the dialogues, so encourage students to focus on what they feel will be useful for them to learn. It will be impossible for them to learn all of the dialogues by heart.

After students have practised the dialogues in pairs, give feedback on their performance and ask them to practise again with another partner, trying to remember your advice.

The words you need

Suggestions are provided in each set of Teacher's notes.

1 Working internationally

Starting up the course

Read the section on Starting up the course on page 10 and decide how you want to:

- introduce yourself
- introduce the students to each other
- introduce the material.

On the agenda

Read about Type 1 units on page 9 and Teaching type 1 units on page 15.

Explain that this is an example of the first of three types of unit. This type normally looks at grammar and pronunciation. Type 1 units also practise listening.

Tell the students the objectives of the lesson:

- to practise **meeting people** and **talking about jobs**
- to revise the **present simple** and **present continuous tenses**. You might need to remind students that although they may have studied these tenses before, you want to concentrate on using them correctly
- to develop their **pronunciation** by focusing on **strong and weak stress**. You might give students one or two examples of this so that they are clear about what this means.

Reinforce this by writing the key words on the board or OHP.

Classroom language

Check now or during the lesson that students understand the meanings of:

present continuous	present simple	true	false	stress
match	check	compare	correct	underline	complete

Warm up

Ask students the questions in the Student's Book. Tell them to ask and answer quickly in pairs and write prompts on the board:

I'd like to work in another country because …

Listen to this

From Jordan to Switzerland

1. • Ask students what they know about Jordan and Switzerland. Look at the picture of Iyad Takrouri. Ask checking questions about what he does and where he lives. You might need to check that students understand the vocabulary in the caption. Do this by asking concept questions or perhaps draw pictures on the board to elicit *crops* and *insecticides*.

- Ask students to read the statements. Play track 1.1 and get them to indicate if they are true or false and then compare their answers with a partner before checking the answers with the whole class.

Answers

1 F 2 T 3 T 4 T 5 F

2. Ask students to read the questions and play track 1.1 again. Once again, get them to compare their answers with a partner before checking with the whole class. Write the answers on the board as you go through so that any weaker students are clear about the correct answers.

Answers

1 Managing new product development
2 Salaries are lower
3 Once a year
4 The countryside
5 Because everybody speaks English

Background briefing: Syngenta

Syngenta is a world-leading agribusiness committed to sustainable agriculture through innovative research and technology. The company is a leader in crop protection, and ranks third in the high-value commercial seeds market. Sales in 2003 were approximately US$ 6.6 billion. Syngenta employs more than 19,000 people in over 90 countries and is listed on the Swiss stock exchange. For more information about Syngenta, go to the *English365* website: www.cambridge.org/elt/english365.

Track 1.1 tapescript ▶▶

INTERVIEWER: So, Iyad, what do you do exactly?

IYAD: I work in Zurich for Syngenta as a technical manager. And, basically, my main responsibility is managing new product development. I work closely with people in our research and development department in Zurich to choose new products which I think – I hope – we can sell in my market areas. I like my job because it's very interesting.

INTERVIEWER: And how's business, Iyad? Is business increasing at the moment?

IYAD: Yes, it's very good in my area. Business is really increasing a lot. In Europe, there's a lot of discussion about the environment, it's very political. And so big farming organisations from Spain, from France and Italy, are transferring their business into places like Egypt and Morocco my area, to grow here. One reason why it makes sense for them to move is because salaries are not so high. But that's business.

INTERVIEWER: Very interesting. And which markets do you work with?

IYAD: The Middle East and North Africa. This means Iran, Iraq, Syria, Lebanon, Jordan, the Gulf countries – that's Saudi, Kuwait, Emirates, Oman and Yemen – and then Egypt, Sudan, Libya, Algeria, Tunisia, Morocco. I really work internationally.

INTERVIEWER: Absolutely. Very international. And do you travel to these countries?

IYAD: Yes, I do. I visit all my sales areas – my countries you can say – once a year for business meetings with local employees and partners who sell our products. So I'm on the road a lot, you can say.

INTERVIEWER: But you live in Zurich now, don't you? Do you enjoy living in Switzerland?

IYAD: Yes, the best thing is the beautiful countryside. I also enjoy living in a country with such a high standard of living. Of course, it's a bit of a change. The Swiss are very precise, you know, about every detail. Time is very important – lunch is always between 12 and 1 – and this can be difficult for me, I'm not so precise. The social life is also very interesting, very different from Jordan. Here people don't mix so much after work. The Swiss like to have a private life alone with the family.

INTERVIEWER: Are you learning Swiss German?

IYAD: Well, I'm learning high German at a local college, which is the written language, for filling in official forms, reading letters, and so on. But the Swiss don't speak that very much – they use Swiss German, which is very different and very difficult for me to understand. You know, there's actually no written grammar. Anyway, I prefer to speak … to work in English because everybody speaks English.

INTERVIEWER: Yes, but you sound happy.

IYAD: Oh, yes. We have a great team which is really international. There's one Swiss, one guy from Russia, South Africa, Romania, Egypt, two guys from the UK and one new guy from Italy.

INTERVIEWER: Really?

IYAD: Yes, so it's very international. Work can sometimes be quite hard, very busy, but the people I work with are fantastic, really nice, that's the best thing, in fact. So I'm very happy, yes!

What do you think?

- Get students to discuss their answers to the questions in pairs or in small groups and write prompts on the board to help them. For example:
  I'd like to travel to different countries because …
  The good thing about travelling is (that) …
- While the students are talking, go round the class and write down any mistakes that you think would be useful for the whole class to consider. It will be especially useful to record any mistakes in the present simple and present continuous tenses.
- Go through the feedback with the whole class. You could write a list of positives and negatives on the board.
- Write some of the students' mistakes on the board – about five should be enough at this stage. Ask students to try and correct the sentences with a partner. Then go over the mistakes with the whole class, asking individual students to provide the correction. If you have some examples of the tenses, it will lead in nicely to the next part of the lesson.

Check your grammar

Present simple and present continuous

- Write examples **a** and **b** on the board and elicit from students the name of each tense. Then draw their attention to the Student's Book and ask them to match the examples of the different tenses with their descriptions.
- Ask students which description describes which tense. You could also draw a timeline for each tense and ask them to decide which line represents which tense. For example:

Present simple

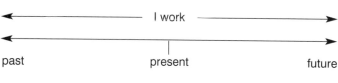

Present continuous

- Explain that with some verbs we do not usually use the present continuous. Ask if they know any verbs that are not normally used in this tense. If they are not forthcoming, draw their attention to the note. Write up an incorrect sentence or two and then draw a line through to highlight the point. You can also refer students to the Grammar reference section on page 112 of the Student's Book, and, if appropriate, go through it with them.

> **Answers**
> 1 (present continuous) b, f   2 (present simple) a, c, d, e

Do it yourself

1 Ask students to correct the sentences. You might want to do the first one with the whole class so that everyone is clear about the task. Ask students to do this individually and give them a time limit of two minutes. Get them to check their answers with their neighbour before checking them with the whole class. Again, write the corrections on the board so that everyone is clear about them. This may not be necessary if you feel everyone is coping with the exercise well.

> **Answers**
> 1 He works in Madrid.
> 2 Where do you come from originally? Are you German?
> 3 Sales are increasing a lot at the moment in China.
> 4 I usually go to work by car.
> 5 This meal is delicious. The meat tastes really good.

2 After going through the answers, students can practise asking and answering the questions. If they are doing this well, you could get them to provide their own answers to the questions. Monitor and write down any mistakes that you think would be useful to correct for the whole class.

Answers

1 What do you do?
2 What are you doing?
3 Do you specialise in project work?
4 How often do you come to Zurich?
5 Where are you staying?
6 Is your business expanding at the moment?

3 Set the scene of two former colleagues meeting in an airport. Ask students to complete the conversation using the verbs in the correct tense. Again, you could do the first one as an example with the whole class. They can compare their answers with a partner before you play track 1.2 so that they can check. Play the track again if necessary. Check the correct answers with the whole class.

Answers

1 are you doing
2 I'm going
3 does he work
4 How often do you see
5 We try to meet
6 Do you know
7 I don't go
8 I'm working
9 things aren't going well
10 your plane is boarding

Track 1.2 tapescript ▶▶|

A: Hi, Marina. Surprise, surprise.

B: Karl! Good to see you. What are you doing here?

A: I'm on my way to Nairobi for a business meeting.

B: Really? I'm going to Paris to meet my brother for the weekend.

A: Oh, does he work in Paris?

B: No. He works in Budapest. Paris is just an easy place for us to meet.

A: OK. How often do you see him?

B: We try to meet twice a year in Paris.

A: Sounds good.

B: It is. Do you know Paris?

A: Not very well. I don't go there very much. Anyway, how's work?

B: Good. I'm working on a new product at the moment. And you?

A: Well, things aren't going well, you know, because it's a very difficult market situation. Oh, I think your plane is boarding.

B: You're right. I've got to go. Bye.

A: Bye. Have a good trip! Really good to see you again.

Sounds good

Strong and weak stress

1 • You could write the first question on the board: *Where do you work?* Say it naturally with 'where' and 'work' clearly stressed. Try to elicit what the students notice about the pronunciation in order to introduce the concept of sentence stress.

• Explain that you are going to focus on improving students' pronunciation, specifically word stress. Then play track 1.3.

• Ask students the questions. Play the dialogues again or repeat some of the sentences yourself in an exaggerated way if they are not forthcoming initially.

• Read through the advice.

• You can now drill the class, making sure the correct words are stressed. Then practise in pairs.

Answers

The underlined words carry the main meaning in the sentences. 'You' is stressed where the speaker wants to give emphasis.

Track 1.3 tapescript ▶▶|

See Student's Book.

2 After students have underlined the words, check the answers before getting them to practise the dialogues in pairs. Once again, monitor and check that they are stressing the correct words.

Answers and Track 1.4 tapescript ▶▶|

A: <u>How</u> <u>often</u> do you <u>travel</u> on <u>business</u>?

B: About <u>once</u> a <u>month</u>. And <u>you</u>?

A: Are you <u>busy</u>?

B: <u>Yes</u>, I'm <u>working</u> on a <u>big</u> <u>project</u> in <u>China</u>.

A: Do you <u>know</u> <u>Madrid</u>?

B: <u>No</u>, I <u>don't</u>. Do <u>you</u>?

A: <u>What</u> are you <u>working</u> on at the <u>moment</u>?

B: A <u>report</u> – the <u>deadline</u> is <u>next</u> <u>week</u>.

A: Did you <u>have</u> a <u>good</u> <u>weekend</u>?

B: <u>Great</u>, <u>thanks</u>. <u>How</u> was <u>yours</u>?

It's time to talk

1 • Tell students that they will now practise what they have learnt in this lesson and have the opportunity to get to know each other better.

• Refer back to the conversation between Marina and Karl and ask if it is a successful conversation and why. Try to elicit the fact that it is dynamic because there are a lot of questions and the speakers show interest in what the other is saying. For example:
Questions
  • What are you doing here?
  • How often do you see him?
  • And you?
Mention that 'and you?' is a good way to ask somebody the same question and to show interest in him/her.
Showing interest
  • Really?
  • Sounds good.
  • You're right.
If students do not come up with these answers, get them to read the information in the Student's Book.

2 • Set the scene and give a time limit for students to make notes and prepare their questions. Remind them of what they should practise before they start.

- You could get students to have conversations in pairs with you monitoring them before you give feedback and get them to correct any mistakes in the target language. They could then have another conversation with another partner, hopefully bearing the feedback in mind.
- At the end, ask the class how successful they felt their conversations were. What were the good and bad points? Finish off with correction of any other mistakes you noted down while you were monitoring.
- You may want to use the Extra classroom activity here (see pages 79 and 85).

What did we do today?
Check the Remember section quickly and remind students of the aims of the lesson.

Follow up
Encourage students to:
1 write sentences about their jobs in the present simple and present continuous tenses
2 write questions they can ask people about their jobs.

2 Power for life

What did we do last time?
Although you may want to do some review work from the previous unit, we recommend that you do the main review work in relation to Unit 1 when you come to the next type 1 unit, i.e. Unit 4. This is more challenging for your students as it involves longer recall, but should ultimately provide more continuity and improve learning effectiveness.

On the agenda: Why are we doing this?
Read about Type 2 units on page 9 and Teaching type 2 units on page 16. Explain that this is the second of three types of unit. This type looks at vocabulary for work and communication skills. The main professional skills in business English are presenting, meetings, negotiating, telephoning, writing and socialising. In *English365* Book 2 we focus on presenting, writing (emails), telephoning and meetings.
Tell students the objectives of this lesson (see On the agenda):
- **talking about your organisation**
- to build **vocabulary** in the area of **business and business organisation**
- to practise **getting through on the telephone and leaving messages**.
Reinforce this by writing the key words on the board or OHP.

Warm up
Ask the students the questions or ask them to ask and answer in pairs. You could ask students if they have heard of Total and what they know about it.

Read on

Total – in the energy business
- Look at the pictures and read the caption. Check understanding of *headquarters*.
- Get students to read the introductory paragraph quickly and set a time limit. Ask some checking questions. For example:
How many barrels of oil do we consume?

1 Get them to read the questions and deal with any vocabulary problems before they do the matching exercise. Give a time limit of a couple of minutes – this will encourage them to read the text quickly and not focus too much on individual words in order to get a general idea of the text. Tell them not to worry if they don't understand any vocabulary at this stage. They will have the chance to read the text in more detail and check new vocabulary later. Check the answers.

Answers
1 B 3 C 4 D 6 A

2 Ask how we say the numbers and then get them to do the exercise. Give them enough time to do this as they need to look for specific information. Check the answers.

Answers
1 The number of barrels of oil we consume every day
2 The number of cubic metres of gas we consume every year
3 The year that Total was founded
4 Total's annual turnover in dollars
5 Total's profit after tax in dollars
6 The number of countries in which Total has employees

Answers
Eight forms of power are mentioned:
oil, coal, gas, electricity, nuclear, solar, wind, gasoline

What do you think?
Ask students to discuss the question in small groups and give prompts. For example:
I think / In my opinion . . . is the most important form of energy, because . . .

You could also ask other questions, such as: *Which is the most dangerous? What problems might there be in the future?* in order to develop the conversation. You could finish by getting some opinions from the whole class.

The words you need ... to talk about business and business organisation

1
- Ask students what they know about General Motors. Explain that they are going to complete a company profile using the words in the box. Go over the meanings of any unfamiliar words before doing the exercise, if you have not already done this. Check pronunciation and drill any words that are causing problems. Check the answers.

- Get the students to make sentences about their organisation or one they know in pairs. Then feed back to the whole class.

Answers

1 Founded   2 sells   3 market leader   4 produces
5 organised into   6 markets   7 employs   8 worldwide
9 share   10 turnover

2 Get students to look at the mind map and do the exercise individually before checking in pairs. Check the answers with the whole class.

Answers

1 do   2 global   3 core   4 big   5 sectors   6 card
7 travel on   8 talk

It's time to talk

- Give students a few minutes to make notes. Quickly go through the questions that they should ask about each point. Get them to work with a partner to ask and answer questions. Monitor the dialogues and record any mistakes to go over later with the whole class.
- You may want to use the Extra classroom activity here (see pages 79 and 86).

COMMUNICATING AT WORK

Telephoning 1: Getting through / Leaving a message

Get students to discuss the questions in pairs. You could also ask them what kinds of problem they have when they use the phone and why.

1 Explain what the students should do and play track 2.1. Play it a second time if necessary.

Answers

Call 1: Leaving a message
Call 2: Getting through
Call 3: The person called is not available
Call 4: Waiting on line

2 Play track 2.1 again. If they are having difficulty you could play the recording and stop at the relevant part. You can highlight some key phrases by writing them on the board and drilling the class on the correct pronunciation. Then erase all but the first letters of the words and see how much students can remember. This will help students with their recall and enable them to do the next task more successfully.

Answers

1 reached   2 leave a message   3 call you back
4 to speak to   5 there   6 put you through   7 moment   8 leave
a message   9 need to talk   10 call me
11 leave you my number   12 experiencing   13 hold
14 becomes available

Track 2.1 tapescript ▶▶

Call 1

Hello. You've reached the voicemail of Eve Warner. I'm sorry I'm away from my desk at the moment. Please leave a message and I'll call you back as soon as I can. Thank you.

Call 2

A: Hello, Amberside Communications. Matthew speaking, how can I help you?
B: Hello, I'd like to speak to Helen Foster, please. Is she there?
A: I'll put you through to her department. One moment, please.
C: Hello, Product Development.
B: Hello, can I speak to Helen Foster, please?
C: Yes, who's calling?
B: My name's Arne Scholte, from Copenhagen.

Call 3

A: Good morning. John Clayton's office.
B: Hello, can I speak to John Clayton, please?
A: I'm sorry, John's in a meeting at the moment. Can I help you?
B: No, it's OK. Will he be there this afternoon?
A: I'm afraid he's not in the office this afternoon. He has a meeting with a client.
B: Can you tell me when I can call him? Does he have a mobile?
A: Well, he does, but I don't think you'll reach him on that. Would you like to leave a message?
B: Well, no, I need to talk to him personally. Perhaps he could call me. Can I leave you my number?
A: Yes, of course, please do. Who's calling please?

Call 4

Hello. Thank you for calling Supex Technical Support. We are experiencing high call load at the current time. For web support, please visit our website at www.supex.com/technical. Otherwise, please hold and an operator will be with you as soon as one becomes available.

3
- At this point it might be a good idea to move students around so that they have a new partner to work with.
- Explain that they will now create a short dialogue using the phrases from the earlier exercise. Give them a few moments to look at the flowchart and think about what phrases they might use and when.
- While students have their conversations, monitor and write down any mistakes to use as models for correction with the whole class. Depending on how they do, you might want to deal with the mistakes and then get them to redo the conversations with a different partner. This will encourage students to think about the kinds of mistake they make and help them to learn from them.

4
- Give students a few minutes to look at the information and check that they are clear about the activity. When they have finished the role-play, again give feedback on their performance, both in terms of communication and linguistically. You can also ask them how they feel they did. Pairs could then reverse roles.
- To finish, select one or two pairs to perform their conversation in front of the whole class.

What did we do today?

Remind students of the aims of the lesson, summarise what they have learnt and reiterate the advice about using the phone.

Follow up

Encourage students to:

1 write down useful phrases for talking about their organisations
2 write down new words in their vocabulary books and record relevant information about the grammar, collocation, pronunciation, etc.
3 write down phrases they could use on the phone.

3 Edinburgh – the festival city

What did we do last time?

Although you may wish to do some review of the work you did in the last lesson, we recommend that you do the main review work in relation to Unit 2 when you come to the next type 2 unit, i.e. Unit 5. This is more challenging for the students as it requires longer recall, but should ultimately provide more continuity and improve learning effectiveness.

On the agenda: Why are we doing this?

Read about Type 3 units on page 10 and Teaching type 3 units on page 16. Explain that this is an example of the third of three types of unit and that this type looks at vocabulary, expression and communication, which are useful to working adults in their lives outside work. In every type 3 lesson, students will learn and practise:

- social phrases which are useful for travel or everyday situations
- vocabulary for travel and everyday subjects of discussion and conversation.

Type 3 units will help students manage better when they travel, and when they meet people socially.

Now tell students the objectives of the lesson (see On the agenda):

- to practise talking about **likes and preferences**
- to learn useful phrases for **arriving in a place you don't know**
- to learn vocabulary to talk about **music, theatre, dance and opera**.

Reinforce this by writing the key words on the board or OHP.

Classroom language

Words to check for understanding before or during the unit are:

cover (verb)	put in order

Warm up

Ask students if they know anything about Edinburgh. Look at the Warm-up questions; they could compare their experiences in pairs. You could also ask them how they manage to solve the problems.

Arriving in a place you don't know

1 • Ask students what they can see in each of the four pictures accompanying the dialogues.
- Ask students to fill the gaps with words and phrases from the list, working alone or in pairs.
- Play track 3.1 so that students can listen and check their answers.
- Check the answers with the group. Ask some vocabulary-checking questions, and check pronunciation, if appropriate.
- Ask students to read the dialogues in pairs, reversing roles if you have time.
- Ask selected pairs to perform for the class and give feedback on their performances.

This will be the standard procedure for handling these social English dialogues in type 3 units; see also the Introduction (page 16).

Answers

1 d 2 g 3 h 4 f 5 a 6 e 7 b 8 c

Track 3.1 tapescript ▶▶

At left luggage

A: Excuse me, can we leave our bags here?
B: Yes, what have you got?
A: We've got a backpack and a large suitcase.
B: OK. That's £4 for the suitcase and £3 for the backpack. The ticket's valid for 24 hours.
A: Fine, thanks. We'll come and get them around 2 this afternoon.
B: That'll be fine. Have a nice morning.

At the accommodation bureau

A: Hello, we've just arrived and we'd like a bed and breakfast for two or three nights, please.
B: Singles or double?
A: Double, please.
B: OK, Edinburgh's very full but I can phone one in Leith for you.
A: Thank you. How far is it and how do we get there?
B: It's about half an hour by bus.

At tourist information

A: Hello, can you help us? We'd like a map of the city.
B: Yes, here you are.
A: And can you give us some information about the festival?
B: This tells you about the official festival. And this has information about the Fringe – the unofficial festival.
A: Thanks. And one last thing: do you have a bus timetable for Leith?
B: Yes, here you are.
A: Thanks for your help.

Getting there

A: Excuse me, we want to get to Leith. Where does the bus leave from, please?

B: Yes, you want a number 37. The stop is just down the road there.

A: Where do we buy the tickets?

B: You don't need to get a ticket in advance. You can pay on the bus.

A: Thank you.

B: You're welcome.

Have a go

Now ask students to make their own dialogues in pairs using the prompts in the Student's Book.

- Ask them to cover the dialogues on the first page of the unit.
- Get students, working in the same or different pairs, to replicate the situation in each of the four dialogues. Stress that they are not expected to remember the exact words of the original dialogues but that they should try to produce *appropriate* language each time. You might want to drill key phrases with the class to ensure good pronunciation first.
- Ask selected pairs to perform for the class and give feedback on their performances.
- You could also ask them to think of other short dialogues for the rest of the class: asking for directions, asking for information at the station, etc. The others can listen and identify the situation and context.

Listen to this

The festival city

The second part of the unit aims to build students' vocabulary for talking about music, theatre, dance and opera.

- Look at the picture and ask checking questions about Joanna Baker. Check the meaning of *marketing*, *public affairs* and *festival*.
- Ask students the pre-listening questions. Also ask them if they have any festivals in their country and what happens at them. If you have time, get students to compare different festivals they have.

1 Give students a few moments to read through the statements. Check the meaning of *formal* and play track 3.2. Then check the answers.

Answers
1 T 2 T 3 F 4 F

2 Give students a few moments to read through the questions before you play the recording again. Check the meaning of *performance*.

Answers
1 about 170
2 about 450,000
3 make money, big audiences
4 £5
5 Going to see dance companies

Background briefing: The Edinburgh Festival

Since the late 1940s Edinburgh has become a major centre for artistic talent. It began with the International Festival and the Fringe. The summer programme of arts and culture has now grown to include the Edinburgh Book Festival, the Edinburgh Film Festival, the Military Tattoo (set in Edinburgh Castle) and the Jazz Festival. The Fringe Festival is intended to give all performers the opportunity to showcase their talents and has launched the careers of many new comedians, artists and playwrights. Over one million people attended the Fringe Festival in 2003. For more information about the Edinburgh Festival, go to the *English365* website: www. cambridge.org/elt/english365.

Track 3.2 tapescript ▶▶

INTERVIEWER: Joanna, what is the Edinburgh International Festival exactly?

JOANNA: Well, the Edinburgh International Festival is the number one European Arts Festival. So we bring world class dance, opera, theatre and music groups, artists and performers to Edinburgh like the New York City Ballet, the Berlin Philharmonic, the Vienna Philharmonic, theatre companies from Austria, France, a dance company from Japan, and so on. We normally have about 170 different performances over three weeks. All this for the people of Edinburgh and the thousands of visitors who come.

INTERVIEWER: How big is the festival?

JOANNA: Well, people now see Edinburgh as 'The Festival City' of the world, because around the International Festival, over August, there's also a Festival Fringe – a big comedy event, there's a book festival, a film festival, a jazz festival, and the Edinburgh Military Tattoo – a big military display in Edinburgh Castle. So, it's five weeks of festivals and 450,000 visitors. This generates around £150 million for the city. So you see, we work with two major objectives, cultural and economic. Festivals are big business.

INTERVIEWER: And what's your role exactly?

JOANNA: Everything from producing tickets to doing the marketing – to sell more of them. I also work with the press, and talk a lot to the sponsors who help to finance the event. My job is to make sure we make money and that we bring in big audiences. And new audiences, young people, and people who don't normally go to see opera or classical music.

INTERVIEWER: Do you think things like opera, classical music, etc. are being enjoyed by more and more people because of your festival?

JOANNA: I think the Edinburgh International Festival is very good for new audiences: it's very open, you can go in jeans and a T-shirt. There's a real buzz about the place. We put shows on at night, 10.30 in the evening, £5 a ticket, so it's cheap, and we get lots of people, all types. We can sell 25 concerts with 2,000 seats at that time of night, no problem. The special thing about our Festival is that it's for everybody. It's very informal. Of course, people jet in from across the world but you can also walk in off the street. It's very easy and very special.

INTERVIEWER: What do you go and see?

JOANNA: My thing is dance. Ballet is my favourite. And, you know, one of the great things about my job is that I actually go and see dance companies during the year to see if we want to bring them to the festival. So it's perfect. Job and hobby together.

What do you think?

Get students to discuss the questions in pairs. You could ask them to make a list of the advantages and disadvantages of combining a job and a hobby. Get them to then compare their opinions with another pair and write prompts on the board:

The advantages/disadvantages of ... are ...
If I had my job and hobby together, I'd ...

The words you need ... to talk about music, theatre, dance and opera

Going out 1

Students can do these exercises in pairs. Check the answers and pronunciation, if appropriate. There are a lot of words to learn at once, so write the most useful ones on the board.

Answers

1 production   2 performance   3 lighting   4 design
5 composition   6 conductor   7 orchestra   8 concert
9 director   10 playwright   11 costume   12 actress   13 Ballet
14 ballerina   15 choreographer   16 contemporary

Going out 2

1 Ask students to put the phrases in the best order. Check the answers and pronunciation and draw their attention to the grammar note.

Answers

From most positive to most negative:

I love ... , I really like ... , I like ... , I quite like ... , I'm not very keen on ... , I don't really like ... , I can't stand ... , I hate ...

2 Look at the sentences and check any pronunciation problems. You could drill some of the questions to encourage good, natural pronunciation, and also write up an example sentence on the board to act as a model for them to follow. Students can then ask and answer in pairs. Monitor and feed back on any key mistakes with the whole class. If you have time, you could do a classroom survey to find out which of the arts is the most popular.

It's time to talk

- Set the scene and get students to look through the programme and think about what might interest them. Go round and help with any vocabulary problems. They can then try to agree on what they would like to do with a partner.
- Encourage them to say why they want to see a particular performance. Explain that they could do something completely different if they wish and remind them to use the vocabulary and structures they have looked at in this lesson. Refer to the vocabulary list that you have built up on the board.
- Each pair could then try to agree on a plan with another pair as a kind of pyramid discussion.
- Monitor and feed back on their performance.
- You may want to use the Extra classroom activity here (see pages 79 and 87).

What did we do today?

Check the Remember section quickly and remind them of the objectives of the lesson. Look again at the vocabulary lists that you have written on the board.

Follow up

Encourage students to:
1 write sentences about the arts and to write any new and useful vocabulary in their vocabulary books. Remind them that they need not record every new word as there may be simply too many to learn at once. They may be better off focusing on the words that they think are the most useful
2 write down sentences that they think will be useful when they arrive in a place that they do not know well.

4 Changing direction

What did we do last time?

Do a review of the last type 1 lesson (see Teacher's notes for Unit 1) and do some quick revision as follows. Ask them:
- what the differences are between the forms of the present simple and present continuous. Choose a common verb like *work* and write the forms (including the negative and questions) on the board
- what the differences are in the use of the two tenses
- to ask and answer questions with a partner in the two tenses (e.g. *What do you do? What are you doing?*).

On the agenda: Why are we doing this?

Tell students the objectives of the lesson:
- to describe **past experiences**
- to revise the **past simple and past continuous** tenses – you might want to write some examples on the board so that students are clear about what they are going to study
- to do some **pronunciation** work on using **intonation to show interest** – you could demonstrate what you mean by *intonation*.

Reinforce this by writing the key words on the board or OHP.

Warm up

Ask the students the questions. You could also ask them what the positive and negative sides to running a restaurant might be.

Look at the picture of Judy Irigoin and ask checking questions about the caption.

Listen to this

Change is fun

1 - Tell students that they are going to listen to Judy talking about her restaurant. Give them a few moments to read the statements and the alternatives.
  - You may want to tell them that in the US, *pancakes* are larger and thicker than pancakes in the UK. Americans would describe a UK pancake as a *crêpe*.

- Check the meaning of *lobster*. You can point out the lobster in the photo of the *crêperie*.
- Play track 4.1 and check the answers.

Answers

1 the USA
2 to give her children a new life
3 with a friend
4 like the *crêperie*
5 didn't make a profit last year

2 Ask students to read through the questions. Check vocabulary like *set up* and *profit* and play track 4.1 again. Check the answers.

Answers

1 She has a sister who lives there.
2 15 days
3 It's beautiful and because there are lobsters.
4 They became stronger and more confident.
5 People only go there in the summer.

Track 4.1 tapescript ▶▶|

INTERVIEWER: Judy, you decided to change your life a couple of years ago. What did you do? And why?

JUDY: Well, I was working for a language school in France when I had the idea. I decided to change my life completely, and so I opened a French *crêperie* called 'Ooh la la' in a place called Kennebunkport, Maine. It's a seaside resort about an hour and 15 minutes north of Boston in the States.

INTERVIEWER: OK. And why did you make the change?

JUDY: Well, the main reason was my two teenage boys. Things were not going well for them at school around this time. I just wanted them to have another experience in life, a real experience. We were living in France at the time and decided to create something for them to have an exciting summer job, and so I thought about the US.

INTERVIEWER: So how did you set up a business in the States? Was it difficult?

JUDY: Well, a *crêperie* seemed good because it didn't need much investment. I wanted to be near Boston, because I have a sister who lives there, and I decided on Kennebunkport because it's just so beautiful. We knew there were a lot of people in summer, and so, after I figured I could make a profit, and the town said we could open a *crêperie*, I set up the place – actually in just 15 days.

INTERVIEWER: Fifteen days? Really, extremely quick!

JUDY: Yes, but I have to say I had a lot of help. I had a good friend in Boston. She was working in the restaurant business and so she came over and she helped design the restaurant and all that. And the place is extremely cute, really it's lovely.

INTERVIEWER: It seems you obviously enjoy running a business.

JUDY: Oh, yeah. It's a lot of fun in the summertime. It's a beautiful place, and in June Kennebunkport is lobster country. People come from all over the world, go out on the lobster boat trip, ride on the ocean, learn about the life cycle of the lobster and things like that. And fish, of course.

INTERVIEWER: Sounds great. And what do the boys think?

JUDY: They love it, they really love it. The *crêperie* is a wonderful

experience for them. They meet and talk to people and make a lot of friends. And you know, in the past they were so quiet, but now they're so much stronger and more confident. It was a good decision.

INTERVIEWER: And, finally, the big question, did you make a profit last year?

JUDY: Well, no! This is a special business in that we really only make money in summer – in June, July, August, maybe September and October. If the trees are beautiful, and the weather is good, we have a lot of people. But the rest of the year there's really no money coming in because there aren't enough people. So we don't make any real profit. But it's great fun! Change is fun. Everyone should have a small business. I really recommend it.

What do you think?

Ask students if they agree with Judy. You could get them to discuss the advantages and disadvantages of owning a small business. Write prompts on the board to help them formulate sentences.

Check your grammar

Past simple and past continuous

- You could get students to look through the tapescript and find examples of different tenses. Elicit what they are and why they are used.
- Check understanding of *figured*.
- Tell students to work through exercises 1 and 2 individually or in pairs, as appropriate. Then check the answers with the whole class. Draw students' attention to the timeline and refer them to the Grammar reference section in their books (page 113) if you wish.

Answers

1 1 I was working (past continuous) for a language school in France when I had the idea. (past simple)
2 When my son saw it, he was really excited. (past simple x 2)
3 We were living in France at the time. (past continuous)
4 After I figured I could make a profit, I set up the place. (past simple x 2)
5 She was working (past continuous) in the restaurant business and so she came over. (past simple)
6 Things were not going well for them at school around this time. (past continuous)
Was is only for first person and third person singular. *Were* is for all others.
2 1 c 2 a 3 b 4 a 5 c 6 b

Do it yourself

1 Give students a few minutes to do the exercise on their own and then check the answers.

Answers

1 James met Sabine in 1998. He was living in New York at the time.
2 I wanted to work in marketing. So I joined a marketing company.
3 I was listening to the radio when you called.
4 I saw Jess a minute ago. She was talking to Sam.
5 Why didn't you answer the phone when I called?

2 • Before doing this exercise you could try to elicit some information about Nina Simone. Write it on the board, making sure students use the correct tenses.

• Students can do this exercise in pairs. Go round the class and help with any vocabulary problems. Check the answers with the whole class.

Answers

1 d   2 c   3 b   4 e   5 a

3 Students can do this exercise individually. Play track 4.2 so they can check their answers. Play it again if necessary and then check the answers with the whole class.

Answers

1 did ... begin   2 was working   3 had   4 took   5 came   6 Was
7 was already writing   8 joined   9 Did ... write   10 was
11 did ... have   12 stopped   13 were doing   14 listened
15 started

Track 4.2 tapescript ▶▶

INTERVIEWER: How did Nina Simone's career begin?

HILARY: Well, she was working in a nightclub when she had the chance to sign for the Bethlehem record label. She took her opportunity with both hands and her first hit came in 1959.

INTERVIEWER: Was Nina part of the black civil rights movement in the US during the 1960s?

HILARY: Absolutely, yes. When the protest actually started she was already writing songs and so she quickly joined the movement.

INTERVIEWER: Did Nina write any specific songs about the fight for equality?

HILARY: Yes. In fact, *Mississippi Goddam* was a direct response to the killing of four black children.

INTERVIEWER: And did her songs have any impact?

HILARY: Absolutely. At that time people always stopped what they were doing and listened when Nina started to sing.

Sounds good

Using intonation to show interest

1 Play track 4.3 and ask students to compare the two versions of the conversation. Read through the different types of response. You can demonstrate the intonation and then drill students.

Answers

In the first exchange, the listener sounds uninterested because his intonation is unenthusiastic. In the second exchange, the listener is more enthusiastic, and uses varied and more dynamic intonation and a wider variety of responses to indicate interest.

Track 4.3 tapescript ▶▶

Conversation 1

A: I went on a boat trip on Saturday.

B: Oh.

A: Yes, it was really good. We sailed along the coast. It was really beautiful.

B: Mmm.

A: Yes, and we saw lots of dolphins.

B: Hmm.

A: I think there were at least 20. It was wonderful!

B: OK.

Conversation 2

A: I went on a boat trip on Saturday.

B: How lovely!

A: Yes, it was really good. We sailed along the coast. It was really beautiful.

B: I'm sure it was.

A: Yes, and we saw lots of dolphins.

B: Dolphins! How many?

A: I think there were at least 20. It was wonderful!

B: Sounds fantastic!

2 Play track 4.4 and get students to decide which type of response the speaker uses. Check the answers by asking students to give the response with the correct intonation and say what type it is. Get them to look at Tapescript 4.4 and practise the conversations in pairs. Play the track again or read it yourself so that students have model intonation patterns to follow.

Answers

1 Type 2   2 Type 3   3 Type 1   4 Type 1   5 Type 1

Track 4.4 tapescript ▶▶

1 A: United won 5–0 at the weekend.

B: 5–0?

2 A: I've decided to leave the company.

B: Why?

3 A: I had a training course on selling last week.

B: Really?

4 A: A new colleague from Italy started work last week.

B: Good.

5 A: Business in China is booming.

B: Great!

3 Students should do this in pairs. Give feedback on their performance.

It's time to talk

• Tell students that they are now going to practise using the language they have looked at in this lesson by talking about something that happened to them in the past. Give them a few minutes to look at the topics and, if necessary, help them with any vocabulary problems.

• With a weaker group, you could demonstrate this yourself. Choose a topic and tell them about it. Encourage them to ask questions and show interest in your answers.

• Get students to choose a topic they would like to talk about. Give them a few minutes to think about it and prepare their stories, focusing on the use of the past tenses in particular.

• In pairs, students talk about their topics. Before they start, encourage the students who are listening to respond, show interest and ask questions. Draw their attention to the possible questions in the Student's Book.

• Monitor and then give feedback on any mistakes.

• They could then choose another topic and talk to another student about it.

- To finish, you could ask selected students to tell the whole class about a story they heard.
- Give feedback on students' performance.
- You may want to use the Extra classroom activity here (see pages 80 and 88).

What did we do today?
Check the Remember section quickly and remind students of the objectives of the lesson.

Follow up
Encourage students to write sentences about their past experiences, using the past simple and past continuous.

5 Job swap

What did we do last time?
Do a review of the last type 2 lesson (Unit 2). Remind students of what they worked on (see Teacher's notes for that unit) and do some quick revision as follows:

Business and business organisation
Ask students to make sentences about their organisation using the following words: *turnover*, *employs*, *founded*, *share*, *organised into*.

Ask them how many words can collocate with the word *business* and get them to make sentences with them.

Getting through / Leaving a message
Ask them to give you useful phrases for getting through on the telephone and leaving a message. If necessary, give them cues to complete, like:
Hello, I'd like ...
Would you like to ...?
I'll ...

On the agenda: Why are we doing this?
Tell students the objectives of the lesson:
- to talk about **professional responsibilities**
- to talk about **jobs and personal development**
- to have a first look at **presenting** and how to **welcome visitors**.

Classroom language
circle

Warm up
Get short answers to the questions from as many students as possible rather than long answers from one or two. The questions are to focus the students on the context of the first part of the unit, not to stimulate extended discussion.

Look at the pictures of Sonia and Ben and ask checking questions about them and their situation.

Read on
Job swapping
Proceed as suggested in the teaching hints for type 2 units in the Introduction (page 16).

Answers
1 1 Job swapping is when two people change jobs for a day or more and learn from the experience.
2 Sonia is a team coordinator. Her duties include organising meetings, travel and documentation.
Ben is a design director. His duties include designing corporate brochures and other documents for outside the organisation.
3 They were both generally very positive about the experience.
2 1 He has to work on a lot of different things, with a variety of tasks.
2 She could do other things and had more creativity than she thought.
3 She'll try to contribute more ideas during team meetings in future.
4 He knew her job was very different from his.
5 He couldn't print some documents.
6 It showed him that organisational skills are essential to achieve targets. He learned more about dealing with pressure.

What do you think?
Do a quick classroom survey to find out how many students think job swapping is a good idea. Brainstorm and write on the board the possible benefits of job swapping. For example: *Developing knowledge of other parts of the organisation.*

The words you need ... to talk about jobs and personal development

Get students to look back through the reading text and underline any verbs that are new for them. Check the meanings and pronunciation, as appropriate.
1 It is important for students to able to describe their own jobs and personal development clearly and accurately. Once they have done the exercise and you have checked the answers it is worth asking them to make their own sentences and then going round the class listening to the sentences they have produced.

Answers

1 build   2 contribute   3 work   4 achieve   5 cope
6 develop   7 improve

2 Ask students to work on their own or in pairs. Play the recording and then check the answers. It is worth spending some time going over some of the wrong answers and explaining the difference between, for example *responsible* and *responsibility*.

Answers

1 responsibility for   2 in charge of   3 responsible for
4 objective   5 tasks   6 deal with   7 take care of
8 involved in

Track 5.1 tapescript ▶▶

BEN: I have responsibility for new designs for our corporate brochure. I'm also in charge of specific design projects. I'm responsible for 25 people. My main objective is to support marketing and sales. One of my other key tasks is to make sure we present a clear brand identity to the customer in our brochures. Another important part of my job is to deal with stores which display and sell our products. Sometimes I take care of visitors from our Spanish office because I speak good Spanish. I'm also involved in the social club at work.

3 Encourage students to focus on the vocabulary which is new to them and try to use it when working in pairs. When you give feedback on their performance, ask how many new words they used.

It's time to talk

1 Set the scene and give students a few minutes to look at the prompts and prepare some notes about their jobs.
2 • This is a good opportunity to mix up the class and get students to work with different partners. When they have finished, get them to tell the whole class which person they would like to do a job swap with, and why. Finally, give language feedback.
  • You may want to use the Extra classroom activity here (see pages 80 and 89).

COMMUNICATING AT WORK

Presenting 1: Welcoming visitors

Get students to discuss the first questions in pairs and ask them what difficulties they have when they give presentations.

1 You might need to play the track more than once.

Answers

Name: Wilkins
Job: Information officer
Morning tour: Production area
Lunch: 12.30
Evening programme: Restaurant

2 After checking the answers, drill some of the phrases with the whole group. If you feel that students need extra help remembering them accurately, write key phrases on the board and rub out all but the first letters of the words. Then see how much they can remember. Get them to say each phrase as a whole group and pay attention to pronunciation.

Answers

1 h 2 g 3 i 4 f 5 e 6 a 7 c 8 b 9 d

Track 5.2 tapescript ▶▶

GEMMA: Hello and welcome to everyone. My name's Gemma Wilkins and I work in the HR department – I'm the information officer in the company. I'd like to give you a short introduction to my job and also to explain the programme for the day. To begin then, I want first of all to say just a few words about me. I'm in charge of all external communication. And I'm also your contact person for the day so please ask me if you have any problems. So, that's my job. That's all I want to say about me for now. Right, now I want to go on to the second part – the plan for the day. As you can see from the programme, we have a tour of the production area with Matthew Durston, our production manager, then lunch at 12.30. After lunch we have a video to show you at 2, then a meeting with our marketing manager. For this evening we have booked dinner for eight o'clock at the Hollies, a fantastic restaurant in the town centre. We'll meet at your hotel at 7.15 and walk there. Right, that's all I wanted to say. Does anyone have any questions before the tour? No? OK, thank you for listening. Now I'm going to hand over to Matthew. So, have a good day!

3 • Set the scene and give students a few minutes to look through the information. Help with any vocabulary problems, if necessary.
  • Play track 5.3. This model will help them with their preparation before they give their own presentation.
  • Give students three or four minutes to prepare their presentations and then give feedback on their performance. If you make notes clearly on a new piece of paper per student, you can give each of them individual written feedback as well.

Track 5.3 tapescript ▶▶

WILLIAM: Good morning, everyone. My name's William Brett and I'd like to welcome you to our company, Le Chat Bleu, with a short introduction about my work and the plan for the day. I also have some information about this evening. To begin then, a few words about myself. I'm the human resources manager here at Le Chat Bleu. I'm responsible for recruitment and also for staff training. Right, the important point is the programme for the day. We begin with a visit to our design studio with Simone Laurent. Then Simone will take you for lunch. And after lunch we have a visit to the sports shoe workshops with John Barnes. At about three o'clock we have a project meeting with different colleagues. Then this evening we would like everyone to meet at half past seven in your hotel lobby. We plan to have a short reception and then dinner in a restaurant, Le Clochard. Well, does anyone have any questions? Is everyone happy with this plan? OK, good, then that's all from me. Thank you for listening. I hope you have a good day! Now let me introduce Simone Laurent from our design team – she'll show you the studio.

What did we do today?

Check the Remember section quickly and remind students of the objectives of this lesson.

Follow up

Encourage students to:
1 write sentences about their jobs and personal development
2 record new vocabulary in a vocabulary book – remind them of the importance of writing both the noun and verb forms and any common preposition, if appropriate
3 write down useful phrases for presentations
4 practise using the phrases.

6 Tourist attraction

What did we do last time?
Do a review of the last type 3 lesson (Unit 3). Remind students of what they worked on (see Teacher's notes for that unit) and do some quick revision as follows.

Arriving in a place you don't know
Ask students to give you some useful phrases for arriving in a place you don't know.
If necessary, give them some cues, like:
left luggage
accommodation bureau
tourist information
buses.
Tell students to make short dialogues using the phrases they remember.

Music, theatre, dance and opera
Give them cues to make complete sentences about the arts, e.g. *production, performance, composer, conductor, director, actor*. Ask them for words to express what they like or don't like and get them to have short conversations using these words.

On the agenda: Why are we doing this?
Tell students the objectives of this lesson:
• to talk about **tourist attractions and locations**
• to learn some key phrases about **health and feeling ill**
• to learn some key **vocabulary about tourist attractions and accommodation**.
Reinforce this by writing the key words on the board or OHP.

Warm up
Look at the questions and get students to discuss their answers briefly in pairs. Get students to feed back to the whole class. Elicit words like *a cold, flu, a broken arm*, etc., and write them on the board.

Health and feeling ill
See the Introduction (page 16): Type 3 units – social English dialogues.

Answers

1 f 2 c 3 g 4 a 5 h 6 b 7 e 8 d

Track 6.1 tapescript ▶▶
Feeling unwell
A: Are you all right?
B: No, actually. I don't feel very well.
A: Yes, you do look pale. Is there anything I can do?
B: No thanks, maybe I'll go home early today.
A: Yes, I think you should.

Fixing an appointment to see a doctor
A: Hello, I'd like an appointment, please.
B: Can I have your name?
A: Yes, it's Raul Ochoa. I'm from Spain. I'm here temporarily, on business.

B: Fine. I'm afraid the doctor is busy all morning. Can you come at 3.15 this afternoon?

At the doctor's
A: Hello, I have an appointment with the doctor at 3.15.
B: 3.15, yes. Can you fill in this form, please?
A: OK. Do you need my insurance details?
B: No, I don't think so. But write your home doctor's details here.

Back at work
A: Ah, you're back! Are you better now?
B: Yes, I'm much better, thanks.
A: Good. We've missed you. Welcome back.

Have a go
See the Introduction (page 17): Type 3 units. You can build a dialogue on the board with the class before students go on to make their own dialogues in pairs. This will give you the opportunity to drill students on their pronunciation. After practising in pairs, get them to perform for the whole class.

Listen to this

Are you looking for somewhere different?
Before turning over the page, and in preparation for track 6.2, tell students that they are now going to listen to someone talking about the place he comes from: Tasmania, Australia. Ask the questions in the Student's Book before you listen.

1 Read the caption and ask checking questions. Check understanding of *wilderness*. Explain the task and give time for students to read through the statements before playing track 6.2. Check the answers.

Answers

1 T 2 F 3 T 4 T 5 T

2 Play track 6.2 again, get students to do this exercise and check the answers. Ask them how different Tasmania is from Europe; or get them to ask and answer the question in pairs.

Answers

1 Tourism, farming and food
2 Half a million people
3 Long and empty
4 Mountains
5 One third
6 It's mostly a natural wilderness; Europe has big cities, many people, a high density of population, and roads and buildings everywhere.

Track 6.2 tapescript ▶▶
INTERVIEWER: When people think of Australia, they probably think of Sydney, or the Outback, or the Great Barrier Reef, but you're from Tasmania, right?

GERRY: Yeah, I was born in Tasmania. Tasmania is an island off the south coast of Australia. It's approximately the size of the Republic of Ireland. And the weather there is much like the south coast of Ireland, or the north coast of Spain. Not very cold and not very hot either, and it rains a fair bit too.

INTERVIEWER: So what's interesting about Tasmania?

GERRY: Well, it used to be a penal colony, a prison for the British Empire. It was a good prison because it's an island. And anyone who tried to escape got eaten by sharks.

INTERVIEWER: Really? Sharks?

GERRY: Yeah, the sea off Tasmania is full of sharks. So there was no escape. But things have improved since the eighteenth century and Tasmania is famous for better reasons. Really, it's a very beautiful place, with a fantastic natural environment. So tourism is a major industry, along with farming and also food, food products. But tourism is a growing industry.

INTERVIEWER: So what is there for people to see in Tasmania?

GERRY: Well, the landscape is very beautiful. And it's got unique animals and unique plants. There are only half a million people, so it's a large island for a small population. There are long beaches, mostly empty, no people at all. You can have a whole beach to yourself. On the west coast it's very mountainous, mountains all down the west. About a third of the state is National Park and complete wilderness. Tasmania is a World Heritage Area and in many places it's possible to walk for maybe ten days without seeing a road or another human being.

INTERVIEWER: How do you find living in Britain compared with being in Tasmania?

GERRY: I like it here, I get to visit the different cultures of Europe and it's been interesting to learn about British culture. But compared with Tasmania, Britain – even the whole of Europe – it's completely different. In Europe there are so many big cities, so many people, such a high density of population, roads, buildings everywhere. Tasmania is mostly a natural wilderness. You can go for miles and all you hear is insects and birds.

What do you think?

Ask students if Gerry confirmed, contradicted or added anything to what they had already thought about Australia.

The words you need ... to talk about tourist attractions and accommodation

1 Get students to look at the advertisement and ask quick checking questions to focus their reading. For example:

What can you see in Sydney?
What can you learn about?
How many nights can you stay in Melbourne?

Encourage students to use English–English dictionaries to check the meanings of the underlined words.

2 Once they have done the exercise, encourage students to produce sentences about their own country using the words.

3 Brainstorm types of accommodation and write them on the board. Students can then look in the book to see how many of the ones listed they had thought of. They can do the matching in pairs and then check the answers.

Ask the question, and if there is time, students could say which one they liked the most and why.

It's time to talk

Do the pairwork exercise and give feedback on students' performance.

You may want to do Extra Classroom activity here (see pages 80 and 90).

Remember

Brainstorm adjectives used to describe a place and check pronunciation. Encourage students to make sentences about a holiday they went on recently.

What did we do today?

Remind students of the objectives of the lesson.

Follow up

Encourage students to:

1 start a new section in their vocabulary book dedicated to words describing health

2 write sentences using words presented in this unit.

7 From Mexico to Germany

What did we do last time?

Do a review of the last type 1 lesson (Unit 4). Remind students of what they worked on (see Teacher's notes for that unit) and do some brief revision work as follows.

Past simple and past continuous
Ask selected students questions like:
What did you do at the weekend?
What were you doing at 9 o'clock yesterday?
Get students to ask and answer similar questions in pairs and go over the uses of the two tenses if necessary.

Using intonation to show interest
Ask students to tell you the different types of response used to show interest. Write them on the board and review the correct intonation.
Get them to have short conversations as above, this time with an appropriate response to show interest.

On the agenda: Why are we doing this?

Tell students the objectives of this lesson:

• to practise **making comparisons**

- to revise the grammar of making comparisons – **adjectives and adverbs: comparative, superlative and** *as ... as*
- to do some work on **pronunciation – stress patterns in long words**.

Reinforce this by writing the key words on the board or OHP.

Warm up

Get students to discuss this in pairs.
Look at the picture of Javier and the caption. Explain that students are going to hear him talking about his time in Mexico and in Germany.

Listen to this

Work is fun

1 Give students time to read the statements before playing track 7.1. Check the answers.

> **Answers**
> 1 F 2 T 3 F 4 T 5 T

2 After students have read the statements, play the track again and check the answers.

> **Answers**
> 1 Two years
> 2 Senior managers
> 3 Mexican Spanish contains older forms of Spanish and some American English words
> 4 An open and friendly style
> 5 Mexican food is closer to Spanish food than German

Track 7.1 tapescript ▶▶

INTERVIEWER: Javier, you've worked internationally in Mexico and Germany, yes?

JAVIER: Yes, I worked in Mexico, but only for two years. Last year I was based in Germany, which was very interesting, but now I'm back in Spain. So, for work, I spent three years abroad. I think it's good to work in different countries. After this, I think you have a better career and, maybe even, you become a better person.

INTERVIEWER: What was Mexico like? Interesting?

JAVIER: Yes, the most interesting place I've worked. OK, in Mexico, as a manager, you have to push sometimes. Things can move a little more slowly than in Spain, and maybe people are not so motivated as in Germany. I know it's a stereotype, but in Germany they often do things very efficiently. But Mexico is another business culture, quite close to the Spanish in some ways so, for me, it was easier to handle.

INTERVIEWER: Interesting analysis. And what about Mexicans and their famous attitude to time?

JAVIER: It certainly wasn't as bad as I expected. Mexicans aren't always late. That's just a stereotype. It's the same as Germany. It's the same everywhere, in my experience. In business, I think it depends on who is having the meeting. If you have a meeting with top management, people at a higher level often come a little later, they have the right to be late.

INTERVIEWER: I have a question about language. In Mexico, is the Spanish the same as that spoken in Spain?

JAVIER: The languages are very similar but I think Mexican Spanish sounds older than the Spanish in Spain. They use a more historical form, with some words that we don't have here any more, and they also use a lot of American English words in their daily conversation. For example, they use 'highway', and other very common words that you hear every day.

INTERVIEWER: What about the working culture? I guess this was very different in Mexico and Germany?

JAVIER: Yes, the culture is very different. Mexican business culture is more about fun. People are more open. They don't think about hierarchy so much, and, also ... maybe in Mexico you can communicate more easily, more freely with your boss, for example. The door is always open, and so on. My style or strategy of management is to be open and friendly, although lots of very good managers have a different style. It's a strategic question. For me, it creates more possibilities to build relationships with people.

INTERVIEWER: And a final question to compare the food. Which was better, Mexican or German?

JAVIER: The food? Well, I prefer Mexican food. The German food was good but I didn't enjoy it as much as the Mexican, it wasn't as spicy as I normally have. But you know, I like Mexican because it's very close to Spanish food, to what I know, so no comparison, for me, no comparison.

What do you think?

Ask the questions and get students to discuss them in small groups. Try to have a range of different nationalities in each group, if possible. If it is a monolingual class, students could think of stereotypes of their country and of any other national stereotypes they know of.

Check your grammar

Adjectives and adverbs

Explain to students that they are going to look at the grammar Javier uses to describe the two countries.
Ask students to look at Tapescript 7.1 at the back of their books and find:
- two examples of comparatives
- an example of the superlative
- an example of *as ... as*.

See if students can make a list of the rules in pairs. Feed back onto the board.

1 Elicit some examples that exemplify each rule and write them on the board. For the answers, refer students to the Grammar reference section on page 114 in the Student's Book. Tell them to look in a dictionary when they are not sure how to form the comparative or superlative.

2

> **Answers**
> badly – worse   well – better

3 b

Do it yourself

Ask students to do exercises 1 to 3 alone or in pairs, and then check the answers. Encourage them to make sentences in pairs about countries or cities they have been to.

Play track 7.2 to check the answers to exercise 2.

Track 7.2 tapescript ▶▶▌

1 In general, people in Germany drive more carefully than they do in Mexico.
2 In Mexico you can get to know people a lot more easily than here.
3 Some people say that status is more important in Mexican business culture.
4 In Mexico people normally have their evening meal later than in Germany.
5 In Mexico prices are generally lower.
6 Most people I met in Mexico knew Germany better than I expected.

3

Sounds good

Stress patterns in long words

1 Write the two words on the board and ask selected students to try to pronounce them correctly. Elicit the fact that the word stress is different and get them to mark it. If they are having problems, get them to look in their dictionaries and highlight the stress marks on each word. Play track 7.3 and get students to repeat the words.

Track 7.3 tapescript ▶▶▌

strategy
strategic

2 Check that students understand the meaning of the words. Play track 7.4 and get them to repeat the words. Do the exercise and play track 7.5. Check the answers. Drill the correct pronunciation of the words. Exaggerate the stress so that it is clear to the students where the main stress falls.

Track 7.4 tapescript ▶▶▌

1 strategy
2 strategic
3 understand
4 motivated
5 comparison
6 competition

Track 7.5 tapescript ▶▶▌

1 Mexico / languages
2 employer / another
3 engineer / underline
4 complicated / educated
5 analysis / competitor
6 absolutely / conversation

Test your partner

Give students a few minutes to look through the Student's Book before testing their partners.

It's time to talk

- Read the instructions and make sure that students understand the situation. Nominate pairs and be clear about which student takes which file card.
- Remind students of the grammatical structures they should use and perhaps write some examples related to this situation on the board.
- Elicit some ways students could start the conversation. For example:
  So, which countries have you been to?
  Which was your favourite?
- Monitor the role-plays and give feedback on the students' linguistic performance, focusing on their use of comparatives and superlatives, as well as examples of word stress.
- You may want to use the Extra classroom activity here (see pages 81 and 91).

What did we do today?

Check the Remember section quickly and remind students of the objectives of the lesson.

Follow up

Encourage students to:
1 write sentences comparing places or people that they know using a range of different adjectives and adverbs
2 always mark the stress on longer words when they write them in their vocabulary book

8 Globalisation

What did we do last time?

Do a review of the last type 2 lesson (Unit 5). Remind students of what they worked on (see Teacher's notes for that unit) and do some quick revision as follows.

Jobs and personal development

Ask students to make sentences about their job using these words: *responsible for*, *in charge of*, *deal with*, *take care of*, *involved in*. Alternatively, you could write the words on the board without the prepositions and ask students for the correct prepositions.

Welcome presentation to visitors

Ask students to give you useful phrases for welcoming visitors. If necessary, give them cues, like:

My name's …
I'd like to give you a short …
Does anyone have … ?
Thank you for …

On the agenda: Why are we doing this?

Tell students the objectives of this lesson:

- to practise speaking – **presenting an argument**
- to look at useful **vocabulary** for talking about **trade and the economy**
- to write **emails** and look at the differences between **formal and informal writing**.

Reinforce this by writing the key words on the board or OHP.

Warm up

Ask the students the questions, but don't spend too long as they will have the chance to discuss this issue in greater detail later in the lesson.

Read on

Can Zac save the planet?

Background briefing: The Ecologist

Founded in 1970, *The Ecologist* is the world's most widely-read environmental magazine; published in four continents, *The Ecologist* is read by over 200,000 people in 150 countries. The magazine has been an important player in major environmental campaigns against GM crops, rainforest destruction, climate change and the impact of globalisation. *The Ecologist* is a non-profit making magazine and is edited by Zac Goldsmith. For more information about *The Ecologist*, go to the *English365* website: www.cambridge.org/elt/english365.

1 Give students a few moments to read through the headings and to ask you about any unfamiliar vocabulary. Set a time limit and do the matching exercise. Tell them that you want them to look for the main ideas at this stage, not to read every word.

Answers

1 B 3 A 4 D 6 C

2 Check that the students know how to say the numbers correctly and ask them to read the paragraphs again. Then check the answers.

Answers

1 100 multinational companies account for 70% of world trade.
2 The national debt of Ghana.
3 The richest 20% of the world's population consumes 17 times more energy than the poorest 20%.
4 580 million people travelled abroad in 1996.
5 By 2020, 1.6 billion people will travel abroad.
6 Zac says that if everyone lived like the average American, we would need six planets to meet the energy needs.

What do you think?

Students can discuss this in small groups before you ask the whole class for their opinions. Give prompts to help students express their opinions:

I think / In my opinion …

The words you need … to talk about trade and the economy

1 Students can do this individually and then check their answers with a partner before you check the answers with the whole class. As you go through, check on their pronunciation.

Answers

1 c 2 d 3 i 4 e 5 a 6 g 7 f 8 b 9 h

Test your partner

If you have a strong group, ask students to make a sentence and say it to their partner, but with the key word missing. Their partner should then work out what the word is from the context. This should help students to realise the importance of learning how to use words correctly in context.

2
- Students do this individually before listening to track 8.1 to check their answers. If you have time, it is worthwhile going over how some of the 'wrong' answers could be used correctly.
- Give feedback on the sentences that students make. Again, stress the importance of knowing how to use vocabulary rather than just knowing the meaning.

Answers

1 environmentally 2 economic 3 politics 4 developing
5 interest 6 invests 7 exporter 8 multinational

Track 8.1 tapescript ▶▶|

1 My company makes products which are environmentally friendly.
2 I think the government has a good economic policy.
3 I'm not very interested in politics.
4 I'd like to work in a developing country like Vietnam.
5 I pay a lot of interest on my bank loan.
6 Our business invests a lot of money in its employees.
7 My country is an exporter of coffee.
8 Ford is a major multinational company.

It's time to talk

- Read the instructions and make sure that students understand the situation. Nominate groups and be clear about which group looks at which information.
- Remind students about how they can introduce their opinions and encourage them to use vocabulary from this lesson.
- At the end, write possible advantages and disadvantages on the board and then give feedback on students' linguistic performance.
- You may want to use the Extra classroom activity here (see pages 81 and 92).

COMMUNICATING AT WORK

Emails 1: Formal and informal writing

Start by asking how often students send emails. Explain that this section deals with writing emails and the differences between formal and informal writing in English.

Before looking at the input in the Student's Book, elicit any features of writing in emails that the students know. You can point out that, very often, emails are more informal than letters.

Answers

1 Neither email is better than the other. The first one is informal, the second is formal.
2 1 i, b   2 l, e   3 h, f   4 a, d   5 j, c   6 k, g

3 Monitor and correct while students are writing their emails. Ask selected students to read their emails to the whole class.

Model answers

Hi Tom,
How's it going?
See attached report and send me your opinion when you can.
See you soon.
Val

Dear Ms Rivers,
I am writing to confirm our meeting on 15 July at 10 am in the SAS Executive Lounge at London Heathrow. I should be grateful if you would send me some product information. Please let me know if you would like me to help you to prepare for the meeting.

I look forward to seeing you again soon.

Kind regards,
Ramón da Silva

What did we do today?

Check the Remember section quickly and remind students of the objectives of the lesson.

Follow up

Encourage students to:
1 write sentences about trade and the economy
2 record new vocabulary in their vocabulary books and to include 'word families' as this will help them to expand their range of vocabulary more quickly.

Remind students that if there are a lot of new words, they should focus on trying to learn the ones that they feel are more useful to them rather than try to learn a large number of new words in one go.

9 Here is the news

What did we do last time?

Do a review of the last type 3 lesson (Unit 6). Remind students of what they worked on (see Teacher's notes for that unit) and do some quick revision as follows.

Health
Ask students to give you some useful phrases for talking about health. If necessary, give them some cues like:
feeling unwell
fixing an appointment
at the doctor's
back at work.
Ask them to make short dialogues using the phrases.

Tourist attractions and accommodation
Give them cues to make sentences about tourist attractions, for example:
cuisine, culture, scenery.
Brainstorm different kinds of accommodation and get them to talk about which they prefer and why.

On the agenda: Why are we doing this?
Tell students the objectives of the lesson:
- to practise talking about **news and current affairs**
- to look at useful phrases for **talking about the news**
- to learn vocabulary connected to the **news and news media.**
Reinforce this by writing the key words on the board or OHP.

Warm up
Get quick answers to the questions.

Talking about news

See the Introduction (page 16): Type 3 units – social English dialogues.

Answers

1 f 2 g 3 c 4 h 5 a 6 d 7 i 8 j 9 e 10 b

Track 9.1 tapescript ▶▶
Breaking news
A: Oh no! Have you seen this?
B: What's happened?
A: There's been a bad crash.
B: That's awful. Where?

Is it really news?
A: Look at this! Rosenberg beat Juventus!
B: Really? What was the score?

A: Three one to Rosenberg.

B: That's a big shock. Who scored?

News at work

A: Chris, did you know about Gemma Hudson? Have you heard that she's leaving?

B: Really? How do you know that?

A: She told me. She's leaving next month.

B: Actually, I'm not surprised. I didn't think she was very happy here.

A: That's right. I think she wants to move back to her home town.

A newspaper article

A: There was a good article in yesterday's paper.

B: What was it about?

A: Problems in schools. Did you see it?

B: No, I didn't see the paper yesterday.

A: You should read it. I'll get a copy off the web and email it to you.

B: OK, thanks. I'll look forward to reading it.

Have a go

See the Introduction (page 17): Type 3 units. You can also ask them to make short dialogues so that the other students have to listen and guess what kind of news is being discussed.

Listen to this

Finding out what's going on

Introduce the class to Elaine by looking at her photo and reading the caption.

Before you listen

If you have time, you could get students to do a quick classroom survey of their own preferences.

Answers

1 1 F 2 F 3 T 4 F

2 1 analysis 2 entertainment 3 interactive 4 research
5 newspapers and the radio

Track 9.2 tapescript ▶▶|

INTERVIEWER: Elaine, you're a print journalist – you write mainly for newspapers – but how do most people get their information about the world in which they live?

ELAINE: I think most people these days – in Britain, anyway – get their information through television. They watch the news on television, but newspapers are still popular in Britain.

INTERVIEWER: But people get news mostly from television?

ELAINE: Yes, I think these days they do. We have 24-hour news coverage. There are many, many channels where you can get news.

INTERVIEWER: How do you compare newspapers and television news?

ELAINE: Well, most of the television news is really terrible. There's no analysis, no detail. If you want to really understand the news, you have to read a good newspaper. In newspapers you get much more analysis. At least, you do in some newspapers.

INTERVIEWER: So you don't like the television, then?

ELAINE: No, not for news. It just tells you a few things and shows lots of pictures, obviously. There's not much information. The

news on TV is presented as entertainment. I think that's what most people want. They want the headlines and a few pictures, they don't want lots of details.

INTERVIEWER: What about other technologies?

ELAINE: I think the internet is becoming more important. And it's good because people can interact with the news. For example, they can write opinions to discussion boards, or there are chatlines about the news. And a second good thing is you can send news items to friends. So yes, the internet is good because it's interactive, people get engaged with it.

INTERVIEWER: Has this technology affected other media too?

ELAINE: I'm sure, yes. Radio and television have become more interactive. They actually invite people to take part in debates.

INTERVIEWER: So in a way that's quite good, people can express an opinion, they can participate in news stories?

ELAINE: Yes, and the internet also means many more people write things, they can put their views across in a way they couldn't before. And also, people can find out more from the internet, they do their own research. It's true, yes, people participate more.

INTERVIEWER: So what you are saying is people do have more choice than ever, more variety.

ELAINE: Oh, yes, massive variety. And more pictures. The internet and newspapers all include a lot of pictures but of course the television provides the most: people get an image of the news, something to remember. Not much detail, but they get a picture to remember something.

INTERVIEWER: And finally, how do you get the news, Elaine?

ELAINE: I read the newspapers and listen to the radio! I don't even have a television!

What do you think?

You could extend this by having a longer speaking exercise on one of the following topics:

• The advantages and disadvantages of the internet

• Should the internet be regulated?

The words you need ... to talk about newspapers and news stories

Bring a newspaper into class and quickly go over some of the key vocabulary: *headline, article, caption, section, front page, back page*, etc. Ask students which English language newspapers they have heard of, know or read regularly.

1 Give students a few minutes to look through the headlines and match them with the sections. Tell them not to worry about any unfamiliar vocabulary at this stage. Check understanding of *obituary* when they look at the cartoon.

Answers

1 f 2 g 3 i 4 h 5 j 6 b 7 e 8 d 9 a 10 c

You could give pairs of students a couple of sections each to invent a headline for. Alternatively, let students invent a headline so that the rest of the class can guess what section they would find it in.

2 Try to elicit some of the words in the list when you ask them what section they like reading and why. Depending on the level of the group it might be worthwhile checking on the difference between *bored* and *boring*.

It's time to talk

- Ask students to work in pairs before getting selected pairs to perform for the rest of the class. Before you begin, point out key phrases from the Remember section and drill them for accurate pronunciation. Also, remind students that they should show interest in a news story and so intonation is important.
- You may want to use the Extra classroom activity here (see pages 81 and 93).

What did we do today?

Remind students of the objectives of the lesson.

Follow up

Encourage students to:
1 write down ways of talking about the news and try to practise using them in real situations
2 record new vocabulary in their vocabulary books
3 read English language newspapers.

Extension

There is a lot of scope for extension when it comes to looking at newspapers and talking about the news. So, depending on interest and time, you could do one of the following:

- Bring in different English language newspapers so students can compare them (tabloid and broadsheet). You can focus on: size of headlines, photos, amount of serious news, etc.
- Compare the presentation of the same story in a broadsheet and a tabloid.
- Students choose an article and present the main points to the rest of the class in order to open a discussion on the topic.

10 Executive search

What did we do last time?

Do a review of the last type 1 lesson (Unit 7). Remind students of what they worked on and do some brief revision work as follows.

Comparatives

Ask students how we can compare two things and then ask them to compare, for example, two cities or companies.

Stress in long words

Write some of the words from Unit 7 on the board and get students to pronounce them correctly. Emphasise the stressed part of the words.

On the agenda: Why are we doing this?

Tell students the objectives of this lesson:

- to talk about **work experience**
- to revise the **past simple**, **present perfect simple** and **present perfect continuous** and *for*, *since* and *ago*
- to improve **pronunciation** – **weak forms of** *have* and *for*.

Reinforce this by writing the key words on the board or OHP.

Warm up

Once you have discussed the Warm-up questions, you could go through the stages of getting a job. Check the vocabulary and collocations, for example, *apply for a job, write a CV, have an interview, accept/reject a job offer.*

Listen to this

Finding the right people

Look at the picture of Henry and read the caption. Explain that students are going to listen to him talking about his work. Check vocabulary like *executive* and *consultancy*. Also check understanding of *vision* before they hear the recording.

Track 10.1 tapescript ▶▶

INTERVIEWER: So Henry, tell us something about your life. You live in Paris, don't you?

HENRY: Yes, I was born in France, but I studied – or was educated – in the USA. After that I joined the US Army and actually I was a soldier in Vietnam.

INTERVIEWER: Really? Did that prepare you for a life in business?

HENRY: No, but it made me grow up. When the war was over, I moved to London. I worked for a strategic consultancy business.

INTERVIEWER: So have you always worked in consultancy?

HENRY: Yes, just about. All my working life. But after London I moved to Paris to join Russell Reynolds Associates. That was a long time ago – in 1979.

INTERVIEWER: 1979. And have you been in Paris the whole time?

HENRY: No, I went to the US for ten years and then came back to Paris.

INTERVIEWER: So can you explain your job? What do you do exactly?

HENRY: I'm an executive search consultant.

INTERVIEWER: An executive search consultant. What does that mean exactly? Is it recruitment?

HENRY: Yes, but it's not really recruitment; it's more than just finding someone to sign a contract. It's a consultancy role because we help companies to solve their specific problems. We help them to find the right people to meet very specific company needs – really the job is essentially about solving problems. It's a very strategic function.

INTERVIEWER: Has the job changed much over time?

HENRY: Oh, yes, it's changed a lot. In the last ten years it has become a job that is relationship-driven. The key thing, the most important thing in my job, is to establish partnerships with the client, working together. You have to understand the needs of the client really well. In fact, we've been looking recently at ways to improve this area of the business further.

INTERVIEWER: So what about the big scandals like Enron in 2002, or the accountancy scandal at WorldCom? I mean, do you think companies now want people with good finance skills, in accountancy, for example?

HENRY: Yes, the various scandals had a big impact and companies have changed a lot since Enron. There's now more focus on everyday management skills. But I don't think that it will continue. Really the strategic vision is much more important; the big ideas matter. It's strategic vision that builds companies. Companies need people at the top with vision and leadership.

INTERVIEWER: You obviously like the work?

HENRY: Very much so. I've been enjoying it very much recently, in fact. Executive search is a great job. I love it because every day it's always different, there's always something new from day to day. This makes it really interesting.

What do you think?

You could do a quick class survey on this and ask students why they would like to change and/or what they like or don't like about their current jobs.

Check your grammar

Past simple, present perfect simple and present perfect continuous

Get students to look at Tapescript 10.1 at the back of their books and underline the tenses. How many different tenses are there? Why are they used?

1 Look at the example sentences and timelines, which you may need to talk through and explain further. Check the answers and, if necessary, give other examples. You could also try to elicit other examples from the students.

Answers

1 1 c 2 a 3 b
2 We form the present perfect continuous with *have* + *been* + the *-ing* form of the verb.
We form the present perfect simple with *have* + the past participle.
3 1 for 2 since 3 ago
for – we can use it with different tenses to describe how long an activity lasted
since – we can use it with the present perfect to indicate the starting point of a past activity which continues to now
ago – we can use it with the past simple to say when something happened

Do it yourself

- Students can work through all four exercises in pairs or you could check the answers after each one.
- Play track 10.2 for the answers to exercise 4.
- Encourage students to think of their own sentences

following the patterns. They could ask and answer *How long …?* questions in pairs or they could do a quick classroom survey. Don't worry too much about the pronunciation at this stage as they will have the chance to focus on this in the next part of the lesson.

Answers

1 1 Maria has lived in London for three years.
2 How long have you had this problem?
3 I came here three years ago.
4 When did you arrive? Last night?
5 How long have you been working for Microsoft?
2 1 has enjoyed 2 joined 3 worked 4 took 5 moved
6 became 7 was 8 has established
9 has been trying / has tried 10 has been building
3 1 for 2 ago 3 for 4 for 5 ago 6 since

Answers and Track 10.2 tapescript ▶▶

4 1 How long has Christopher Gent worked in business?
2 When did his career begin?
3 How long did he work in banking?
4 How long was he CEO of Vodafone?
5 When did Vodafone buy Mannesman?
6 How long has the mobile phone sector been experiencing problems?

Sounds good

Weak forms of *have* and *for* with the present perfect

Tell students that you are going to focus on the correct pronunciation of *have* and *for* with the present perfect in fast speech.

Play tracks 10.3, 10.4 and 10.5 and ask students:
- what they notice
- to repeat what they hear as accurately as possible.
You might need to repeat the sentences yourself a few times.

Answers and Track 10.3 tapescript ▶▶

1 How long <u>have you</u> worked in Paris?
How long <u>have you</u> <u>been</u> living here?
How long <u>has he</u> <u>been</u> working in sales?

Answers and Track 10.4 tapescript ▶▶

2 I've worked in Paris <u>for</u> five years.
I've <u>been</u> living here <u>for a</u> few months.
He's <u>been</u> working in sales <u>for the</u> last four months.

Answers

3 We link 'for' and 'a' because a consonant precedes a vowel.

Track 10.5 tapescript ▶▶

for five years
for a few months

4 When they have completed the phrases, get students to try to repeat them accurately.

1 for a few months
2 for four weeks
3 for a year
4 for a couple of days
5 for ten hours
6 for the last two weeks

5 Demonstrate this for students first. Tell them that this time they are focusing on the correct pronunciation rather than the grammar as they did earlier.

It's time to talk

- Set the scene and give students a few minutes to read through the job advertisement. You can deal with any vocabulary problems that come up at this stage. Organise the students into pairs and check that they know what they are going to do. You might point out that the salary is mentioned in the advertisement and that this is common practice in the UK. Is it the same in their country? Do they think the salary should be included? Why? Why not?
- Remind students of the grammatical structures and pronunciation features they need to practise. You might also go through the typical structure of an interview (including some initial small talk). Give students a few minutes to prepare – you could put all the Student As and the Student Bs together for this.
- After the interview, ask if Student B got the job and why and give feedback on students' performance.
- If you have time, ask students to reverse roles.
- You may want to use the Extra classroom activity here (see pages 81 and 94).

What did we do today?

Check the Remember section quickly and remind students of the objectives of this lesson.

Follow up

Encourage students to:
1 write sentences about their own work experience
2 practise their pronunciation, even when they are on their own! Emphasise that this can really help them to improve.

11 Making money

What did we do last time?

Do a review of the last type 2 lesson (Unit 8). Remind students of what they worked on (see Teacher's notes for that unit) and do some quick revision as follows.

Trade and the economy

How many words can students remember from Unit 8 to talk about trade and the economy? Elicit the words (you could give definitions if they are having trouble) and get them to make sentences. With words like *environment* and *export*, get them to give you the whole word family.

Emails

Ask students to recall the different parts of an email and elicit formal and informal phrases for each stage. Build up possible emails on the board or OHP.

On the agenda: Why are we doing this?

Tell students the objectives of this lesson:
- to talk about **personal finance**
- to build **vocabulary** to talk about **finance and investments**
- to practise having **meetings: asking for and giving opinions**.

Reinforce this by writing the key words on the board or OHP.

Warm up

- Get students to discuss this in pairs quickly. One pair could then compare their ideas with another pair before feeding back to the rest of the class. Write the ideas on the board or OHP.
- Look at the picture of Philip and read the caption.

Read on

Alternative investments

1 Give students a time limit for this. Ask them how many of the same ways of investing they thought of in the Warm up.

Answers

1 Put money in the bank or invest in stocks and shares
2 Buy a second house to let; buy a share in commercial property
3 Any of the following: buy art; invest in furniture or antiques; play the lottery; gamble on horse racing

2 Get students to read the questions before reading the text in more detail.

Answers

1 Check that the rent will cover the mortgage and maintenance, and give you a profit
2 Location and demand for property
3 Someone who invests money in a new business
4 You have to know about art and art fashions
5 It's high risk and you need to know about fashions here too
6 It is very rare that you win anything

What do you think?

You could also ask if students have had any success with their investments.

The words you need ... to talk about finance and investments

1 Students can do this individually or in pairs. While checking the answers, also check pronunciation.

> **Answers**
>
> 1 d 2 h 3 j 4 a 5 c 6 g 7 i 8 b 9 f 10 e

Test your partner

With a strong class, get pairs to make sentences but omitting the key word. The other students should work out what the word is from the context.

2 After the exercise, encourage students to make their own sentences with words they think will be useful for them.

> **Answers**
>
> 1 property 2 mortgage 3 interest rates 4 bonds, investment
> 5 shares 6 shareholders, dividends 7 assets
> 8 commercial property

It's time to talk

- Make sure that students are clear about what to do. Help with any vocabulary on the File cards.
- At the end of the activity, see who made and lost the most money. If there is time, you could also highlight some of the key collocations in the File cards. For example: *invest in*, *make a profit*, *take out a mortgage*, *bet on*.
- You may want to use the Extra classroom activity here (see pages 81 and 95).

COMMUNICATING AT WORK

Meetings 1: Asking for and giving opinions

Get students to discuss the questions in small groups and ask them what problems they have, if any, during meetings in English.

1 Get students to read the possibilities before playing track 11.1.

> **Answers**
>
> Alex does not make his points very well because he sounds aggressive and too direct. The phrases *I disagree* and *You're wrong* can often sound too direct in a business meeting. *Yes, but ...* or *I'm not sure about that ...* or *Don't you think ...?* are more usual ways to disagree.

2 When you check the answers, check pronunciation and, if necessary, drill some of the phrases.

> **Answers**
>
> | | |
> |---|---|
> | What do you think ... ? | I think ... |
> | (*Using a name*) Alex? | But ... |
> | That's true, (yes). | I'm not sure about that. |
> | | Yes, but ... |

Track 11.1 tapescript ▶▶

JON: So, what do you think is the best way for the business to grow in the long term?

ELEANOR: I think we have to export. We have to find new markets.

WAYNE: Actually, I'm not sure about that. Not at the present time. That's only one way. It could be better to find a partner in another country, or different partners. That has cost and marketing advantages. Alex?

ALEX: I disagree. You're both wrong – the discussion is a waste of time. We can't do anything like that. We should forget all about increasing sales at this time.

JON: One moment, Alex. I think it is important to talk about these things. It's part of developing a strategy for the future. We have to consider the long term.

ELEANOR: That's true, yes. It's important to look ahead.

ALEX: Well, when the economy is doing badly there's no way you can build up sales in any meaningful way.

WAYNE: But there are plenty of examples of businesses doing well when the competition is having a hard time. Look at Ryanair, for example. Ryanair increased its market share during a downturn for the whole airline industry after September 11th.

ALEX: Yes, but we don't work in the airline business ...

3

> **Possible answers**
>
> 1 My view is 2 What do you think 3 In my opinion / I think
> 4 Actually, I don't agree 5 What about
> 6 I'm not sure about that 7 You're probably right

4 Put students into small groups and get them to take it in turns to briefly present their opinion on a topic to their group, and then ask for others' opinions. This will serve as a starting point for their discussion. Remind students to use the phrases from exercise 2. Give feedback on students' performances. If they did not use many of the phrases, you could repeat the exercise, but get them to present opinions on a topic of their choice.

What did we do today?

Check the Remember section quickly and remind students of the objectives of the lesson.

Follow up

Encourage students to:

1 record new vocabulary in their vocabulary books

2 write down useful phrases for giving opinions.

12 Ecotourism

What did we do last time?

Do a review of the last type 3 lesson (Unit 9). Remind students of what they worked on (see Teacher's notes for that unit) and do some quick revision as follows.

Talking about news

Ask them for useful phrases for: *introducing a news story, showing surprise at a story, talking about news at work* and *talking about a newspaper article.*

Talking about newspaper stories

Ask students what the different parts of a newspaper are. Ask for different adjectives they could use to react to news stories. In pairs, get them to make up short dialogues about the day's news stories.

On the agenda: Why are we doing this?

Tell students the objectives of this lesson:
* to talk about **the environment**
* to learn phrases for **getting directions**
* to learn vocabulary for talking about **environmental problems**.

Reinforce this by writing key words on the board or OHP.

Warm up

* Get students to discuss this in pairs and explain that you are going to look at phrases for asking for and giving directions.
* Ask if any of them have ever got lost or couldn't find their way and what happened.

Getting directions

Ask students to look at the photos and tell you as much as they can about them.

Answers

1 j 2 i 3 e 4 a 5 g 6 h 7 c 8 f 9 d 10 b

Track 12.1 tapescript ▶▶|

By car

A: Excuse me. Is this the right road to the Sculpture Park?
B: Yes, it is. Go straight on to the roundabout. Turn right. Then it's about four miles on the left.
A: So, straight on to the roundabout and right. Four miles.
B: Yes, it's easy. You can't go wrong.

Where is it?

A: Hello, I think I'm lost. Can you tell me where the *Age d'Or* restaurant is?
B: I'm sorry, I'm not from here.
A: OK, thanks. I'll ask someone else.
B: Just a minute! I can see it, it's just over there!
A: Oh yes, so it is! Thanks a lot.

Understanding the map

A: Excuse me. Can you show me where we are?
B: Of course. We're here, next to King's College. Where do you want to go?

A: I'm looking for Bank Street. Do you know where it is?
B: It's not far, I'll show you. I'm going that way.

Getting around a big building

A: Sorry to bother you, this is the fifth floor, isn't it?
B: Yes, it is. Where do you want to be?
A: I'm looking for the Brunel Room. Is it near here?
B: Yes, down this corridor and through that door, then it's on the left.

Have a go

Check pronunciation and drill some of the key expressions.

Listen to this

Tourism and the environment: the Eden Project

Get students to look at the picture of the Eden Project and ask if they know where it is and what they know about it.

Background briefing: the Eden Project

The Eden Project, brainchild of Tim Smit, opened in 2001. Its primary purpose is to educate people about the natural environment. Situated in Cornwall, UK, the main focus of the site is two huge biomes, or greenhouses – two of the largest in the world. The Humid Tropics biome, which is 200 metres long and 50 metres high is maintained at a constant 30º C, and is home to tens of thousands of tropical plants from South America, West Africa and Asia. In the Warm Temperate biome there are plants from the Mediterranean, California and South Africa. There are plans for a third Semi-Arid biome. The Eden Project attracts two million visitors every year. For more information about the Eden Project, go to the *English365* website: www.cambridge.org/elt/english365.

Before you listen

Get students to discuss this in pairs.

Answers

1 1 T 2 F 3 T 4 F 5 T
2 1 You can learn about the natural environment
   2 Think about the relationship between plants and people
   3 Money
   4 It has created jobs, tourism, and brought money to the local community; helped to rebuild an area badly damaged by industry; an educational benefit as well as a leisure resource
   5 He created the Eden Project.

Track 12.2 tapescript ▶▶|

INTERVIEWER: Chris, tell us what the Eden Project is about.
CHRIS: Well, it's in Cornwall, in the south-west of England, and basically it's a number of what we call biomes. Biomes are very big structures made of transparent hexagons on a steel framework. And inside these huge biomes we grow different kinds of plant, all kinds of plant from all over the world, from hot regions, mild temperate regions and cold regions. And we control the temperature and the amount of water in the air – the humidity – in each biome so that all these different kinds of plant can grow.
INTERVIEWER: So is it a theme park like Disneyland?

CHRIS: ② No, not at all. It's much more than that. The most important thing about the Eden Project is that you can learn about the natural environment. ①②

INTERVIEWER: So it has an educational objective.

CHRIS: Absolutely. One of the many good things about the Eden Project is that it makes people think about the relationship between plants and people. ②②

INTERVIEWER: So is it ecotourism?

CHRIS: Definitely, if we mean a form of tourism that increases our understanding of the natural environment. Yes, that's really very true for the Eden Project.

INTERVIEWER: Do you think there are any problems with the concept of ecotourism?

CHRIS: Well, in some ways, yes. At the Eden Project the number of visitors has been extraordinary, so there's the physical problem of traffic, cars, visitor numbers, that can be a ③ problem. But the real danger in ecotourism is if money becomes the priority, the most important thing. If visiting a natural environment, for example rainforests or special habitats like the Galapagos Islands, becomes all about money, that can damage the environment that really we want to protect. Yes, money's the biggest danger. ③②

INTERVIEWER: And what has the Eden Project done for the local community?

CHRIS: Well, there are lots of benefits. It has created jobs, tourism, ④② and brought money to the local community. It has helped to ⑤ rebuild an area which was badly damaged by industry. It's an educational benefit too as well as a leisure resource. So it's really good for the environment.

INTERVIEWER: Who first thought of the idea?

④ CHRIS: ⑤② The Eden Project is the vision of one man, Tim Smit. He thought of the Eden Project. He took a damaged industrial environment in Cornwall with a lot of economic problems. It had an old industry – clay mining – and a lot of people who didn't have jobs. He had a vision, an idea. He wanted to make a difference. The wonderful thing is he achieved that. He made a real difference, not only to this area but to everyone who comes here. I think we can all carry that idea, we can have a vision and we can all help to make a difference.

What do you think?

Have the students themselves contributed to the way their organisation works? Is this something any individual can do or does change have to be implemented from above?

The words you need ... to talk about the environment

1 Students can do this individually or in pairs. Check on pronunciation when you go through the answers.

Answers

1 c 2 h 3 b 4 a 5 e 6 f 7 d 8 g

2

Answers

1 fossil fuels   2 energy consumption, global warming
3 farming   4 pollution   5 infrastructure
6 the natural environment

Ask the whole class the questions quickly. They will have more time to talk about this in the next exercise.

It's time to talk

- Brainstorm things that people do to help the environment and then get students to look through the list and see how many of the things they had thought of. Help with any vocabulary, if necessary.
- Individually they can choose the things that they do, will do or won't do, before asking their partner. Ensure that students ask questions. For example: *Do you use public transport to get to work?*
- You could do a quick survey of what the students do already in order to find out who is the 'greenest' student.
- You may want to use the Extra classroom activity here (see pages 81 and 96).

What did we do today?

Check the Remember section quickly and remind students of the objectives of the lesson.

Follow up

Encourage students to:
1 write down phrases for getting directions
2 write down new vocabulary in their vocabulary books
3 write sentences about the environment.

13 Changing culture

What did we do last time?

Do a review of the last type 1 lesson (Unit 10). Remind students of what they worked on and do some quick revision as follows.

Describing work experience

Ask students to recall the main tenses we use to talk about past experiences and get them to give you examples. Then get them to talk about their recent experiences in pairs. Monitor for the correct use of the tenses. You could give them question prompts like:
What have you done this week?
What did you do last week?
What have you been doing recently?
Check the difference between *for, since* and *ago*.

Weak forms

Write questions and answers on the board or OHP like:
How long have you been in England?
For a few months.
Get students to underline the weak forms and then practise saying them in pairs.

On the agenda: Why are we doing this?

Tell students the objectives of this lesson:
- to discuss **future plans**
- to learn how to talk about **the future**: *will, going to* **and the present continuous**

- to practise **pronouncing contractions with pronouns and auxiliary verbs**.

Reinforce this by writing the key words on the board or OHP.

Warm up

- Ask the Warm-up question or get students to ask each other in pairs. You could also ask them what could be done to remedy this situation.
- Look at the headline and ask students what they think it means.
- Look at the pictures of Terje, Ingrid and Pierre and read the caption. Check understanding of *boardroom*.

Listen to this

Norway sets female quota for boardrooms

Explain that you are going to focus on ways of talking about the future and that first of all they are going to listen to Terje, Ingrid and Pierre talking about a new law in Norway and the effects they think it will have.

Answers

1 1 T 2 F 3 F 4 F 5 T
2 1 More women will mean better corporate leadership.
    2 Companies need time to find the right women.
    3 Less than 10%
    4 He doesn't think there are enough qualified women to fill a 40% quota.
    5 You can't make a cultural change quickly.

Track 13.1 tapescript ▶▶|

INTERVIEWER: According to the article in the newspaper, it seems that companies in Norway are going to fix quotas for women in management. They're planning to have 40% women at board level. What do you think about this, as a Norwegian, Terje?

TERJE: Well, I agree with the idea in principle. In a company with only men taking decisions, I think you miss opportunities. Women see things differently. So, for me, more women in top positions means better leadership for companies. And that's why we're introducing this change.

INTERVIEWER: Are you going to push this process in Norway immediately?

TERJE: No, we are going to run this process over a period of two years so that companies can manage things efficiently. They need the time to find enough good women, for one thing.

INTERVIEWER: Ingrid, what do you think?

INGRID: It's interesting. In fact, in my company we've been discussing equality recently and we're going to take some decisions later this month.

INTERVIEWER: Really? Well, I'll call you at the end of the month to find out what you've decided. Pierre, what are your thoughts?

PIERRE: Of course, I agree with the general objective. In France there are also very few women in top management. In the IT business, there are fewer than 10% women. I know Hewlett Packard is led by a woman but this is an exception.

INTERVIEWER: So where's the problem?

PIERRE: In France, we tried quotas with political parties and it didn't work. The parties were happier to pay fines and penalties than to try to have the right quotas. A quota is not a solution, believe me.

INTERVIEWER: Interesting. Is there going to be a penalty system with this, Terje?

TERJE: I'm not sure. I'll check and I can get back to you on that.

INTERVIEWER: Yes, I'd like to know.

INGRID: I think a quota is a good idea, because women can give another point of view at all levels of a company. So it's good to help women to get onto the boards of companies.

PIERRE: But there's another problem. I think 40% is too high. It'll create real recruitment problems for companies. It just isn't possible because we don't have enough women to take this 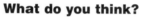 responsibility.

INGRID: There aren't enough women because men normally only recruit men because they know women have other responsibilities with the family. For me, the problem is one of culture and starts in the home.

TERJE: I agree. And I think Scandinavian countries are a little ahead of the rest of Europe. For example, when couples have a child, the man has the same amount of time off as the woman.

INGRID: Yes, the problem is that we need a change in the whole psychology of countries – a big change in culture – to see a long-term change in the position of women at work. You can't change a culture in six months.

What do you think?

You could get students to list the advantages and disadvantages of a quota system.

Check your grammar

Future 1: *will*, *going to* and the present continuous

Play track 13.1 again and ask students to note the different ways in which the speakers refer to the future and write them on the board or OHP. Try to elicit the different uses. Establish the three <u>main</u> ways of talking about the future.

1 and 2

Students can work through these exercises individually or in pairs. Give more examples if necessary. Students may have difficulty grasping the difference between *going to* and the present continuous. One simple and clear distinction is that we can use the present continuous for something we write in a diary.

Answers

1 1 <u>I'll call</u> you at the end of the month.
    2 <u>Are you going to</u> push this process in Norway immediately?
    3 <u>I'm seeing</u> our directors tomorrow.
    4 <u>I'll check</u> and I can get back to you on that.
    5 Companies in Norway <u>are going to</u> fix quotas for women in management.
    6 <u>We're introducing</u> this change next year.
2 *will* c   *going to* a   present continuous b

Do it yourself

Students can do all three exercises individually or in pairs.

Answers

1 *Suggested answers*
   1 Don't worry. I'll solve the problem immediately.
   2 Sorry, that's my phone ringing. I'll turn it off.
   3 I can't come to lunch with you. I'm going to do some training in the gym.
   4 You look stressed. I'll help you with that report, if you want.
   5 I'm flying to Brussels tomorrow at 8.55.
2 1 I'm going to watch 2 I'll do 3 I'm going to work
   4 I'm going to discuss 5 I'll do 6 I'll have
3 1 I'll help 2 am I presenting 3 I'll change
   4 Everyone is staying 5 I'll tell
   6 I'm going to send / I'm sending / I'll send
   7 I'll let 8 we're meeting
   9 I'm just going to finish / I'm just finishing
   10 I won't forget

Track 13.2 tapescript ▶▶

EMMA: Hi, Mark. It's Emma. Can you give me some details about the workshop next month?

MARK: OK. I'll help if I can.

EMMA: Well, firstly, according to the schedule, when am I presenting?

MARK: Your presentation is on Tuesday 8 September at 10 am. Is that OK?

EMMA: Wednesday at 10 would be better for me.

MARK: Fine. I'll change your time to the Wednesday. OK?

EMMA: Thanks. And what about hotel accommodation?

MARK: It's all arranged. Everyone is staying in the Manor. It was the cheapest.

EMMA: That's fine. I'll tell Rachel and Sam. They asked me this morning.

MARK: You can also tell them that I'm going to send everybody an information pack with the hotel details, probably at the end of next week, I'm not sure yet.

EMMA: OK, I'll let them know. In fact, we're meeting later today at 4 so I can tell them then, if I don't forget.

MARK: Right. So, any plans for the rest of the morning?

EMMA: Not really. I'm just going to finish a few reports and then it's lunch.

MARK: Sounds good. Thanks for your call. And don't forget to tell Rachel and Sam!

EMMA: Thanks, I won't forget. Bye.

MARK: Bye.

Sounds good

Contractions with pronouns and auxiliary verbs

1 Ask the students if they found the listening easy or difficult. Elicit that they may have found it difficult because of the use of contractions and that this is a very common feature of spoken English. Explain that the use of contractions in their own speech will help them to sound more fluent and that becoming familiar with contracted forms will help significantly with their understanding.

Answers

1 haven't 2 Didn't 3 don't 4 I'm 5 Don't 6 I'll

We use contractions, which generally have weak stress, in order to speak more fluently and so that we can place the main stress on other key words in the sentence.

Track 13.3 tapescript ▶▶

EMMA: I still haven't had the workshop schedule. Did you send it?

MARK: Yes. Didn't you receive it by email last week?

EMMA: No. I don't have any information and I'm a bit stressed.

MARK: Don't worry. I'll send you another schedule right now.

2

Answers and Track 13.4 tapescript ▶▶

Contracted forms in **bold**.

MARK: Hello, **I'm** calling to check you got the schedule. Have you got it?

EMMA: Yes, I have. **It's** here in my mailbox but I **can't** open it.

MARK: **I don't** understand.

EMMA: **It's** very strange. **I've** never had any problems with emails from you before.

MARK: Did you save the document first?

EMMA: Yes, I did. It **didn't** make any difference. Can you resend it?

MARK: OK, **I'll** send it again straightaway. Please phone me if it **doesn't** open.

EMMA: **Don't** worry. I will!

It's time to talk

- The objective here is to practise using the different ways of talking about the future, so make sure students are focused on this.
- Check the students are clear about their roles and give them a few minutes to prepare.
- Give feedback on their performance, with particular attention to their use of the future forms. If there is time, students could change roles.
- You may want to use the Extra classroom activity here (see pages 81 and 97).

What did we do today?

Check the Remember section quickly and remind students of the objectives of this lesson.

Follow up

Encourage students to write sentences about their future plans and intentions.

14 The customer is always right

What did we do last time?

Do a review of the last type 2 lesson (Unit 11). Remind students of what they worked on (see Teacher's notes for that unit) and do some quick revision as follows.

Talking about finance and investments
Write key words from the unit on pieces of paper and in pairs get students to test each other. One student looks at the word and gives a definition or synonym and the other has to say what the word is.

Asking for and giving opinions
Ask students to give you phrases for the following functions:
asking for opinions
giving opinions
agreeing
disagreeing.
In small groups, give topics for them to make statements about, for example: global warming, the government, the economy, etc.

On the agenda: Why are we doing this?

Tell students the objectives of this lesson:
- to talk about **customer satisfaction and customer service**
- to look at useful expressions for **telephoning – making and changing arrangements**.
Reinforce this by writing the key words on the board or OHP.

Warm up

Students can discuss this in pairs and write their ideas on the board or OHP.
Look at the pictures of Sam Walton and the store, read the caption and ask students what they know about Wal*Mart.

Read on

Ten foot attitude

Background briefing: Wal*Mart

Wal*Mart is a US discount retailer offering a wide variety of general merchandise. Wal*Mart stores have a range of departments including family clothing, health and beauty aids, household needs, electronics, toys, fabrics and crafts, lawn and garden, jewellery, shoes, a pharmacy, garden centre and snack bar or restaurant. The stores operate on an 'Every Day Low Price' philosophy and maintain their price structure through expense control. Wal*Mart Associates, i.e. employees, aim to provide exceptional customer service, and to make it a characteristic unique to the chain. Wal*Mart has recently made moves into other countries, and bought, for example, the Asda supermarket chain in the UK. For more information about Wal*Mart, go to the *English365* website: www.cambridge.org/elt/english365.

1 Give students a few minutes to read the paragraphs and set a time limit.

> **Answers**
>
> **1** 1 C 3 A 5 D 6 B
> **2** 1 Associates (This word gives the idea that the company values them as equal partners and as an important part of the company.)
>   2 Sheila who jumped in front of a car to stop a little boy from being hit, and Annette who gave up the toy she wanted for her own son so that a customer's son could have it for his birthday
>   3 The fact that associates show they are grateful to customers for their business
>   4 Whenever associates come within ten feet of customers, they should look the customer in the eye, greet them and ask if they need any help
>   5 At university, Sam Walton spoke to everyone near him and soon got to know more students than anyone else
>   6 It helps in ways that its customers want, for example, it gives help to local schools, hospitals and groups in need

What do you think?

You could ask students what their organisation's approach to customer service is. Do they have any guidelines that they have to follow?

The words you need ... to talk about customer service

1 Write their ideas on the board or OHP.

> **Answers**
>
> 'Service' occurs four times:
> extra service; the service was as simple as a smile; better service; customer service

2 and 3

Students can do these individually or in pairs. Check their pronunciation when you go through the answers. Get students to make sentences about their organisation using words from the exercises.

> **Answers**
>
> **2** great: exceptional, five star
>   poor: unsatisfactory, below standard
>   cheap: low cost
>   expensive: pricey, costly
>   rapid: fast, quick
>   individual: personal
> **3** 1 at your 2 offer 3 range 4 tailor 5 station 6 charge
>   7 agreement 8 sector 9 standards

It's time to talk

- Give students a few minutes to think about an experience that they would like to talk about before they interview each other.
- You may want to use the Extra classroom activity here (see page 82 and 98).

COMMUNICATING AT WORK

Telephoning 2: Making and changing arrangements

Explain that this part of the unit is about language for making and changing arrangements on the telephone and ask the whole class the question.

> **Answers**
>
> 1 Wednesday 10th May: Oakwood House, Smith Square at 10 am
> 2 Referring to last contact: I sent you an email about our meeting.
>   Suggesting a meeting: Can we meet next week sometime?
>   Fixing a time: What day would suit you?
>   Confirming: I'll send an email to confirm.

Track 14.1 tapescript ▶▶

CHAMINDA: Hello, I'd like to speak to Charlotte Bennett, please.

CHARLOTTE: Speaking. Hello.

CHAMINDA: Ms Bennett, good morning. My name's Chaminda Jay. I sent you an email about our meeting. Can we meet next week some time?

CHARLOTTE: Yes, that's right. What day would suit you?

CHAMINDA: Wednesday or Thursday, if possible. I'm in London till Thursday evening, so any time really.

CHARLOTTE: Well, we can meet here in my office at Oakwood House at 10 on Wednesday the tenth. Is that OK?

CHAMINDA: 10 am. Fine. Where is that exactly?

CHARLOTTE: Oakwood House is on Smith Square, and Smith Square is easy to get to.

CHAMINDA: That's fine. OK, I'll send an email to confirm, and a few ideas for our meeting.

CHARLOTTE: Very good. Thanks for calling. See you on Wednesday morning at 10.

CHAMINDA: Thanks. Bye.

3 and 4 You will need to pause the recording so students can write their answers.

> **Answers**
>
> 3 Problem: Charlotte can't make the meeting on Wednesday because she has to be out of the office all day.
>   Solution: They change the appointment to Thursday at 12 noon.
> 4 I've got a problem now
>   I have to be out of the office
>   the following day
>   is that all right with you
>   it's not a problem for you

Track 14.2 tapescript ▶▶

CHARLOTTE: Hello, is that Mr Jay?

CHAMINDA: Yes, speaking.

CHARLOTTE: Hello, it's Charlotte Bennett here. Thanks for your email, but unfortunately I've got a problem now.

CHAMINDA: Oh, what's that?

CHARLOTTE: I'm afraid I have to be out of the office all day on Wednesday. Could we meet the following day instead?

CHAMINDA: The day after? OK, that's no problem. What time would suit you?

CHARLOTTE: If we say Thursday morning, is that all right with you?

CHAMINDA: Yes, that's fine. 10 o'clock?

CHARLOTTE: A bit later, if you don't mind. Could we make it 12 o'clock?

CHAMINDA: That's OK. Same place?

CHARLOTTE: Yes, same place, Thursday the eleventh at 12 noon. And sorry about the change. I hope it's not a problem for you.

CHAMINDA: Not at all. Have a good week.

CHARLOTTE: OK, thanks very much. I'll email the new details.

CHAMINDA: Thanks. Bye for now.

5 Before doing this exercise, it might be a good idea to drill some of the key phrases. You could also build up a model dialogue on the board or OHP and get them to practise it in pairs.

What did we do today?

Check the Remember section quickly and remind students of the objectives of the lesson.

Follow up

Encourage students to:
1 write sentences about customer service in their organisation
2 write down key phrases for telephoning.

15 An interesting place to live

What did we do last time?

Do a review of the last type 3 lesson (Unit 12). Remind students of what they worked on (see Teacher's notes for that unit) and do some quick revision as follows.

Getting directions

Ask students for useful phrases for getting directions in a car, when trying to understand a map, when trying to find where something is and when getting round a big building.

The environment

Brainstorm useful vocabulary for talking about the environment and get students to talk about what they do to help protect the environment.

On the agenda: Why are we doing this?

Tell students the objectives of this lesson:
• to talk about **homes**
• to look at useful phrases for **visiting someone's home for dinner**
• to learn and practise **vocabulary for homes and houses.**
Reinforce this by writing the key words on the board or OHP.

Warm up

Ask students to describe the backdrop photo (what is it?) and briefly to answer the Warm-up questions. Check the meaning of *DIY*. You could build up a list of types of home on the board: *flat/apartment*, *detached house*, etc.

Visiting someone's home for dinner

Get students to describe the photos and say what they think the situation is in each one before doing the exercises.

Track 15.1 tapescript ▶▶❘
Welcome
A: Hello, nice to see you.
B: Thank you. I'm sorry we're a bit late.
A: No, not at all. Perfect timing. Let me take your coats.
B: Thank you.

Two small gifts
A: Did you have any problems finding us?
C: No, it was easy. Here, we've brought you some flowers.
A: Oh, that wasn't necessary – but they really are beautiful. Thank you very much.
C: And these. I hope you like chocolates.
A: Oh, that's very kind. In fact, we both love chocolate!

The home
C: What a beautiful house. Have you lived here long?
A: Yes, we've been here ten years now. It didn't look like this when we moved in!
C: It's beautiful. And you have some lovely photographs too.
A: Yes, Peter loves taking pictures. Do you like photography?

Saying goodbye
B: It's been a wonderful evening. Thank you for having us.
D: Not at all. It was our pleasure.
B: And the meal was delicious. Thank you so much.
D: Don't mention it. It was great to see you.

Have a go

Build a dialogue on the board as a model and check pronunciation.

Listen to this

Living in a windmill

Look at the picture, read the caption and ask the Before you listen questions. Ask if students can think of any other alternative places to live and what the good or bad points about living there might be.

Track 15.2 tapescript ▶▶❘
INTERVIEWER: Susanna, how did you find your windmill?
SUSANNA: I saw a photograph of it in the paper, about 15 or 16 years ago.
INTERVIEWER: Was it in a good state? Did you move in straightaway?
SUSANNA: It was possible to live in it but there was a lot of work to do, yes. The staircase was in, which was I suppose an important

thing, and the floors were in, but there was no heating and there was no modern kitchen or anything like that. And we had to have new windows put in.
INTERVIEWER: So did you do a lot of work yourself? Are you a DIY person?
SUSANNA: No, no, I can't even put a screw in the walls. We designed it ourselves but we got the builders to do the work.
INTERVIEWER: How many floors does it have? Can you describe it a little?
SUSANNA: It has five floors – ground floor and then first floor, second floor, third floor and fourth floor. And then it has a roof you can get on to. On the ground floor it's a round room and I think it's more than eight metres across. The top floor I think is about four metres across, so the rooms get smaller as you go up. So the walls aren't straight, and it's not just round but it's not straight either. It means we've got problems with hanging pictures, hanging curtains, putting up shelves, everything, it's very difficult.
INTERVIEWER: What's the best thing for you then about your home?
SUSANNA: I like where it is, the location. It's not in a village. It's a really nice spot. And I like it because it's different. We don't have to think a lot about furniture and all that because it already looks completely different.
INTERVIEWER: And what do other people think?
SUSANNA: Well, people like it, but not everyone likes sleeping at the top because the room is round and you can't find the door because the door's in the floor and that sort of thing. And if we have children sleeping over, they wake up in the night wanting to go to the loo, and you shut the door because you're frightened that they'll fall down the stairs, and then they can't get out. It's awful – like Rapunzel. Actually, my favourite fairy story was Rapunzel when I was young.
INTERVIEWER: But do your children like it?
SUSANNA: They love it. I think it was a joy from start to finish for the children.
INTERVIEWER: Do you have much land with the windmill?
SUSANNA: We bought a field next door, so we've got a field and the garden.
INTERVIEWER: And are there any disadvantages?
SUSANNA: The main one is that it's expensive because you have to have everything made to fit it. And the rooms are small because you know, with a round room, once you've put a bed and something else in a round room you've lost huge amounts of space.
INTERVIEWER: But basically it sounds wonderful. Susanna, thank you very much indeed.

What do you think?
Students can discuss these questions in pairs.

The words you need ... to talk about houses and homes

1 Ask students how many rooms they can name before looking at the list. You could also ask them to say what they do in each room. In pairs, they could then say what they do while their partner listens and then says the name of the room.

2 To consolidate these words, ask students to describe these features in their houses. A student could describe a feature in their house while the others listen and then say what it is. For example:

I keep my books on these. They are made of wood.

Answers

1 c 2 h 3 a 4 f 5 g 6 d 7 e 8 i 9 b

3 • Students could brainstorm different jobs before doing the exercise.
 • Ask the follow-up questions and supplement them by asking who does the different jobs in their home.

Answers

1 washing 2 washing-up 3 housework 4 ironing
5 put ... away 6 lay 7 clear 8 make 9 take 10 put out

It's time to talk

Get students to work individually at first so they can think of questions they can ask. The Student As could work in a group in this first stage, as can the Bs. Go round the class and help with any unfamiliar vocabulary.
You may want to use the Extra classroom activity here (see pages 82 and 99).

What did we do today?

Check the Remember section quickly and remind students of the objectives of the lesson.

Follow up

Encourage students to:
1 write a short description of their house
2 choose carefully which new words they would like to learn.

Extension

Time permitting, get students to work in pairs and describe their home to a partner. Their partner listens and draws a plan. Not only will this recycle a lot of vocabulary from this lesson, but it will also provide a good opportunity to practise listening and speaking.

Revision 1 Units 1–15

ANSWERS

Grammar

1 1 work, manages, provides
 2 am / 'm planning, is, are coming
 3 was just reversing, heard
 4 have / 've been writing, has just crashed
 5 have / 've worked, have / 've been working, is almost finished

2 1 Seville is hotter than Paris in summer.
 2 Bill Gates is the world's richest man.
 3 London is not as big as Tokyo.
 4 The 2002 World Cup was the worst ever.
 5 Wal*Mart has the biggest turnover of any retail business in the world.
 6 Yesterday I played squash but I played badly.
 7 My friend Sam plays squash better than I do.
 8 The weather in northern Spain is not as hot as in the south.

Pronunciation

1 1 ✓ ↑ Oh, really?
 2 ✓ ↑ Three? Only three?
 3 ✗ ↓ I'm sure.
 4 ✗ ↓ Is it?
 5 ✓ ↑ Oh, right.
 6 ✓ ↑ The Snowball? Fine.

Track R1.1 tapescript ▶▶

1 A: I saw a film yesterday.
 B: Oh, really?
2 A: There were only three people in the cinema.
 B: Three? Only three?
3 A: It was a really good film as well.
 B: I'm sure.
4 A: It's still on if you want to see it.
 B: Is it?
5 A: Or we could go somewhere else – go to a club?
 B: Oh, right.
6 A: What about the Snowball?
 B: The Snowball? Fine.

2 Where do you work?
 I work for a film company in Bristol.
 What do you do?
 I'm an editor.
 How long have you been working there?
 For about six years.
 How long have you lived in Bristol?
 For ten years.

Track R1.2 tapescript ▶▶

A: I saw a film yesterday.
B: Oh, really?
A: There were only three people in the cinema.
B: Three? Only three?
A: It was a really good film as well.
B: I'm sure.
A: It's still on if you want to see it.
B: Is it?
A: Or we could go somewhere else – go to a club?
B: Oh, right.
A: What about the Snowball?
B: The Snowball? Fine.

Business vocabulary

1 1 founded 2 produces 3 factories 4 turnover
5 worldwide 6 market share 7 organised 8 employs

2 1 g 2 c 3 e 4 i 5 d 6 a 7 b 8 f 9 h

Business communication

1 like to speak to
2 you through
3 could I speak
4 to leave a message
5 got a problem now
6 Could we meet
7 it's not a problem
8 ask him to phone

Social phrases

1 f 2 a 3 j 4 c 5 i 6 d 7 e 8 g 9 b 10 h

General vocabulary

1 culture, scenery
2 performance
3 travel
4 recycle
5 housework, washing-up
6 contemporary
7 bed and breakfast, hotel
8 wonderful
9 switch off
10 shelves

16 Taiwan – still a tiger

What did we do last time?

Do a review of the last type 1 lesson (Unit 13). Remind students of what they worked on (see Teacher's notes for that unit) and do some quick revision as follows.

The future

Ask students to tell you something about their future plans and check the difference between *going to* and the present continuous.

Give students prompts to elicit this use of *will*. For example:
It's too hot in here. Answer: *I'll open the window.*
I need the report. Answer: *I'll get it.*
You will probably need to demonstrate this to students so that they can get the idea.

Contractions

Write the following sentences on the board:
I will call you later.
We are very busy at the moment.
I am sorry.
I cannot open the file.
I do not know.
She has worked very hard this week.
It is a difficult problem.
Get students to mark on the contractions and practise saying the sentences correctly.

On the agenda: Why are we doing this?

Tell students the objectives of this lesson:
- to talk about **quantities** using different **quantifiers**
- to develop **pronunciation** – **linking**.

Reinforce this by writing the key words on the board or OHP.

Warm up

- Get students to discuss the questions in pairs. Compare answers for the whole class and write any examples of quantifiers on the board or OHP.
- Look at the picture of Vanessa and read the caption. Explain that they are going to hear her talking about her job and the Taiwanese economy.

Listen to this

Real competitive advantage

Answers

1 1 T 2 F 3 F 4 T 5 F
2 1 30%
  2 The hotel is in a banking district
  3 10%
  4 The US
  5 It keeps personal information on a database

Track 16.1 tapescript ▶▶|

INTERVIEWER: Vanessa, how much of your work in the hotel is with the corporate sector, big companies?

VANESSA: All my work is with the corporate sector. I'm responsible for corporate accounts. So I don't spend any time with tour groups or things like that. I should say that the job is quite important because most of our clients are businesses.

INTERVIEWER: How big is the hotel?

VANESSA: We have 350 rooms including 46 suites.

INTERVIEWER: 350? That's a lot. How many guests are from overseas? Quite a lot, I imagine.

VANESSA: Yes, the overseas market is extremely important to us. So about 30% of our guests come from Japan, 20% from the US and Canada, and just over 8% from Europe. About 40% are from Asia, meaning mostly Hong Kong, Malaysia and the Philippines.

INTERVIEWER: Do you have any guests from Singapore?

VANESSA: We have some people from Singapore, not so many.

INTERVIEWER: And are people mostly on business?

VANESSA: Just over 50% of the guests are corporate, about 30% individuals, and a small part is tour groups. We always have a little tour group business at the hotel. Also we do a few weddings most weeks and a lot of conference work.

INTERVIEWER: What kind of corporate clients do you have?

VANESSA: Well, in Taipei there's a lot of IT. For example, in Taipei there are large subsidiaries of Intel and Hewlett Packard, so a lot of people come from overseas for meetings here. Of course, in Taiwan the economy is very IT-based. But there's also some banking. In fact, in this district there are a lot of banks so the hotel gets lots of – you can say – banking business, because the banks are close.

INTERVIEWER: And how's business nowadays in Taiwan? Is Taiwan still a tiger economy?

VANESSA: Yes, I think so. As I said, the main industry sector here is IT and Taiwan produces 10% of the world's semiconductors. There are a few problems in the world economy but we have no big worries about business in the future. We're always optimistic. China, Japan and Hong Kong are very important economies for Taiwan. But the US is the biggest market. And with the American economy quite strong and the economy here going well, we're very confident and optimistic about business in the future.

INTERVIEWER: What's the most important attraction of the Sherwood Taipei hotel? Why should I stay there?

VANESSA: Well, firstly, we have the facilities people need, business services, like, for example, every room has a full internet service. And we have a gym, a spa and an indoor swimming pool. But the real difference in our business – the real competitive advantage – is in the great level of customer service we offer to each customer. We have excellent personnel training. No staff are allowed near guests until they're properly trained. And the other thing we offer is a very personalised service. So, for example, all guests have a personal profile on the hotel database. We keep a record of what people like, so when each guest returns to the hotel we know exactly how to keep him or her happy.

What do you think?

Quickly get an answer from each student about their organisation.

Check your grammar

Quantifiers

- Explain that you are now going to look at quantifiers. You may wish to write some examples on the board so that students know exactly what they are.
- Get them to look at Tapescript 16.1 and find other examples. They could also categorise them according to the amounts they refer to.
- Look at the examples and get students to answer the questions. Elicit other examples from the class.
- Read the note and also mention that we can use *any* in negative sentences. Give an example.

Answers

1 most / a lot of 2 a lot of / most 3 much 4 Most / A lot of
Most and *a lot of* combine with both plural countable and uncountable nouns.
5 a little 6 a few
A little combines with uncountable nouns.
7 any 8 no

Do it yourself

As you check the answers to all three exercises, ask students to explain why they have chosen that particular answer.

Answers

1 1 How many years have you lived here?
2 How much information do you have about Taiwan?
3 We only have a little information about our customers. We need more for our database.
4 We have many / a lot of things to talk about.
5 There are no / aren't any tourists here in the winter.
2 1 All 2 Each 3 many 4 Much 5 some 6 Most 7 a few
3 1 any / a lot of 2 many / all 3 a lot of / much
4 much / a lot of 5 many / a few

Test your partner

Students could also ask similar questions about each other's country or region.

Sounds good

Linking

You could begin by asking students what problems they have when listening to English speakers and what causes these problems. Guide them to the fact that linking often makes it more difficult because two or more words can sound like just one. Explain that this part of the lesson will not only help to improve their pronunciation but also their listening skills by raising their awareness of some of the features of fast speech.

1 You could write the dialogue on the board and mark the links clearly. You will probably need to demonstrate the pronunciation a few times for the students and drill them as a class before they practise in pairs.

Answers and Track 16.2 tapescript ▶▶

A: Shall we go and get some lunch? I need something to eat.
B: Sorry, I don't have a lot of time. I've got an important report to finish.
A: OK. Don't work too hard. I'll see if Jo's free for a little lunch.

2 Give students some other examples of each way of linking. Drill the sentences with the whole class and give time for students to practise alone for a few moments if they wish.

Answers and Track 16.3 tapescript ▶▶

1 Did it cost a lot of money?
　→　　→　　→
　　　/j/　/r/　　/r/
2 Shall I order a taxi for Anna?
　→　→　　　→　　　→
3 Do you need any help?
　→　　　　→
4 Did you have a nice evening?
　→　　　　　→
　　/j/　　/w/
5 Could I ask you a few questions?
　→→　　　　→
　　　/w/
6 Are you interested in art?
　→　　　　　→　→

It's time to talk

- Handle this in the normal way for File cards (see Introduction page 14).
- You may want to use the Extra classroom activity here (see pages 82 and 100).

What did we do today?

Check the Remember section quickly and remind students of the objectives of the lesson.

Follow up

Encourage students to:
1 write sentences about their organisation using quantifiers
2 practise their pronunciation; explain it is important to improve pronunciation outside the classroom, as well as in, and regular practice is the way to do this.

17 RoboDog

What did we do last time?

Do a review of the last type 2 lesson (Unit 14). Remind students of what they worked on (see Teacher's notes for that unit) and do a quick review as follows.

Customer service
Brainstorm vocabulary useful for talking about customer service and get students to make sentences about the customer service in their organisation.

Telephoning
Ask students to make complete sentences used for making and changing arrangements, using these key words:

meet (e.g. *Can we meet sometime next week?*)
suit (e.g. *What time would suit you?*)
confirm (e.g. *I'll send an email to confirm.*)
afraid (e.g. *I'm afraid I have to be out of the office all day on Wednesday.*)
instead (e.g. *Can we meet on Friday instead?*)
hope (e.g. *I hope it's not a problem for you.*)

They could practise making quick calls to make and then change an arrangement.

On the agenda: Why are we doing this?

Tell students the objectives of this lesson:
- to talk about **technology**
- to learn **vocabulary** connected with **technology and gadgets**; check understanding of *gadget*
- to practise writing emails – dealing with customer enquiries.

Reinforce this by writing the key words on the board or OHP.

Warm up

- Get students to describe the picture and quickly ask the questions. Write any suggestions about what it does on the board.
- Look at the photo of Nick and read the caption.

1 Set a time limit and see how many functions for RoboDog the students thought of in the Warm up.

Answers

Receive emails, play football, greet the kids, balance, understand its location, hear and see, make decisions, find its way around a house or office, do useful tasks, understand and act on up to 60 instructions

2

Answers

1 T 2 F 3 F 4 F 5 T 6 F

What do you think?

You could also get students to discuss other questions: How useful or necessary is this invention? Do they think it will become popular? Is there any other new technology they would prefer? What would they like to have done in the house?

The words you need ... to talk about technology and gadgets

Before doing the exercise, get students to look back at the reading text and quickly find some of the dog's technical features. For example: *It has an on-board camera.*
Explain that now you are going to look at words for talking about such features of new technology and gadgets.

1 Try to elicit possible questions about the specifications before completing the questions in the Student's Book.

Answers

1 colour 2 high/tall 3 long 4 wide 5 weigh 6 cost

2
- Get students to look at the picture of the camera and to describe it in as much detail as possible. Ask them to say what it might be able to do. Elicit possible questions they might ask about it before doing the exercise.
- Students could then practise asking and answering similar questions about a gadget or item that they own, for example, a laptop. Tell them that it does not matter about the exact dimensions and they should just focus on forming grammatically correct questions and answers. Selected pairs could then perform for the whole class while the others have to guess what is being discussed.

Answers

1 b 2 f 3 c 4 e 5 a 6 d

It's time to talk

- Explain that students are now going to ask and answer questions about the gadgets on the File cards and that they should use language from the previous exercises.
- Give them a few minutes to look at the information and prepare their questions. Help with any vocabulary while they are doing this.

- Students could change roles when they finish.
- You may want to use the Extra classroom activity here (see pages 82 and 101).

COMMUNICATING AT WORK

Emails 2: Handling customer enquiries

Ask students the questions. They could compare what their recent emails were about, for example, *asking for information*, etc.

1 Before they start, ask them to brainstorm possible reasons for sending emails. Elicit useful language that they looked at in Unit 8, for example, *opening and closing emails*. As you check the answers, help with any vocabulary problems.

> **Answers**
>
> 1 f, g 2 a, h 3 d, l 4 e, i 5 c, k 6 b, j

2

> **Answers**
>
> 1 e *or* i 2 k 3 d *or* f 4 a 5 c 6 b 7 g 8 d *or* f 9 l

3 Ensure that students write a full email and do not make it too short. If available, a computer or overhead projector may be useful for giving class feedback.

> **Model answers**
>
> Dear Sam,
> I'm sorry about the late delivery. This was due to a production problem. I can assure you that the goods will be ready for despatch on Monday. We are confident that you will have them by the end of the week.
> Best wishes,
>
> Dear Mr Amis,
> I would like to apologise for the wrong delivery. I can assure you that we will collect and replace the goods this week. Our courier will telephone you later today.
> Thank you for your understanding.
> Kind regards,
>
> Dear Susanna,
> We have good news about the production problem we told you about. I am pleased to tell you we have now resolved this, so everything is running normally again.
> Regards,

What did we do today?

Check the Remember section quickly and remind students of the objectives of this lesson.

Follow up

Encourage students to:
1 write sentences describing the specifications of gadgets or equipment they use
2 keep a record (or copies, if possible) of emails they write in English to show you and the rest of the class.

18 Learning styles

What did we do last time?

Do a review of the last type 3 lesson (Unit 15). Remind students of what they worked on (see Teacher's notes for that unit) and do some quick revision as follows.

Visiting someone's home for dinner
Ask students to give you complete phrases to:
welcome somebody
talk about gifts
comment on somebody's house
say goodbye.

Houses and homes
Ask them in which rooms they do the following:
cook
eat
watch TV
listen to music
keep the car.
You can also ask them for various household chores and who does them in their home (e.g. *doing the washing-up, making the beds, ironing, etc.*).

On the agenda: Why are we doing this?

Tell the students the objectives of this lesson:
- to practise useful phrases for **asking for and giving help**
- to practise vocabulary connected to **learning a language**.
Reinforce this by writing the key words on the board or OHP.

Warm up

You could also ask if students helped someone or asked for help in English and some of the phrases they used to do this.

Asking for and giving help

Get students to describe the photos and say what they think the situation or problem is in each one before doing the exercises.

> **Answers**
>
> 1 g 2 c 3 f 4 d 5 a 6 h 7 e 8 b

Track 18.1 tapescript ▶▶|
Technical problems

A: Excuse me. Can you help me? What does this mean exactly?
B: Let me see. OK, there's a technical problem with the network.
A: Sorry, I don't understand. Can I access the intranet?
B: Yes, you can. But you can't send emails or use the internet just now.

Lost or stolen?

A: Oh no! I think I've lost my bag.
B: How? Where did you last see it?
A: I put it down here, but now it's gone.
B: Oh dear. Shall I call the police?

Using equipment

A: I need to make a photocopy of this. Can I use this machine?
B: No problem. Do you know how to use it?
A: Could you show me how to do double-sided?
B: I'm not sure. I'll ask someone to show you.

Getting information

A: I can't remember Phil's phone number. Have you got it?
B: Sorry, I haven't. Cathy will probably know. Shall I give her a quick call?
A: No, it doesn't matter. I'll see her at lunch.
B: Are you sure? It's no problem.
A: No, it's OK. I'll see her later.

Have a go

- Build a dialogue on the board as a model and check pronunciation.
- Students could also invent other dialogues and perform them in front of the rest of the class. The class should listen and try to guess what the problem is.

Listen to this

Teaching people to learn

Look at the picture of Nicholas and read the caption. Ask the question and get students to discuss what makes a good learner.

> ### Answers
>
> **1** Thinking positively
> Different kinds of learners
> Working with companies
> Teaching memory techniques
> Good teachers
> **2** 1 Nicholas talks about people's lack of confidence about speaking in front of people – they say, 'I can't speak in front of 20 people'; and about learning languages, they say, 'I'm no good at languages.'
> 2 Students learn about themselves and their learning styles by doing this.
> 3 Microsoft has a visual culture; Marks & Spencer has a more practical culture.
> 4 It shows people how good their memory can be.
> 5 Learners, though teachers can help.

Track 18.2 tapescript ▶▶|

INTERVIEWER: Can you say something about how you help or teach people to learn?
NICHOLAS: Sure. We start with people's ideas about learning. Unfortunately, people often have very negative ideas. For example, they say 'I can't speak in front of 20 people,' or British people often say 'I'm no good at languages.' So we need to get people thinking positively about what they can achieve as a start to the learning process.
INTERVIEWER: And after that?
NICHOLAS: Stage two is to concentrate, to understand what you want to learn. And finally, the third stage, we look at the best techniques to learn it. So, those are the three processes, learning ideas, concentrate, and know the best techniques. Then you can become an effective learner.
INTERVIEWER: You talk about learning techniques. What do you mean?

NICHOLAS: People learn in different ways. So you have visual learners, and physical learners, people who want to do and touch things, and you have auditory learners, people who need to hear things, etc. And others. We help learners to understand their own learning style and so learn faster.
INTERVIEWER: How do you do that?
NICHOLAS: One exercise we have is to ask people to teach others something they are good at. This helps people to find out about themselves. So for example, a special skill, say cooking. Some people describe their kitchen and how everything is organised on tables, etc. They are visual thinkers. Others say, 'Right, I've got a carrot and I cut it up …' That's the physical type. So people learn about themselves with us.
INTERVIEWER: Interesting. And do you work with companies much?
NICHOLAS: Yes, and I find companies have different learning cultures. In Microsoft, people think with pictures. In fact, a lot of IT people are visual learners. Marks & Spencer's culture is more practical, it's about doing things. And companies have different ideas of failure. For some organisations, making mistakes is not an option. But mistakes can be good for learning. People who don't like making mistakes don't make good learners.
INTERVIEWER: Do you think you could help language learners?
NICHOLAS: I think so. Memory is important. So sometimes I teach them something like 50 Egyptian hieroglyphs in an hour with simple memory techniques and positive thinking. People think it's amazing. And why do we do that? It shows people how good their memory can be. Also things like mind maps which I use, these could be really good for vocabulary learning.
INTERVIEWER: But at the end of the day, is learning also about good teachers?
NICHOLAS: Yes and no. I tell my students that learning is not just about good teachers. Teachers help, but learners have to take responsibility for learning. Taking responsibility is really important. You have to understand how you learn, and how to stay motivated and to create learning space in your own life. It's really up to each individual to build a personal learning plan and use it over the long term.

What do you think?

What helps the students to learn faster? Is there anything that they would recommend to the rest of the class? How do they learn new words, for example?

The words you need ... for eating and drinking

1 When you check the answers it is worthwhile explaining the use of some of the 'wrong' answers: *skills*, *remind*, *translate*, etc. You may want to use Better learning activity 8 here (see pages 116 and 125).

> ### Answers
>
> 1 knowledge   2 remember   3 revise   4 translation
> 5 memory   6 mean   7 made   8 study

Test your partner

Students could also make up original sentences and do the same.

2 Encourage students to use English–English dictionaries while they do this individually or in pairs. Also check on their pronunciation.

It's time to talk

- Give students time to read through the plan and help with any vocabulary.
- To make this more interactive, you could get students to interview each other in order to create their learning plan. They could then discuss their learning plans in groups of four.
- Do quick feedback with the whole group by asking selected students about aspects of their plan.
- You may want to use the Extra classroom activity here (see pages 83 and 102).

What did we do today?

Check the Remember section quickly and remind students of the objectives of this lesson.

Follow up

Encourage students to:
1 record new vocabulary and phrases
2 stick to their learning plan.

19 Britain at work in 2010

What did we do last time?

Do a review of the last type 1 lesson (Unit 16). Remind students of what they worked on (see Teacher's notes for that unit) and do some quick revision as follows.

Quantifiers

Ask students which of the following quantifiers can be used with countable nouns and which with uncountable nouns: *all*, *most*, *many*, *much*, *a lot of*, *a few*, *a little*, *some*, *any*. Then get them to make sentences or questions about their organisation using these quantifiers.

Linking

Write the following sentences on the board and get students to identify the links:
We have a lot of visitors to our company.
I've been here for a few days.
I ate a little salad at lunchtime.
Get students to pronounce the sentences correctly and perhaps write their own.

On the agenda: Why are we doing this?

Tell students the objectives of this lesson:
- to talk about **predicting the future**
- to look at **future forms**: *will, can, may, might* **and the first conditional**
- to do some **pronunciation** work on **stressing syllables in sentences**.

Reinforce this by writing the key words on the board or OHP.

Warm up

- Look at the picture of Richard and read the caption.
- Look at the opinions and check understanding of *stressful* and *retire*.
- Get students to tick the ideas that they agree with.

Listen to this

Vision of the future

1

2 Give students a few minutes to read the questions. Check understanding of *self-employment*, *retirement* and *focus*.

Track 19.1 tapescript ▶▶|

INTERVIEWER: Richard, I've read your book with great interest. I'd like to discuss some of the ideas you write about. So, what's the future for Britain in 2010, starting first with the economy?

RICHARD: Well, I think the internet will be very important, more important than now. Through that we'll see many new connections across continents and we'll see lots more global trade. Also, and this is happening already, a lot of manufacturing activities from Britain, Europe and the United States will move to South East Asia, especially China. In Europe and the States, we'll see more focus on design and development, the activities which create real value in products and services.

INTERVIEWER: That's interesting. And what about work – how will our working lives change?

RICHARD: I think we'll see many changes. The first thing to say is that working life may become much more unstable for many people. It's very likely that large companies will no longer give us job security as in the past. If this happens, we'll see a lot more self-employment and people moving between companies to find new opportunities. But with lots more change, working life will become more stressful.

INTERVIEWER: What about home working? Do you think more people are going to work from home in the future?

RICHARD: Well, what we'll see is a redefinition of the workplace. The workplace will still be important, for developing ideas, for building teams, and so on. But if you have to write a report and do all the administration, you can do that at home. And I think this is really important because people travelling to work create big lifestyle problems with heavy traffic and pollution. It makes really good sense for people to stay at home more. Of course, you'll still have some workers, like shop staff and cleaners, who have to go to a workplace from 9 to 5. But I think if people get the opportunity – especially many office staff and managers – they will choose to work from home, perhaps up to 50% of their working time.

INTERVIEWER: We're living longer now. Do you think we'll work later in life?

RICHARD: No, I don't think people will work later in life, definitely not. As now, people will quit their jobs at around 55, as soon as they can. The pressure of work will make people retire – the stress factor again. And in the south of England, if the pension situation doesn't change enormously, we'll see people selling their houses to move to cheaper parts of the country as a way to pay for retirement. In fact, if it becomes easier to buy houses abroad, many people from Britain might actually emigrate to France or Spain. We see it now a little. And retirement will be different too. People will stop work in order to do things, to travel and generally enjoy life more.

INTERVIEWER: In the book you talk a little about enjoyment and pleasure in the future. Is that the future for us all, to enjoy life more?

RICHARD: It's an interesting point about western society. In 2010, in this new global situation, people may feel that they have no strong voice, no impact on politics. If this happens, people may adopt a 'live for today' lifestyle. They won't think about the future, they'll live for the moment. In 2010 the new focus in people's lives will be on personal life, on pleasure and enjoying what they can.

What do you think?

Get students to give examples of what a 'live for today' lifestyle might mean, before they discuss this. You could write suggestions on the board and they could then say which ones they might do themselves.

Check your grammar

Future 2: *will, can, may* and *might*

- Explain to students that you now want to look at the grammar forms that Richard uses to talk about the future.
- Get them to look at Tapescript 19.1 and find examples. They should find the following: *will*, *won't*, *might*, *may*. You can also ask how Richard often introduces his predictions: *I think*, *I don't think*.
- Look at the example sentences and get students to answer the questions.

Answers

1 Sentences a and c   2 Sentences b and d

The first conditional

- Get students to look through Tapescript 19.1 and find examples of the first conditional. Elicit the grammatical structure before looking at the Student's Book and then getting them to answer the questions.

- You could get students to give you their own examples.

Answers

1 *Will* expresses certainty that the action in the clause will happen.
Can expresses the idea of ability.
May and *might* both express the idea of possibility. Some grammar books state that *might* indicates that the speaker feels an action is more improbable than when using *may*. However, most native speakers indicate their expectation of probability by emphasising uncertainty with appropriate intonation and voice tone rather than through the selection of either *may* or *might*.
2 The present simple
3 *If* indicates that the action in the *if* clause is only a possibility.
When indicates that the action in the *when* clause is sure to happen.

Do it yourself

1

Answers

1 I'm sure we won't have any problems.
2 I'm not sure where Juan is. He may / might be in the canteen.
3 If we take more time, we might not make so many mistakes.
4 If you don't send me a new brochure, I can't place an order.
5 When I have time, I promise to send you the report.

2 Write other possible examples on the board to go through with students.
3 You could also get students to make their own examples about their lives.

Answers

In sentences 1 and 3 *when* is the most realistic choice. In the other sentences, both *if* and *when* are possible depending on the person's work–life context.

Possible answers

1 When I retire, I'll be able to travel more.
2 If my organisation offers me the chance to work abroad, I'll definitely go.
3 When I go home this evening, I may watch TV.
4 If my company moves to offices 150 kilometres from our current location, I might leave my job.
5 When I have to use English for my next meeting at work, I can try out some new expressions.
6 If I drive to work tomorrow, I might get stuck in heavy traffic.

Sounds good

Using stress when giving opinions

1 You might need to play track 19.2 more than once or repeat the sentences yourself with exaggerated stress. Get them to mark the stressed words – you can suggest ways of doing this: by highlighting, underlining, etc. In the answers below, the speakers stress the underlined words in the sentences.

SPEAKER 1: But if we cut marketing by <u>twenty</u> per cent, we can save <u>more</u> money.

SPEAKER 2: But if we cut <u>staff</u> by just <u>one</u> per cent, we can save even <u>more</u> money.

2 Play track 19.3 and get students to mark the stressed words.

Answers

1 SPEAKER 2: But if we increase salaries by <u>twenty</u> per cent, staff will be <u>very</u> happy.

2 SPEAKER 2: But if we invest <u>more</u>, we can increase <u>turnover</u>.

3 SPEAKER 2: But if we <u>keep</u> the party, staff will be <u>really motivated</u>.

4 SPEAKER 2: But if we <u>reduce</u> quality just a <u>little</u>, we can save <u>millions</u>.

Track 19.3 tapescript ▶▶|

1

SPEAKER 1: If we increase salaries by ten per cent, staff will be happy.

SPEAKER 2: But if we increase salaries by twenty per cent, staff will be very happy.

2

SPEAKER 1: If we invest less in sales training, we can reduce costs radically.

SPEAKER 2: But if we invest more, we can increase turnover.

3

SPEAKER 1: If we cancel the Christmas party, we can save thousands.

SPEAKER 2: But if we keep the party, staff will be really motivated.

4

SPEAKER 1: If we increase quality, we can increase our prices.

SPEAKER 2: But if we reduce quality just a little, we can save millions.

3 • Explain to students that they will complete some Speaker 2 sentences themselves and then read them to a partner. You could do the first example. Write the sentences on the board and discuss how you should stress Speaker 2's words. Ask a pair of students to model the process: the first student reads Speaker 1's opinion and the second student reads his/her own sentence using stress to indicate a different opinion.

SPEAKER 1: If we increase our prices by <u>twenty-five</u> per cent, we will increase turnover <u>significantly</u>.

SPEAKER 2: I'm not sure. I think if we increase our prices <u>so much</u>, we will <u>reduce</u> turnover.
(Because people will stop buying our products.)

or

SPEAKER 2: I'm not sure. I think if we <u>reduce</u> our prices by just <u>five</u> per cent, we can <u>really</u> improve turnover.
(Because so many more people will buy the product because it is cheaper.)

• Go round and monitor while pairs are doing this. First, check the sentences they have written. Then encourage them to listen carefully to each other so they hear the stress in their partner's sentences when reading their answers aloud.

• For the final activity, making sentences about their own organisation, you could ask students to prepare short dialogues in pairs. They then read out their examples and the other students have to identify the changes in stress which they hear.

It's time to talk

• Explain what students should do, get them to read through the predictions and help with the meaning of any unfamiliar words.

• Remind them of useful phrases when they are discussing if they agree with the predictions or not. For example:
I agree.
I'd go along with that.
I disagree, I think ...
I don't think that will happen. I think ...

• On the board, go through an example of how students can make first conditional sentences when they discuss the possible results of these predictions.

• Give students some time to think of their own predictions before they discuss them with a partner.

• Ask selected students to give you their predictions and the consequences.

• You may want to use the Extra classroom activity here (see pages 83 and 103).

What did we do today?

Check the Remember section quickly and remind students of the objectives of this lesson.

Follow up

Encourage students to:

1 write six predictions about the future

2 write the possible results of these predictions

3 practise using sentence stress to emphasise different points.

20 How the rich travel

What did we do last time?

Do a review of the last type 2 lesson (Unit 17). Remind students of what they worked on (see Teacher's notes for that unit) and do some quick revision as follows.

Technology and gadgets
Ask students to make questions about the following specifications:
dimensions
weight
colour
price.

Emails – dealing with customer enquiries
Get students to give you phrases for the following functions:
giving good news
giving bad news
giving assurances
saying sorry
giving reasons
expressing urgency.

On the agenda: Why are we doing this?
Tell students the objectives of this lesson:
- to talk about **selling and the sales process**
- to practise **leading a meeting**.
Reinforce this by writing the key words on the board or OHP.

Warm up
- Get students to list the advantages and disadvantages of working as a salesperson and perhaps ask them what kinds of tasks a salesperson performs.
- Then look at the picture of Sylvia and read the caption.

Read on

Selling jet travel for €8,000 an hour
1 • Get students to read the summaries and give them a time limit to complete the task as they should be reading for gist.
  • When they have finished, ask them what parts of the text helped them to decide on the best summary. Elicit the idea that very often the first sentence of a paragraph acts as a kind of summary or 'topic sentence'.

Answers

1 1 c
2 1 Paying by the hour for a jet aircraft to fly where you want
  2 If it helps you to win a big contract
  3 A game of golf and a dinner, or a gastronomic evening, with a short presentation to promote Flexjet
  4 A man wanted to get off at 7,000 metres because a fly stopped him from sleeping
  5 It was harder because Germans prefer not to show they have a lot of money
  6 A 'killer instinct' (to be completely focused on reaching your objective)

What do you think?
Ask the question and elicit answers. What would they like to sell? Do they have any tips for successful selling?

The words you need ... to talk about sales and selling

Explain that you are now going to look at some of the vocabulary associated with sales and selling. Get students to look through the reading text and look for related words. Check understanding of these.
1 • Check pronunciation and get students to test each other before they do the pairwork exercise, especially if you have a weaker class.

- It might also be worthwhile highlighting how we use the words, e.g. 'X is an up-market product', 'to do/carry out market research', etc., and eliciting example sentences.

Answers

1 b 2 c 3 h 4 a 5 g 6 d 7 f 8 i 9 e

2 You could also mention that two-part verbs tend to be more informal. After the exercise, get students to make their own sentences.

Answers

1 keep down 2 break into 3 come down 4 take off
5 look through 6 put up 7 give away 8 sold out

It's time to talk

- Give students a few moments to look through the questions and alternatives in the Sales quiz and go round and help with any vocabulary. Before they look at the answers, they could swap roles so that both students in the pair get to ask and answer the questions.
- Get some feedback from the whole class on who would make a good salesperson.
- Most people can be successful sales representatives. However, the quiz can reveal a lot about people's motivation.

Scores
Less than 13 points
People who mostly choose the second answers have a strong Win–Lose mentality which will stop them being successful in the longer term. If this was your score, change your ways!
13–16 points
People who mostly choose the first answers are strong on motivation and energy but not so strong on how business works. If this was your score, you need to develop more knowledge of business or you will be quickly frustrated by poor results. Good luck!
17–21 points
Bravo! People who mostly choose the third answers should do well. If you scored 17 or more you have clear thoughts about the selling process, the customer focus, and the balance necessary for success. Well done!

- You may want to use the Extra classroom activity here (see pages 83 and 104).

COMMUNICATING AT WORK

Meetings 2: Leading a meeting

- Start by doing some quick revision of the work you did in Unit 11 on giving opinions in meetings. Ask them for phrases you can use: *to ask for an opinion, to give an opinion, to agree* and *to disagree.*
- Ask the questions and brainstorm key vocabulary related to meetings: *chairperson, participants, agenda, items, action points,* etc.

1 Meeting 1

OBJECTIVE: To fix location and date of next sales workshop

DECISION: Greece; date to be agreed

Meeting 2

OBJECTIVE: To decide on colour for brochure

DECISION: Red

2 Meeting 1

Opening

Shall we get started?

Does everyone have a copy of the agenda?

We need to discuss ...

What do you think?

Controlling

Thanks for that.

So you want to ...

Closing

So we've decided to ...

Meeting 2

Controlling

Sorry to interrupt.

Can we let (Stefan) finish?

Closing

Can we agree to ...?

I think we can finish there.

Track 20.1 tapescript ▶▶

PAOLO: OK, shall we get started? Does everyone have a copy of the agenda? Yes? Good. Right, we need to discuss where and when we hold the next sales workshop. Stefan? What do you think?

STEFAN: I think we should go to the Athens office. Greece had a very good year and we should show that by travelling there.

PAOLO: OK, thanks for that. So you want to go to Greece. Julie? What's your view?

JULIE: I agree with Stefan. I know it might be expensive but I think our Greek colleagues have something to teach us. They had such a good year.

PAOLO: OK, I agree with you. Good, so we've decided to go to Greece. The next question is when. So can we …

Track 20.2 tapescript ▶▶

PAOLO: Right, now the last thing we need to decide. We just need a quick decision on which of these two colours to use for the new brochure, the red or the deep blue. Stefan? What are your thoughts?

STEFAN: Definitely the red. We've always had red as a basic colour in our promotional literature and advertising. I think we should stay with that, to be honest. No reason to change something that works. I think …

JULIE: That's just wrong. You can't say that. The blue design is much …

PAOLO: Sorry, Julie. Sorry to interrupt. Can we let Stefan finish?

STEFAN: OK, as I was saying, I think we have to focus on maintaining a clear brand image in the market. Our red window is a very well-known logo. I think it confuses our identity if we start changing the colours. Not now – it's not the right time. We should go for red.

PAOLO: Julie?

JULIE: I don't know. Maybe you're right. I just feel that we should be open to change and be ready to do something new in the market, to

make people sit up and say 'Wow'! But I can see I'm in a minority here. It was just a feeling. Red is good.

PAOLO: OK. Good. So, we've decided to go for red this time. I think it's a safe and sensible choice. But perhaps we can also all agree to look at this issue further for next year – maybe that's the time to make a change. Can we agree to that?

JULIE: OK.

STEFAN: OK.

PAOLO: Right. Thank you both very much. If there's nothing else, I think we can finish there.

3 Get students to discuss this in pairs.

Julie wants a new colour – blue – to make more impact in the market. The chairman handles the disagreement well, firstly, by politely stopping Julie's interruption and, secondly, by taking Julie's opinion into account for discussion in the future.

4 • Before doing this, drill key expressions and encourage students to use them. Make sure that they understand the exercise and be firm about them taking turns in leading the meeting: a potential problem is that more confident students could dominate the discussion. One possibility would be for students to present and lead a meeting to discuss their own work-related problem with the rest of the group.

• Give feedback on their performance.

What did we do today?

Check the Remember section quickly and remind students of the objectives of this lesson.

Follow up

Encourage students to:

1 write sentences about sales and selling

2 write down key expressions for meetings.

21 Great cinema

What did we do last time?

Do a review of the last type 3 lesson (Unit 18). Remind students of what they worked on (see Teacher's notes for that unit) and do some quick revision as follows.

Asking for and giving help

Ask students to brainstorm phrases that can be used to ask for help. Give them the following prompts:

technical problems

lost or stolen

using equipment

getting information.

Learning a language

Brainstorm useful vocabulary for talking about learning a language. Check the difference in meaning between *remind*, *remember*, *memory*, and *knowledge* and *skills*. Get them to make sentences. Ask for techniques that can be used to record vocabulary.

On the agenda: Why are we doing this?

Tell students the objectives of this lesson:
- to practise talking about **film and the cinema**
- to practise useful phrases for **making recommendations and giving advice.**

Reinforce this by writing the key words on the board or OHP.

Warm up

Ask the question and perhaps get students to draw up an itinerary for an evening out. Get them to look at the backdrop photo: can they identify the film? Do they like it? (It shows Clark Gable and Vivien Leigh in *Gone with the Wind*, 1939, directed by Victor Fleming.)

Recommendations and advice

Answers
1 f 2 c 3 h 4 a 5 j 6 i 7 e 8 b 9 d 10 g

Track 21.1 tapescript ▶▶

Suggesting entertainment

A: I have to take some clients out tonight. Any ideas?

B: There's a film festival on this week. I would take them to that.

A: That sounds interesting. I'll do that. Thanks.

B: It would be a good idea to book in advance. It's really popular.

A: OK. Thanks for the tip.

Recommending restaurants

A: I'm eating out tonight. Can you recommend a good Indian restaurant?

B: Yes, I can. I think the best one is the Bengali Palace on Coney Street.

A: OK, thanks. Any others? What do you think of the Mogul, near the river?

B: I'm not sure about that one. Sometimes it's almost empty.

A: OK, I'll try the other one. Thanks.

Giving advice about hotels

A: I'm going to Bonn in May. Do you think I need to book a hotel before I go?

B: I think so, yes. I think you should book somewhere on the internet.

A: OK, I'll do that.

B: But why don't you talk to our travel department first? I'm pretty sure they have some special deals with hotels in Bonn.

A: Good idea. I'll speak to them today. Thanks.

Shopping problems

A: I'm going shopping. Do you know anywhere which sells films on DVD with English and French subtitles?

B: Probably the best place to look is Waterstones. It's a bookshop in the city centre.

A: OK. Anywhere else?

B: I'm not sure. You might find something in the record shops as well. Try HMV or Virgin, for example.

A: OK, thanks. Could you write those down for me, please?

Have a go

Can students make dialogues recommending things to do in their town or city?

Listen to this

The big screen experience

Look at the picture of Clare, Anna and Ron and read the caption.

Before you listen

Get students to discuss the questions in pairs briefly. Write up kinds of films on the board, for example: *comedy*, *thriller*, *horror*, etc. You could also get students to talk about the last film they went to see. What was it? Who was in it? What was the plot? etc.

1 Check the meaning of *kill off* before students listen to track 21.2.

Answers
1 F 2 T 3 T 4 T 5 F

2 Get students to describe the still from *North by Northwest* (directed by Alfred Hitchcock, starring Cary Grant, 1959) and ask if any of them have seen it and what they know about it. Check understanding of *dubbing* and *subtitles*.

Answers
1 Nice films about relationships with happy endings
2 About 50 times
3 De Niro and Jack Nicholson
4 When you change the actors' voices by dubbing, you change the feel of the film
5 The big screen, the community atmosphere, the experience of going out and meeting friends for a drink

Track 21.2 tapescript ▶▶

INTERVIEWER: What kinds of film do you like? Clare?

CLARE: Well, I want to watch films that are entertaining. I need to be entertained. So I quite like most Hollywood films. I hate depressing films.

INTERVIEWER: What about you, Anna?

ANNA: I like to watch thrillers, especially psychological thrillers with a twist in the tail – you know, an ending which is a complete surprise. And things with Jean-Claude Van Damme, action films. And I hate nice films about relationships with happy endings.

INTERVIEWER: What about James Bond? Anna?

ANNA: James Bond? I like to watch them sometimes. I wouldn't go to the cinema to see one. They're a little bit predictable now. The plots are always the same. I suppose I'd watch one on video if I didn't have anything else to do, though.

INTERVIEWER: What about a favourite film of all time? Ron?

RON: For me, it has to be a classic Hitchcock film, maybe *North by Northwest* or *Psycho*.

ANNA: Yes, I like Hitchcock.

RON: I think I've seen *North by Northwest* about 50 times because we've got digital television and they keep showing it. But it's brilliant, great dialogue, and because it's that sort of

Technicolor, every frame looks fantastic, the colour is amazing.

INTERVIEWER: Have you got any favourite actors or actresses? Clare?

CLARE: I like watching De Niro. For me, he's maybe the best actor of our generation. And Jack Nicholson, of course, as well. He's really funny.

ANNA: I go more for the director. So I love Tarantino's films, for example.

RON: Do you? I hate all that violence. It's too much. It's not really my idea of entertainment.

ANNA: Yes, but Ron, gangster movies like *The Godfather*, it's classic cinema.

RON: Maybe for you. I prefer quieter films about more ordinary people. I watch a lot of French and Italian films, even though I don't speak French or Italian.

INTERVIEWER: Do you prefer subtitles or if the film is dubbed?

RON: Definitely subtitles.

ANNA: No, dubbed films. In Germany and Italy they do it very well.

RON: I don't like dubbing. I think it changes the feel of a film if you change the actors' voices. Subtitles are far better.

INTERVIEWER: So, how often do you all actually go to the cinema? Ron?

RON: Not much, maybe once a month. I get videos and DVDs now more than I go to the cinema.

INTERVIEWER: Really? And do you think videos or new movies on the internet will kill off cinema in the future?

RON: I'm not sure. Maybe.

CLARE: Oh, come on, Ron. No way. People said the same about television. But cinema is a different experience. I mean, just seeing it on the large screen is great.

INTERVIEWER: Do you think so?

CLARE: Definitely. You can't really compare it.

ANNA: I agree.

CLARE: It's a really different thing. There's something special about watching a film with other people in a sort of community atmosphere. And it's not just seeing the film; it's the going out and meeting your friends for a drink before and afterwards. Cinema is great and it's here to stay!

What do you think?

Ask the students if they download films from the internet, or if they would want to.

The words you need ... to talk about film and cinema

Get students to look at the stills and see if they can identify any of the films.

1 Can students add any films they know to the list? What films have been made in their country recently?

Answers

1 g   2 h   3 j   4 a   5 l   6 f   7 d   8 b   9 i   10 c   11 k   12 e

2 • Get students to complete the sentences and then check the answers by listening to Tapescript 21.3.
  • Ask them to make similar sentences of their own using some of the vocabulary, e.g. *plot, twists, cast, violent*, etc.
  • Perhaps tell students that some women prefer to be called *actors*.

• The picture is of Jack Nicholson in *The Shining*, directed by Stanley Kubrick, 1980.

Answers

1 actor   2 actress   3 entertaining   4 plot   5 plays   6 cast
7 character   8 directed   9 set   10 ending   11 violent
12 subtitles

Track 21.3 tapescript ▶▶

1 It was a great performance. Jack Nicholson is my favourite actor.
2 She's a real star. I think Meryl Streep is my favourite actress.
3 We had a great evening out. The film was really entertaining.
4 I saw a good thriller recently. The plot was a bit complicated but I enjoyed it.
5 Tom Cruise plays the role of a successful New York lawyer who learns that life is not as simple as he thought.
6 Go and see the latest Spielberg movie. It has a great cast – all the top names are in it.
7 I went to see *Taxi Driver* with some friends last night. The main character is played by Robert De Niro.
8 There's a festival of films directed by Kurosawa on at the local cinema this week. I've only seen *The Seven Samurai*. I'd like to see some of his others.
9 His new film is set in Japan in the year 2020.
10 It was a romantic film. It had the usual happy ending but it was quite moving.
11 It was so violent that I had to close my eyes on several occasions. I just couldn't watch what was happening on the screen.
12 The film was dubbed. I prefer subtitles so you can hear the original language.

It's time to talk

• Give time limits for this and think ahead about how to organise the class so that each student knows who they should interview.
• You may want to use the Extra classroom activity here (see pages 83 and 105).

What did we do today?

Check the Remember section quickly and remind students of the objectives of this lesson.

Follow up

Encourage students to:
1 keep a list of useful phrases for recommending and giving advice and for talking about film and cinema
2 write down new vocabulary in their vocabulary books.

22 Your personal brand image

What did we do last time?
Do a review of the last type 1 lesson (Unit 19). Remind students of what they worked on (see Teacher's notes for that unit) and do some quick revision as follows.

The future
Ask students for their predictions about the future. Get them to say what they think is certain and what is only possible. Then ask what the consequences might be. Remind them, if necessary, of the form of the first conditional. For example:
People will communicate via videophone.
If people communicate by videophone, they won't travel to meetings so often.
Review the difference between *when* and *if*.

Sentence stress
Write the following sentences on the board, say them and ask students to identify where the main stress falls and hence what is being emphasised. Then ask them to say the sentences in pairs, emphasising different key words to focus their meaning.
If we increase productivity, we will save money.
If profits don't increase, there will be job losses.

On the agenda: Why are we doing this?
Tell students the objectives of this lesson:
• to talk about **personal image**
• to look at *must, have to* and *need to*
• to practise **strong and weak stress with modal verbs**.
Reinforce this by writing the key words on the board or OHP.

Warm up
• Get students to look at the pictures and describe them before answering the questions. Ask them what kind of image they think they have. Is it something they think about? Does their company have any guidelines about image or a dress code?
• Look at the picture of Jenny and read the caption.

Listen to this

Image Counts
1 Check understanding of *etiquette* before playing track 22.1.

2

Track 22.1 tapescript ▶▶

INTERVIEWER: Jenny, what is Image Counts and what do you do?

JENNY: Well, I'm an image consultant and I work with people who want to change something about themselves – their image, in fact.

INTERVIEWER: And who are your clients?

JENNY: Well, they're mostly men and a lot of them seem to be 37 or 29 or 49! Many men think, 'I'm nearly 30 – or 40 or 50 – and I haven't got the right job or the right life.' That's when they pick up the phone.

INTERVIEWER: I see. So how do you help people?

JENNY: Well, I help people in three ways: firstly, with their appearance – the way they look; secondly, their voice – the way they talk; and finally, their behaviour – the way they are with other people, in a restaurant, and so on. I help people to brand themselves, to market themselves professionally.

INTERVIEWER: Is the voice important?

JENNY: The voice is very, very important, personally and professionally, and a lot of men do actually have quite a boring voice. I work with two voice coaches. One is called Doctor Voice. He goes all around the world with famous pop groups. OK, you don't have to become a pop star, but an interesting voice helps you in life, and it takes time to improve. You need to be patient.

INTERVIEWER: OK. And what about etiquette?

JENNY: Well, we develop 14 different kinds of etiquette: business etiquette, email etiquette, social etiquette, and so on. You don't need to learn everything immediately – people just choose the key things for them.

INTERVIEWER: And restaurant etiquette?

JENNY: Yes, if a company wants to make someone a director, they often take him or her to a restaurant. A director has to know how to behave and we help clients to pass the test. I had to do a lot of work with a client on this last week, in fact.

INTERVIEWER: Do you go into detail? Do you talk about how to hold a wine glass?

JENNY: Yes, and sometimes we explain that you mustn't butter bread like it's a picnic. And we look at language: things you must and mustn't say.

INTERVIEWER: And clothing?

JENNY: We talk a lot about what people mustn't wear, that's the important thing, to know what they mustn't wear.

INTERVIEWER: Do you brief clients on working internationally?

JENNY: Yes, I have experts for this. Like you absolutely mustn't write on someone's business card and you shouldn't put it in your back pocket, that sort of thing.

INTERVIEWER: What about body language?

JENNY: I think the most important thing to begin with is shaking hands. I always, always teach everybody how to shake hands and almost nobody knows how to do it.

INTERVIEWER: So can you tell us one or two golden rules?

JENNY: Oh, I've got lots! I must show you the brochure which has our golden rules. But first, what's really important … well, I constantly say to our clients you really must listen to people better, try to listen more than you talk. And another basic one – you need to be nice to look at. That always makes people think 'Ah that's such a nice person.'

What do you think?

You could also ask students if they already follow Jenny's advice. What do they do with business cards? What is the best way to shake hands? How much time do they spend on their appearance?

Check your grammar

Must, have to and *need to*

- Ask students to recall any sentences from the interview with *must, mustn't, have to, need to* and *don't need to*. If this proves difficult, get them to look through Tapescript 22.1 for examples.
- Elicit the meaning of the different modal verbs before checking with the examples in the Student's Book, completing the sentences and answering the questions.
- You might want to give extra examples for these, especially for the difference between *must* and *have to*. For example:
  I want to lose weight. I must do more exercise.
  My doctor told me to lose weight. I have to do more exercise.

Answers

1 must   2 have to, need to
3 don't have to, don't need to / needn't   4 mustn't
With *mustn't*, the speaker expresses the idea that he/she opposes the person going to the meeting OR that it is forbidden for the person to go to the meeting.
With *doesn't have to*, the speaker expresses the idea that it is not necessary for the person to go to the meeting.
The past of *must* and *have to* is *had to*.

Do it yourself

After doing the exercises, students could make sentences about the rules or guidelines in their organisations.

Answers

1 1 I really must stop smoking.
2 Do you have to go to the meeting tomorrow?
3 She doesn't have to go to the meeting if she doesn't want to.
4 Did you have to take a later plane yesterday because of the delay?
5 We don't have to work late on Friday after all.
2 1 don't have to 2 must 3 have to 4 have to 5 have to
6 doesn't have to 7 didn't have to   8 had to
3 1 mustn't 2 don't have to, need to 3 mustn't, need to
4 mustn't 5 don't have to 6 don't have to, need to
7 mustn't 8 don't have to

Sounds good

Strong and weak stress with modal verbs

1 You might need to play the recording more than once or demonstrate the examples yourself.

Answers

In the second sentence the speaker uses *really* and stresses *should*; stressing the modal gives it more urgency.

Track 22.2 tapescript ▶▶|

1 I think you should go to the meeting, not the workshop.
2 I think you really should go to the meeting, not the workshop.

2 Ask the students why the modal verb has been stressed. Elicit that this stress changes the focus of the sentence and highlights the importance of the modal verb.

Answers

1 A: W, B: S   2 A: W, B: S   3 A: S, B: W   4 A: W, B: S

Track 22.3 tapescript ▶▶|

1 A: Our organisation can help people to develop themselves and their careers.
   B: Believe me. Our organisation *can* help people.
2 A: You shouldn't use your car. Use a company car.
   B: I didn't say it's illegal to use your car but you really *shouldn't*.
3 A: Some people don't want to accept criticism. But they *must* if they want to mprove.
   B: People must accept criticism every day they are with us.
4 A: You mustn't forget that there are only three golden rules to learn.
   B: I didn't say you shouldn't forget. I said you *mustn't* forget.

3 Students could use the sentences they made in Do it yourself above for this.

It's time to talk

- Get students to do this activity with a new partner.
- Encourage them to ask and answer questions, rather than just show each other what they have written.
- When students come to give each other advice, write prompts on the board, for example:
  I think you should …
  You could …
  Why don't you … ?
- You may want to use the Extra classroom activity here (see pages 83 and 106).

What did we do today?

Check the Remember section quickly and remind students of the objectives of the lesson.

Follow up

Encourage students to write sentences about what they have to and don't have to do at work, etc.

23 Managing people

What did we do last time?

Do a review of the last type 2 lesson (Unit 20). Remind students of what they worked on and do some quick revision as follows.

Sales and selling vocabulary

Ask students to brainstorm different words connected with sales and selling. If necessary, ask prompting questions, like:
How can you describe exclusive, high quality products?
What is the name for money paid to sales representatives for sales made?
Aim to elicit words like: *up-market, commission, mailing, sales forecast,* etc.
Can students think of two-part verbs that mean: *enter the market, increase a lot, read,* etc.?

Leading a meeting

Ask students to give you phrases to:
open a meeting
control a meeting
close a meeting.

On the agenda: Why are we doing this?

Tell students the objectives of this lesson:
- to talk about **human resources**
- to learn vocabulary for **managing people**
- to practise **writing emails – making travel arrangements.**
Reinforce this by writing the key words on the board or OHP.

Warm up

- Check understanding of the vocabulary before students do the task.
- Write a list of HR activities on the board.
- Look at the photo of Anke and read the caption.
- Ask students to describe the appraisal photo. What do they think is happening?

Read on

We listen to what they say

1 Give students a time limit for this activity. They should see how many of the activities on the board are mentioned in the text.

Answers

HR activities: attracting, developing and keeping the best people; recruitment; staff development; negotiating with works councils and unions on working conditions and salaries; pensions planning; company strategy; staff appraisal; downsizing; expatriation

2

Answers

1 Laying people off or downsizing
2 A system of monitoring employees' performance at work by interviewing them
3 Two-way communication, to listen to employees
4 Staff moving abroad to work
5 Because of relationship problems, especially if the employee's partner is unhappy
6 Women like the personal aspects and the communication

What do you think?

Get students to summarise in their own words what Anke says about women at work before they answer the question. They could also tell a partner their experiences of their appraisal system.

The words you need ... to talk about managing people

1 Check pronunciation of the words when you go through the answers. Ask students to make sentences about their organisation using the words. You could also ask what staff development activities are offered by their organisation. Do they think there is enough? What would they like to see introduced? Check understanding of *works council*, which also occurs in the File cards.

Answers

1 e 2 h 3 g 4 f 5 i 6 c 7 d 8 a 9 j 10 b

2

Answers

1 lay off 2 unemployment 3 early retirement
4 voluntary redundancy 5 recruit 6 development
7 skills 8 training 9 trade unions 10 works councils
11 policies

It's time to talk

- Set the scene and explain what the students have to do.
- Before they begin, get them to recall useful expressions for giving opinions and making recommendations and give them time to prepare their strategy.
- You may want to use the Extra classroom activity here (see pages 83 and 107).

COMMUNICATING AT WORK

Emails 3: Making travel arrangements

Explain that you are going to look at useful language for making travel arrangements by email and that even if they don't make the arrangements themselves at the moment, they might have to in the future!

1 First, elicit the kind of things you might have to write in an email when making travel arrangements.

Answers

1 h 2 f 3 g 4 d 5 a 6 c 7 i 8 e 9 b

2 Ask checking questions to guide students through the email. For example:
What time is the flight?
What time does it arrive?

Model emails

Dear Get There Travel,
Please book three flights from London Heathrow to Budapest on 14 March. Dep. 10.00, arr. 12.30. Names Anthony Bowden, Ingrid Kepper, (*your name*). Return 15 March. Dep. Budapest 14.00.

Thank you.

Hello Janina,
Anthony, Ingrid and I will arrive on March 14 at 12.30 at Budapest Airport. Flight No. CR1663. Please arrange for a car to meet us.

Thanks. See you soon.

Dear Hotel Ibis,
My colleague Anthony Bowden booked three single rooms for the night of 15 March in your hotel. Please change the reservation to 14 March, for one night only.
Sorry for any inconvenience. Thank you.

Best wishes,

Dear Ingrid,
Here are details for the Budapest trip.
LHR – Budapest 14 March Dep. 10.00, arr. 12.30
Return 15 March Dep. Budapest 14.00
Hotel Ibis, Budapest, 14 March (same hotel as last time)
See you soon,

What did we do today?
Check the Remember section quickly and remind students of the objectives of this lesson.

Follow up
Encourage students to:
1 keep a record of useful vocabulary to talk about managing people
2 keep examples of their emails about travel arrangements to show you and the rest of the class.

24 Social issues

What did we do last time?
Do a review of the last type 3 lesson (Unit 21). Remind students of what they worked on (see Teacher's notes for that unit) and do some quick revision as follows.

Making recommendations and giving advice
Ask students to make useful phrases for the following situations:
suggesting entertainment
recommending restaurants
giving advice about hotels
giving advice on shopping.

Film and cinema
Get students to talk about a film they have seen recently, using at least three of the following words:
set, plays, character, violent, ending, thriller, cast, entertaining, directed, actor, fantasy.
For example:
I recently saw Buffalo Soldiers. *It is* set *in Germany, on a US army base. Joaquim Phoenix* plays *the main* character. *Parts of it are quite* violent *but it has a good* ending.

On the agenda: Why are we doing this?
Tell students the objectives of this lesson:
• to learn and practise useful vocabulary for talking about **social problems and solutions**
• to practise useful phrases for **receiving international colleagues**.
Reinforce this by writing the key words on the board or OHP.

Warm up
• Ask the questions. What do students show their visitors?
• Ask the students to describe the photos and get them to say what they think is happening in each one.

Receiving international colleagues

Answers
1 g 2 j 3 i 4 h 5 a 6 c 7 b 8 e 9 d 10 f

Track 24.1 tapescript ▶▶
Welcome
A: Welcome to head office. We hope you enjoy your stay.
B: Thanks a lot. I'm really looking forward to working with you.
A: Did you have a good trip? Was everything OK?
B: Yes, it was fine, thanks. No problems at all.

Security
A: OK, we need to do a couple of things first. You need to fill in your details here.
B: Fine. Shall I do that now?
A: Yes, please. And you have to wear this badge all the time.
B: Do I give it back when I finish in the evening?
A: No, you can keep it until you leave.

Work space
A: So this is your office. I hope you don't mind sharing.
B: Not at all. I'm used to it!
A: Fine. And you can use this computer. It's connected to the internet.
B: Thanks. Do I need a password?
A: Yes, just type 'visitor' for user name and password.
B: And how about the phone?
A: You just press 1 for an outside line.

Outside work
A: And this is my home number, just in case you need anything in the evening.
B: Oh, I wouldn't disturb you at home.
A: No, really, feel free. You can always reach me at home or on my mobile.
B: That's very kind. I hope I won't have to.
A: Well, I think that's everything.
B: Thanks. Everything is very clear.

Have a go

Can students role-play other situations involving talking to visitors?

Listen to this

Social issues in Britain

- Get students to describe the photos.
- Look at the pictures of Rajid, Bill, Mary, Maurice and Joyce and explain that the students are going to hear these people talking about social issues they think are important in Britain today.

Before you listen

Check understanding of these words. Can students tell you more about the problems?

> **Answers**
>
> **1** 1 d 2 c 3 e 4 a 5 b
> **2** 1 Football 2 More jobs and more money 3 Three million
> 4 Better education, more hi-tech industries
> 5 Incredibly high 6 Houses and flats people can afford
> 7 At weekends 8 More police, more black police
> 9 Single parent families and divorce
> 10 More tax for the rich, more spending on the poor

Track 24.2 tapescript ▶▶|

Rajid

INTERVIEWER: Rajid, what do you think is the biggest social problem in Britain today?

RAJID: Britain is supposed to be a multi-ethnic society but I think racism is still a huge problem. We just don't get treated the same. It's more difficult for non-whites to get jobs, to do well at school. There's still an incredible amount of racism in football. Politicians talk a lot about racism but they don't do anything about it really.

INTERVIEWER: And what's the answer to the problem?

RAJID: Maybe if we had more jobs and more money in Bradford, things would be better and there would be fewer problems.

Bill

INTERVIEWER: Bill, what, for you, is the biggest social problem in Britain today?

BILL: Well, if you'd asked me that question 20 years ago – in the eighties, say, I would have said unemployment straightaway. We had three million people unemployed then. Today it's much better but jobs are still a big problem. Far too many jobs today are low paid, part-time jobs in service industries – cleaning, hotels, fast food, things like that.

INTERVIEWER: And what's the answer?

BILL: We need better education, a better educated workforce. And more hi-tech industries – that's the way ahead economically.

Mary

INTERVIEWER: Mary, what's your view on the biggest social problem in Britain today?

MARY: The thing I worry about most is homelessness. House prices are so incredibly high. It can be a real problem for young people. If they've got problems at home and have to move away from their family, there's sometimes nowhere for them to go, there's nowhere they can afford, and some of them end up sleeping on the streets begging. And it can be a real problem for people who lose their jobs too – they often can't pay for their homes and then they have nowhere to go either.

INTERVIEWER: And what do you think the answer to this problem is?

MARY: I think the government has to build houses and flats that ordinary people can afford – a reasonable price or a reasonable rent.

Maurice

INTERVIEWER: Maurice, in your opinion, what's the biggest social problem in Britain today?

MAURICE: Personal safety definitely. It's definitely not safe on the streets at nights, especially at the weekends. There's too much violence, so much aggression sometimes. Every day you read about something in the papers, someone got attacked, and there's more knives and guns. And hooliganism and vandalism – at least where I come from.

INTERVIEWER: And what's the answer to the problem?

MAURICE: I know a lot of people who say the police are the problem but for me the answer is more police, definitely. More police and more black policemen.

Joyce

INTERVIEWER: Joyce, tell me what you think is the biggest social problem in Britain today.

JOYCE: All our problems come from poverty, from social deprivation, people not having enough to live on. We have so many children living in poverty because they're in single parent families, and they're living in poverty because there's so much divorce. And the rich are getting richer and the poor are getting poorer.

INTERVIEWER: And what's the answer?

JOYCE: Britain's a very rich country and we need more equal distribution of the country's wealth. More tax for the rich and more spending on the poor, I think.

What do you think?

Write any other problems on the board or OHP. Can students elaborate on the problems? What are the possible causes and solutions?

The words you need ... to talk about social problems and solutions

1 Get students to say whether these are problems in their country too, and how serious they are.

> **Answers**
>
> **1** 1 unemployment 2 street crime 3 ethnic violence
> 4 homelessness 5 begging 6 poverty 7 car theft
> 8 football hooliganism
> **2** 1 improve 2 better 3 conflict 4 solve 5 make
> 6 worse 7 solution
> **3** Can students suggest any other possible solutions?

> **Answers**
>
> 1 e 2 d 3 f 4 a 5 c 6 b

It's time to talk

- Give students a few minutes to look at their File card.
- Ask them to look at the Remember section for useful language for making suggestions.
- Encourage them to suggest solutions of their own.
- You may want to use the Extra classroom activity here (see pages 84 and 108).

What did we do today?

Check the Remember section quickly and remind students of the objectives of the lesson.

Follow up

Encourage students to:
1 write down key phrases for welcoming visitors
2 write sentences describing social problems in their country.

25 The coffee business

What did we do last time?

Do a review of the last type 3 lesson (Unit 22). Remind students of what they worked on (see Teacher's notes for that unit) and do some quick revision as follows.

Must, have to *and* need to

What advice would students give to someone starting work for their organisation? Get them to use *must*, *have to*, *need to*, *don't have to* and *mustn't*. For example:
You need to dress smartly.

Strong and weak stress with modal verbs

Say these sentences twice, stressing the modal verb and then the underlined word. Elicit the fact that it alters the focus of the sentence and then get students to practise saying them.
You shouldn't make private telephone calls.
You must be on time for the meeting tomorrow.
We can help you with any problems.
You mustn't forget that the customer is always right.

On the agenda: Why are we doing this?

Tell students the objectives of this lesson:
- to talk about **possibilities**
- to look at the **second conditional**
- to do some **pronunciation** work on **silent letters and difficult words**.

Reinforce this by writing the key words on the board or OHP.

Warm up

- Also ask them what measures organisations can take to be ethical. What does it actually mean in practice?
- Look at the picture of Arnauld and read the caption.
- Explain that students are going to listen to him talking about the coffee business.

Listen to this

Douwe Egberts – coffee producer and seller

Get students to describe the photos.

Answers

1 1 F 2 T 3 T 4 F 5 F
2 1 Receiving the correct data
   2 The price would rise
   3 It guarantees enough production, more producers means more coffee
   4 By paying market or higher prices
   5 Because they don't publish or communicate the fact that they work ethically

Track 25.1 tapescript ▶▶

INTERVIEWER: So, Arnauld, who do you work for?

ARNAULD: I work for Douwe Egberts in Paris as a financial controller. My main responsibility is to set budgets, to prepare and then update them and to explain results, for the company in general.

INTERVIEWER: Do you have a lot of contact with other departments to get figures?

ARNAULD: Yes, communicating with other departments is important in my job. But the biggest problem or challenge I have is receiving the correct data. I can then set a realistic budget. Business units have to give me figures on their sales for the next three years, to give me a forecast. To be honest, it's very difficult for them to estimate accurately the level of sales. It's not a precise science. If we were able to see into the future, life would be a lot easier.

INTERVIEWER: The market for coffee at the moment – is it tough?

ARNAULD: The global coffee situation is good for us. Production worldwide is still over the level of consumption, so the price of coffee is fairly stable, cheap in fact. That's very good for our company, as we have about 10% oversupply.

INTERVIEWER: What would happen if demand were greater than supply? Or, if world coffee stocks decreased?

ARNAULD: It's clear, if stocks decreased or demand were greater than supply for whatever reason, the price would increase, I don't know how much, but sure, our margin would decrease. It's very difficult to pass on any price increases to the consumer. You have to take care of market share.

INTERVIEWER: What about coffee production, the coffee producers?

ARNAULD: Coffee production depends on the weather. When it's bad, it can cause damage. But that hasn't happened for three or four years. What's new in the market is the arrival of a new producer, Vietnam.

INTERVIEWER: Vietnam – really?

ARNAULD: Yes, and now they've climbed their way up to be one of the five biggest producers of coffee in the world. This is good for us: it guarantees enough production – more producers means more coffee. It's good for us but not for the coffee producers because it won't help the price to go higher. But at Douwe Egberts we also have to take care of the coffee producers. It's an ethical question for companies to think about developing countries. They should do something.

INTERVIEWER: Does Douwe Egberts really take this ethical question seriously?

ARNAULD: Absolutely. They've decided not to communicate this – what they are doing or what they've done – but they do a lot to take care of … to help producers.

INTERVIEWER: So if the prices totally crashed at some point in the future, would Douwe Egberts help coffee producers by continuing to pay a normal price to producers, to pay above the market price?

ARNAULD: Definitely, yes, we would. We would pay above the market price in some situations. We'd try to support producers through any big crisis. No doubt.

INTERVIEWER: It's good to hear about a company with an ethical attitude.

ARNAULD: Yes, but I think there's a trend. Each big American company is beginning to do something in this area, to be ethical, to be more responsible. Many companies I know have a policy in place.

INTERVIEWER: When you said this, I thought it was just public relations, customer psychology.

ARNAULD: No, it's not 'just public relations' because these companies don't really communicate it. They don't publish information about it or anything. So I really think they just do it out of a feeling of ethical responsibility, which is good.

INTERVIEWER: Absolutely.

What do you think?

What should companies do? Do students know of any examples of ethical policies adopted by companies? Is this something that should be left to companies or should governments intervene?

Check your grammar

The second conditional

Answers

1 The first conditional suggests that the idea in the *if* clause is possible.
The second conditional suggests that the idea in the *if* clause is less likely.
2 The past simple
3 *would* indicates certainty: (if A, then B is sure)
could indicates ability: (if A, then someone/something is able to do B)
might indicates possibility: (if A, then B is possible)

Do it yourself

1

Answers

1 If we increased her salary, she would be more motivated.
2 If we did that, we would meet the target.
3 If we changed our office around a little, people could work more efficiently.
4 If we decreased our prices, I think it would start a price war.
5 Would you work on Saturday if we gave you next Monday off as a holiday?

2 Check understanding of the vocabulary before doing the exercise.

Model answers and Track 25.2 tapescript ▶▶|

1 If we banned motor cars in major cities, we would reduce urban pollution significantly.
2 If we introduced a 35-hour working week, employees could create a real work–life balance.
3 Companies would be able to find qualified people more easily if we had a better education system.
4 If we made criminals wear microchips, we could stop a lot of crime.
5 If we had to give 2% of our income to developing countries, we would reduce poverty significantly.
6 Our staff would be much healthier if they did 30 minutes of regular exercise every day.
7 If we worried less about money and material possessions, we might be happier.
8 If politicians listened to the people, the world would be a much better place.

3 Can students think of their own sentences to talk about improving working conditions in their companies?

Answers

1 pay   2 did   3 will   4 would   5 will   6 created
The man uses the first conditional to suggest that the ideas are possible. The woman uses the second conditional to make them seem less likely, and to communicate her disagreement with the man's ideas.

Track 25.3 tapescript ▶▶|

1
A: If we pay for staff membership of the local fitness centre, everyone can take some regular exercise.
B: Yes, but if we did that, it'd cost a lot of money.

2
A: If we offer better quality food in the canteen, people will eat more healthily.
B: Yes, but if we offered better quality food at lunchtime, it would have little impact on their general diet.

3
A: If we create more open spaces, people will feel less stressed.
B: Yes, but if we created more open spaces, we wouldn't have enough room for all our employees.

Sounds good

Silent letters and difficult words

1 Check understanding of the words before doing the exercise and encourage students to say why the words are difficult, for example *would* because we don't pronounce the 'l'.

Track 25.4 tapescript ▶▶|

would
might
climb
who
doubt
know
honest
science

2

3 Students can write the notes in pairs. Demonstrate possible notes with the class. For example:
half – we don't pronounce the 'l'
hour – we don't pronounce the 'h'

Track 25.5 tapescript ▶▶|

half
scissors
island
knife
whole
hour
chemist
business
guide
steady
listen
autumn
lamb
wrong
thought

It's time to talk

- Check the meaning of *hypothetical*.
- Give students prompts to answer the questions:
  I'd ...
  I think I'd ...
- Give students some examples and check pronunciation.
- After they have finished the activity, get them to feed back to the class, saying what their partner would do in some of the situations.
- You may want to use the Extra classroom activity here (see pages 84 and 109).

What did we do today?

Check the Remember section quickly and remind students of the objectives of the lesson.

Follow up

Encourage students to:
1 write sentences about the future, using both first and second conditionals; how likely they feel something is will be reflected in their choice of form
2 record pronunciation when they learn new words.

26 Intelligent skis

What did we do last time?

Do a review of the last type 2 lesson (Unit 23). Remind students of what they worked on (see Teacher's notes for that unit) and do some quick revision as follows.

Managing people
Ask students to define vocabulary like: *personnel, appraisal, laying off employees, pensions, early retirement, recruit.*

Emails – Making travel arrangements
Ask students what they would write in an email in order to:
enquire about accommodation
book flights
inform someone of your plans
inform someone of a change in plans
suggest an alternative time to meet someone.

On the agenda: Why are we doing this?

Tell students the objectives of this lesson:
- to describe **products and their selling points**
- to practise **dealing with complaints on the telephone**.

Reinforce this by writing the key words on the board or OHP.

Warm up

- Look at the questions in the Student's Book and get brief replies to the following questions:
  Where do they go skiing?
  Are they good at it?
  What problems do people have when they go skiing?
- Write suggestions for what 'Intelligence' skis might be on the board.
- Get them to describe the photos. Look at the photo of Shannon and read the caption.

Read on

Intelligent ski technology

Background briefing: Head
Head NV is a leading global manufacturer and marketer of premium sports equipment. It is a technology-driven company. Howard Head, the inventor of the first metal ski, founded the company in 1950. The Tyrolia bindings and Mares diving brands were added in the 1970s and more recently the Penn balls and Dacor diving brands were acquired during the 1990s. Head NV has been under its present management since 1996 and was listed on the New York Stock Exchange and the Vienna Stock Exchange in September 2000. Their current operations are organised into four divisions: Winter Sports, Racquet Sports, Diving and Licensing. For more information about Head, go to the *English365* website: www.cambridge.org/elt/english365.

- First, you could get students to skim all the paragraphs quickly in order to find out who was the closest in suggesting what 'Intelligence' skis meant.

- Check understanding of *wide* and *narrow* before getting them to do the exercise.
- When you check their answers, ask students to say why they chose a particular heading to go with the paragraph.

Answers

1 1 C   2 B   4 E   5 D   6 A
2 1 They make it easier to turn and increase speed
2 They vibrate more
3 Adapt to different conditions
4 They send an electrical signal to the computer chip and the fibres become hard and stiff
5 The skis are very expensive

What do you think?

Can students think of any other technological advances in sport? Has this benefited the sport or not (e.g. lighter footballs, body suits in swimming, etc.)?

The words you need ... to talk about products

1 Before doing the exercise, get students to look through the reading text again and find any expressions that describe the product. Then explain that you are now going on to look at other ways of doing so.

Answers

1 c   2 g   3 d   4 h   5 a   6 f   7 b   8 e

2
- Get students to describe the photo of the handheld computer. Ask them what they think it can do and what functions it has.
- Ask some comprehension questions to encourage the students to read through the text quickly before they do the task. Don't worry too much about the grammatical accuracy of their answers at this stage. For example:
  Who is it for?
  What are the main functions?
  How accurate is the GPS system?
- To try and activate the new vocabulary, you could get students to work in small groups and quickly describe a product they own while the others listen and guess what it is.

Answers

1 designed for   2 includes   3 user-friendly   4 enables
5 You can   6 ensures

Track 26.1 tapescript ▶▶|

Find your way with the Compaq handheld computer with Navigator. The new Compaq iPAQ 3800 is designed for the international business person who is always on the move. It includes a top quality diary with computing functions and built-in MP3 player. The GPS navigating system, when installed, is very user-friendly and enables you to pinpoint your location anywhere in the world to within 10 square metres. You can be sure that you will make that next meeting on time with turn-by-turn voice directions. The Compaq iPAQ 3800 ensures stress-free travel and gives you the confidence to relax.

It's time to talk

- Give students a few minutes to prepare for the activity. Perhaps elicit a few possible sentences to describe something in the classroom, e.g. the tape recorder or CD player:
  It is designed for teachers.
  It comes with top-quality speakers.
- You may want to use the Extra classroom activity here (see pages 84 and 110).

COMMUNICATING AT WORK

Telephoning 3: Handling complaints

Ask the questions and get students to tell a partner what happened last time they had to deal with a problem, or last time they made a complaint on the telephone.

1

Answers

1 D   2 B   3 C

2 Drill some of the key phrases and get students to make up short dialogues using them.

Answers

1 I'm very sorry about that   2 Let me check   3 get back to you
4 There was a computer error   5 Is that OK?   6 Sorry again
7 I really do apologise   8 We had a lot of problems
9 We'll talk next week

Track 26.2 tapescript ▶▶|

Call 1

OSCAR: Oscar Hansen.
DANIELA: Oscar. Hi, it's Daniela Beermann.
OSCAR: Hi, Daniela. How are you?
DANIELA: Well, not so good, actually. We've just received the last order of paint from you – order number E258 – and found that it's 5,000 litres short.
OSCAR: Really. I'm very sorry about that. Let me check. You said E258, yes?
DANIELA: That's right. We ordered 15,000 litres at the start of last week and we've just taken delivery of 10,000.
OSCAR: Yes, I have it on screen. You're right. The order was 15,000 litres. I do apologise. I don't really understand why this has happened. I'll check with dispatch and get back to you within the hour. Is that OK? Then we can organise a new delivery as soon as possible.
DANIELA: Fine.
OSCAR: OK, Daniela. Very sorry about this. I'll call you back shortly.
DANIELA: Thanks. Bye.
OSCAR: Bye.

Call 2

DANIELA: Daniela Beermann.
OSCAR: Hi, Daniela. Oscar calling back.
DANIELA: Hi, Oscar. So, any news of what happened?
OSCAR: Yes, it seems there was a computer error in the warehouse which caused the problem. I've asked them to investigate and give me a

report. Anyway, we've dispatched another 5,000 litres today and that will be with you tomorrow morning. Is that OK?

DANIELA: Yes, that's fine.

OSCAR: Sorry again for the inconvenience, Daniela.

DANIELA: It's OK. These things can happen. Thanks for sorting it out so quickly.

OSCAR: No problem. Can you send me an email to confirm the arrival of the goods tomorrow?

DANIELA: OK, will do. Thanks, Oscar. Bye.

OSCAR: Thanks, Daniela. Bye.

Call 3

JACK: Hello. Jack Sansom.

ANGELA: Jack. It's Angela. There's a problem.

JACK: What's wrong?

ANGELA: Sam's just told me that there's a delay with the API project. You told me everything would be finished this week.

JACK: Yes, I really do apologise. I know I promised, but the project is very complex. We had a lot of problems last week with the software installation.

ANGELA: But you didn't tell me, Jack.

JACK: I was going to call you this afternoon. But it's not a big problem. We'll finish things off by Tuesday next week – so it's only a two-day delay. OK?

ANGELA: OK, that's not too bad.

JACK: I'll call you on Tuesday afternoon when everything's finished. OK?

ANGELA: Right. That's fine.

JACK: Sorry about the delay. We'll talk next week. Have a good weekend.

ANGELA: OK, you too. Bye.

JACK: Bye.

3 Encourage students to use the language presented in the previous exercise.

What did we do today?

Check the Remember section quickly and remind students of the objectives of the lesson.

Follow up

Encourage students to:

1 write sentences about a product they are familiar with

2 write a dialogue between a customer who has a complaint and someone who is good at handling complaints.

27 You are what you eat

What did we do last time?

Do a review of the last type 3 lesson (Unit 24). Remind students of what they worked on (see Teacher's notes for that unit) and do a quick review as follows.

Receiving international colleagues
Ask students for phrases to do the following:
welcome a visitor

enquire about their journey
ask someone to complete a form
show someone their office or workspace
explain how to use the phone
give your home number.

Social problems and solutions
Elicit social problems from the students like: *homelessness, begging, vandalism, poverty, street crime*, etc. and then ask for possible solutions to these problems using words like: *solution, worse, make, solve, improve* and *better*.

On the agenda: Why are we doing this?

Tell students the objectives of this lesson:

- to practise useful phrases for **the restaurant**
- to learn and practise useful vocabulary for talking about **food**.

Reinforce this by writing the key words on the board or OHP.

Warm up

- Get students to describe the backdrop photo. Can they recognise any of the food and dishes? Then ask the questions in the Student's Book.
- Do they know any expressions that could be used in a restaurant?

Food talk

Answers

1 b   2 g   3 c   4 f   5 a   6 i   7 d   8 e   9 h

Track 27.1 tapescript ▶▶

Understanding the menu

A: Excuse me, can you help me? What exactly is *coq au vin*?

B: *Coq au vin*? It's chicken cooked in wine, madam.

A: I see. How is it cooked?

B: It's done in a casserole dish in the oven with red wine, onions, bacon, mushrooms and garlic. It's one of the chef's specialities.

A: It sounds delicious. I'll try it.

Complimenting the chef

A: That was very good. You have an excellent chef.

B: Thank you. And we try to cook mainly with local ingredients.

A: That's good. Where do you get them?

B: We have good contacts with all the local farmers.

A: Yes, everything tastes very fresh.

Explaining the name of a local dish

A: This soup is excellent. What's it called?

B: We call it *miso* soup with *wakame*. *Miso* is a kind of bean paste and *wakame* is a kind of green seaweed. We use it a lot in soups.

A: It's very good.

B: Yes, but my wife's is better. She got the recipe from her grandmother.

Describing how something is cooked

A: This fish is delicious. I'd love to know the recipe.

B: I make it with wine, ginger, garlic and herbs and then cook it in a hot oven.

A: It sounds complicated.

B: No, it's really easy. The most important thing is not to overcook it.

A: Well, it's just perfect.

Have a go

Can students role-play any other dialogues, e.g. dealing with a problem?

Listen to this

How do you like our food?

Look at the picture of Lesley (and her book) and read the caption.

Before you listen

- Have students ever been in a situation where they had to eat something they didn't like?
- Get students to describe the photos.

1

Answers

Food is really important to the Japanese.

2

Answers

1 A beautiful picture.
2 Fresh food, top quality and presentation.
3 She used to send him boxes and boxes of food from Japan.
4 'How do you like our food?'
5 Because the Japanese eat whale meat (some of which, the people who get angry believe, comes from endangered species).

Track 27.2 tapescript ▶▶|

INTERVIEWER: Lesley, why do you think food is so important?

LESLEY: I think food is incredibly important in every culture. Very often when Japanese people travel abroad, the very first thing that they think about is the food because Japanese food is incredibly different from western food and lots of Japanese that I know take food with them when they go abroad.

INTERVIEWER: So what's the most important thing about Japanese food?

LESLEY: It's got a fantastic variety of ingredients. The freshness is the most important thing and the presentation – how the food looks on the plate. Japanese food looks like a beautiful picture, it looks just wonderful. So the three things that matter are fresh food, top quality and the presentation. A really special thing in Japan is the Buddhist vegetarian cuisine which is prepared in Buddhist temples and is based on things like tofu and *miso* and lots of soya bean products, all very healthy. Of course it tastes wonderful as well.

INTERVIEWER: Do you think visitors to Japan like Japanese food when they go there, or do they tend to stay with their own western ideas?

LESLEY: These days most people know Japanese food from restaurants. But I must say there are people that don't fancy raw fish, though I have to say they are very silly if they don't try it. It's wonderful. But I know that some Japanese can have problems when they go abroad. I remember a Japanese student in Oxford. He told me that his mum sent him boxes and boxes and boxes of Japanese food. Things like noodles and seaweed. He absolutely couldn't live without them. I think he actually felt sick when he first came to London because he couldn't stand the food and then she started sending him boxes of food.

When you talk to Japanese in Japan the very first thing they say is 'How do you like our food?' And if you say you like it very much they are really happy and then you can go on and have the rest of your conversation.

INTERVIEWER: Is there anything you won't eat in Japan – I hear people talk about raw fish, or live fish, whale meat and things like that?

LESLEY: In fact I have – and you won't like me for this – eaten whale because I got so incredibly tired of environmentalist types who whenever the subject of Japan comes up, even at Christmas parties when I'm trying to relax and have a nice time, they start attacking me because Japanese eat whale! So I thought 'I will have some whale.' Now, when people mention whale, I can tell them it tastes really good, rather like tuna, and I enjoyed eating it very much. It makes people really mad with rage! I've never had live food, and there is live food in Japan, there are things like live little fish and live prawns which move around in one's mouth apparently. But I personally don't think I could eat live food, so it's either dead and fresh or it's dead and cooked. Then it's OK!

What do you think?

What do foreigners think of the national food of the students' countries? Is it popular?

The words you need ... to talk about food and cooking

1 See if students can tell you the cooking methods in English before they look at the words.

Answers

1 d + v   2 c + vii   3 f + viii   4 g + vi   5 h + i   6 i + iv   7 e + ii
8 j + x   9 a + ix   10 b + iii

2 When you have checked the answers, you could get students to say what kind of food they like.

Answers

1 overcooked   2 spicy   3 rare   4 medium   5 ripe   6 rich
7 tender   8 salty   9 off   10 sweet   11 savoury   12 sour

It's time to talk

- Read the rubric and make sure that students understand the task.
- Give them time to prepare for this and allow them to use their bilingual dictionaries to look up any ingredients that they are not sure about in English.
- Get selected students to describe their dishes to the whole class.
- You may want to use the Extra classroom activity here (see pages 84 and 111).

What did we do today?

Check the Remember section quickly and remind students of the objectives of this lesson.

Follow up

Encourage students to:
1 write phrases for use in a restaurant
2 write sentences to describe ways of cooking food.

28 That's entertainment!

What did we do last time?
Do a review of the last type 1 lesson (Unit 25). Remind students of what they worked on (see Teacher's notes for that unit) and do some quick revision as follows.

The second conditional
Ask students questions like:
What would you do if you got promoted?
What would you do if you were the CEO of your organisation?
How would you feel if you had to move to another country?
Make sure that students use the second conditional in their answers. Write some of the answers on the board and quickly go over the form and use.

Silent letters and difficult words
Write the following words on the board:
would, might, comb, honest, know, who, debt, chemist, Wednesday, thought, guide.
Get students to pronounce them and say why they are difficult.

On the agenda: Why are we doing this?
Tell the students the objectives of this lesson:
- to talk about **processes**
- to revise using the **passive** – ask students if they recognise the passive and perhaps write some examples on the board, e.g. *Computers are made ..., A new factory was built ...*
- To do some **pronunciation** work on **corrective stress** – again, you might need to give students an example:
  A: So, you've lived here for three years.
  B: No, I've lived here for four years. (stress on *four*)
  Write this on the board and demonstrate the corrective stress.
Reinforce this by writing the key words on the board or OHP.

Warm up
- Ask students the questions and get them to describe any PR events that their organisations have put on. You could also ask how companies launch new products and what kinds of things they do to maximise publicity.
- Look at the picture of Janie and read the caption. Explain that students are going to listen to her talking about her job.

Listen to this

From strongmen to look-alikes
Ask students what they think the title of the listening might mean and then get them to describe the pictures. Help with vocabulary if necessary.
1 Check understanding of *casting, corporate, product launch, promotion* and *freelance* before you play the recording.

Answers

1 1 T 2 F 3 T 4 T 5 F

2 1 Product launches and promotions
2 A product launch with a fireworks display
3 One day
4 The heat
5 Every week

Track 28.1 tapescript ▶▶

INTERVIEWER: What do you do exactly, Janie?

JANIE: I run – I suppose I'm managing director of an entertainment agency, but it's quite different to most agencies. We use singers, dancers, musicians, models, acrobats, strongmen, jugglers, look-alikes – we do absolutely anything and everything.

INTERVIEWER: So what kinds of event do you organise and for which clients?

JANIE: We mainly do corporate events: product launches and promotions for companies. That means we do the design, the music, the show, everything.

INTERVIEWER: And how old is your company? How many people?

JANIE: Well, I've been working here for 14 years. I started off working from my living room but it was just myself and my assistant Katy then. But we're still a small organisation and we run really on a project basis using freelance people.

INTERVIEWER: So is it a problem to get the right people for each project?

JANIE: Well, firstly, any possible contract is discussed internally. Then, if we think it's interesting, performers are contacted to check their availability. If they're available, they're hired immediately so we can then go ahead with the project. In fact, two singers were recruited this morning for a new project.

INTERVIEWER: OK. So it's very much a virtual organisation with contacts you bring in?

JANIE: Yes, that's right. I mean we've got around 500 people on our books, artists, etc., so it's a huge family here, but, as I said, the actual organisation is very small.

INTERVIEWER: What's the most interesting event you've organised?

JANIE: We did a really interesting project last year. It was a product launch, and we actually organised a fireworks display for the event – we created a really big bang effect for the launch of the product.

INTERVIEWER: How long do these events typically last?

JANIE: Well, that one was a day event, from first thing in the morning until late at night. Most events are one day, in fact. But that one took three months to plan.

INTERVIEWER: OK. And what's the most difficult event you've ever had to organise?

JANIE: Probably the most difficult events are the ones we do in India for the film business just because they work in such a different way to here. Changes are often made at the very last minute in India, people are replaced, new ideas are added, so you have to be extremely patient. And it's so hot – the heat's the hardest thing. One of the most difficult things, I remember, was when I had 50 dancers for a movie scene, with one song, and it took three and a half weeks and we were working 12 to 14 hours a day in heat of well over 40 degrees. That was tough!

INTERVIEWER: Just one last question I have to ask. You mentioned look-alikes. Who's your most popular look-alike?

JANIE: I knew you'd ask that. Well, with look-alikes, it's changing. Britney Spears and Kylie Minogue were always requested by everyone in the past, but at the moment we have a lot of Frank Sinatras. I think our top Frank Sinatra is booked every week at the moment. So old Frank is really making a comeback.

INTERVIEWER: You enjoy the job, I can see, don't you?

JANIE: Oh, absolutely. I love the variety, because every single day is different. There are lots of challenges but lots of fun projects. And I get the chance to travel a lot, which is something I really enjoy doing.

What do you think?

What kind of entertainment would students like to provide? Why? How would they like to organise a product launch or corporate event?

Check your grammar

The passive

- First, see if students can find any examples of the passive in Tapescript 28.1. Alternatively, you could play selected parts of the recording and get them to listen for examples.
- Remind them that it is not always necessary to add 'by + agent' after the passive.
- Ask for examples of processes in their organisations, using the passive.

Answers

Describing processes
Firstly, any possible contract is discussed internally.
Then performers are contacted.
If they are available, they're hired immediately.

We form the present simple passive using the verb *to be* + the past participle.
We use the passive when we focus on the action more than on the person.

Other uses of the passive
Speaker A uses the passive because it is not important to say who recruited the singers or who gave them the wrong music (or it is not known).
Speaker B uses the active because it is important to specify who is responsible for the action.
We form the past simple passive with the past simple of the verb *to be* and the past participle.

Do it yourself

1

Answers

1 The coffee is normally made by our secretary.
2 The report was prepared by a colleague yesterday.
3 He was asked by his boss to meet a client at the airport.
4 I am fascinated by your ideas.
5 The email was sent yesterday.

2 Do the first one on the board as a model.

Answers

1 Firstly, a meeting is arranged with the client to identify needs.
2 Secondly, the freelance people we want to use are contacted.
3 Thirdly, a second meeting is organised to discuss the proposal.
4 Then a detailed schedule is agreed.
5 After that a price is negotiated.
6 Finally, the contract is signed.

3 Get students to describe the photo of the carnival and then get them to read through the text quickly, without worrying about the gaps. Ask some quick comprehension questions to guide their reading. For example:
What are the origins of the carnival?
How many visitors are there every year?
What does the festival celebrate?

Answers

1 was established 2 were used 3 was started 4 was also seen
5 is normally held 6 are turned up 7 is now managed
8 were trained 9 were also used 10 is expected

Track 28.2 tapescript ▶▶|

The Notting Hill Carnival is the biggest street event in Europe and has roots going back hundreds of years. Historically, the Carnival was established by black slaves. Song, dance and costume were used by the slaves to protest about social conditions and celebrate black culture. The modern London Carnival was started over 30 years ago by the Trinidadian community newly arrived in London. At the beginning it was also seen as a form of social protest by black people living locally who were facing racism and social inequality. Now it is a fully multicultural event attracting over one million visitors every year. It is normally held on the last weekend of August with Sunday and Monday as the main days. The Carnival is a festival of music and dance. Music systems are turned up so that dancing can go on all night. The event is now managed by London Notting Hill Carnival Ltd. Last year 200 personnel were trained in health and safety because of the large crowds. Hundreds of police were also used to guarantee the event went smoothly. This year organisers are hoping to build on the success of last year and it is expected that visitor figures will reach 1.5 million.

Sounds good

Corrective stress

1
- Read the rubric and make sure students are clear about the situation and the task.
- After you have checked the answers, get them to practise the dialogues in pairs while you check for the correct stress. You may need to provide a clear model and drill the whole class first.

Answers

Actually, it's fourteen years.
No, she runs the company.
She was, but now it's Sinatra.

Speaker B stresses these words in order to draw attention to mistaken information used by speaker A and to give the correct details.

Track 28.3 tapescript ▶▶|
See the Student's Book.

2 Get students to practise the dialogues in pairs.

Track 28.4 tapescript ▶▶|
See the Student's Book.

3 Demonstrate this with the class before doing the activity.

It's time to talk

- Give time for preparation of this. Perhaps you could present an aspect of your institution. You could talk about the process of student enrolment. For example:
  Students are assessed.
  They are interviewed by the Director of Studies.
  They are put into an appropriate level class.
- Encourage them to ask you further questions and write them on the board as a model for what you want during their presentations.
- Ask students to take notes during the presentations and to ask at least two questions. When they have finished, selected pairs could describe a process that they heard about to the whole class.
- You may want to use the Extra classroom activity here (see pages 84 and 112).

What did we do today?

Check the Remember section quickly and remind students of the objectives of this lesson.

Follow up

Encourage students to write sentences in the passive to describe processes in their organisation.

29 Life coaching

What did we do last time?

Do a review of the last type 2 lesson (Unit 26). Remind students of what they worked on (see Teacher's notes for that unit) and do some quick revision as follows.

Products
Ask for antonyms for the following:
old-fashioned, simple, narrow, standard, badly, built, weak.
Get students to describe a product they have using these words and the following verbs:
include, enable, designed for, ensure.

Handling complaints on the telephone
Ask for phrases to do the following:
check reasons for a problem
give reasons for a problem
apologise strongly
give assurance
check the customer is happy
refer to next contact.

On the agenda: Why are we doing this?

Tell students the objectives of this lesson:
- to talk about **change**
- to learn and practise vocabulary to **describe changes and trends**
- to practise **handling questions in presentations**.

Reinforce this by writing the key words on the board or OHP.

Warm up

- Look at the pictures of Linda and Sue and read the caption.
- Ask the Warm-up questions. What else would students like to have done? What do they want to do in the future? Do they plan to stay in the same job? Where do they see themselves in five years' time? Do they have a career plan?

Read on

Do you need a change?

Look at the pictures and elicit the jobs that the people have. Would students like to follow any of these careers? Why? Why not?

1 When they have finished the exercise, check their answers and ask what key words or phrases helped them to do the task (e.g. 'Together we work out a clear action plan' in A, 'Better working relationships with colleagues and reduced stress are often significant benefits' in B, 'the advice isn't cheap' in C and 'Coaching has grown sharply' and 'now there are 400' in D).

2

What do you think?

Would a life coach benefit students? What would a life coach say to them? If you have time, they could talk about their jobs in pairs and role-play a life coach advising a client. Stress that this is not intended to be a particularly serious activity as some students may be sensitive about this.

The words you need ... to talk about changes and trends

1 First get students to find any words or phrases connected with change in the reading text (e.g. 'falling motivation' in A, 'reduced stress' in B, 'Coaching has grown sharply' in D).

Answers

Verb (infinitive)	Past simple	Past participle	Noun	Adjective
reduce	reduced	reduced	reduction	reduced
fall	fell	fallen	fall	falling
grow	grew	grown	growth	growing
rise	rose	risen	rise	rising

2 Quickly elicit what tenses should be used when they make their own sentences after doing the exercise.

Answers

1 b 2 c 3 a 4 e 5 f 6 h 7 d 8 g

3 When you check the answers, quickly go over how the 'wrong' answers can be used. For example:
1 Increased focus on quality *led to* a decrease in the number of customer complaints.
Explain that these words are followed by a noun phrase.

Answers

1 due to 2 resulted in 3 due to 4 a result of 5 lead to

Track 29.1 tapescript ▶▶

As you can see from the graph, the number of customer complaints decreased significantly last year. I think this was mainly due to our increased focus on quality. You can see here that quality was much better, up 50% on last year. So we should be happy that the investment in new machinery has resulted in better quality and more satisfied customers. If I can now turn to profits, I'm afraid that the figures are not so good due to the higher investment costs we've just discussed. It is also partly a result of a slight drop in sales of 3%. We expect things to improve next year. Finally, I would like to say that our new focus on the Central and Eastern European markets will lead to a lot of new business next year. So we should go forward with confidence. Thank you.

It's time to talk

- Quickly draw some graphs on the board and revise ways in which they can be described.
- Read the instructions and ask each pair to describe their graphs. You could make this more interactive by asking the students to listen and draw the graph as it is being described.
- As a follow up, students could draw a graph that relates directly to their organisation and describe that either to the whole class or to their partner.
- You may want to use the Extra classroom activity here (see pages 84 and 113).

COMMUNICATING AT WORK

Presenting 2: Handling questions effectively

Before looking at this section, ask if students can think of any techniques or language for dealing with questions.

1 When you check the answers, you could ask what the question actually was, and highlight how a question can be introduced, e.g. 'I have a question about training.'

Answers

1 Budget 2 Training 3 Upgrade costs

2 Check pronunciation and drill these phrases if necessary.

Answers

1 Does anyone have any questions?
2 OK, if there are no more questions, I'd like to go to the next point.
3 Does that answer your question?
4 It's an important question.
5 Right, if there are no more questions, I'll finish there.

Track 29.2 tapescript ▶▶

KURT: OK. So, that's all I want to say about costs. Does anyone have any questions?

COLLEAGUE 1: Just one question. Are we on budget?

KURT: Thanks for that question, Maria. Well, as I said, costs have increased and are a little over budget. This is mainly due to problems with staff, as I explained. But I am sure we will be under budget at the end of the project. Is that OK?

COLLEAGUE 1: Yeah, fine. Thanks.

KURT: Good. OK, if there are no more questions, I'd like to go to the next point. Let's think now about something else that we …
***

KURT: OK, so that's all I wanted to tell you about the software part of the project. Are there any questions on that?

COLLEAGUE 2: Yes, I have a question about training. Are we going to have training?

KURT: Well, we've organised training courses for everybody involved so I really don't see any problems here. Does that answer your question?

COLLEAGUE 2: OK. I'd be interested to discuss it more later, if possible.

KURT: Fine, we can talk about training over coffee. Good. Are there any other questions about the software? One thing I forgot to mention …
***

KURT: Right. That's all I wanted to say about technical questions. Does anyone have any questions?

COLLEAGUE 3: Well, just a quick question about upgrades. The new system sounds great, and much cheaper than the current one. But when we need to upgrade this new system, costs will rise sharply. Will the budget cover this?

KURT: It's an important question. Thank you. No need to worry. I can tell you that we've already agreed an excellent price for the first upgrade. Is that OK?

COLLEAGUE 3: Well, I think so, yes. Thanks.

KURT: Right, if there are no more questions, I'll finish there. Thank you.

3 Give feedback on their performance and ask them to give another presentation on the other topic if appropriate. You could get selected groups to perform for the rest of the class.

What did we do today?

Check the Remember section quickly and remind students of the objectives of this lesson.

Follow up

Encourage students to:
1 write sentences to describe changes in their organisation
2 write down useful phrases for handling questions.

30 Work or lifestyle?

What did we do last time?

Do a review of the last type 3 lesson (Unit 27). Remind students of what they worked on (see Teacher's notes for that unit) and do some quick revision as follows.

Food talk
Ask students for phrases to use in the following situations:
they don't understand something on a menu
they want to ask how something is cooked
they want to compliment the chef
they want to explain a local dish
they want to describe how something is cooked.

Food and cooking
Ask students the differences between the following pairs of words:
steamed / boiled
baked / roasted
grilled / fried
raw / barbecued
rare / overcooked
ripe / off
sweet / savoury
spicy / rich.

On the agenda: Why are we doing this?

Tell students the objectives of this lesson:
- to talk about **work and lifestyle**
- to revise **vocabulary about learning**
- to revise and practise **saying goodbye** (as is appropriate for the last unit of the book). You can explain that, because of this, you will do the social English dialogues at the end of the lesson rather than at the beginning.

Reinforce this by writing the key words on the board or OHP.

Warm up

- Would students like to become vegetarians or vegans? Why? Why not?
- Look at the picture of Tony and read the caption. Point out the slogan on his T-shirt.

Listen to this

Work, belief and lifestyle

1 Check understanding of *leather* before you play the recording.

Answers

1 No   2 Yes   3 Yes   4 Yes

Track 30.1 tapescript ▶▶|

INTERVIEWER: So, you work for the Vegan Society, Tony. What do you do exactly?

TONY: Well, I'm in charge of media and marketing and that sort of thing. So my job is really to promote our organisation and the ideas of what it is to be a vegan, to help people learn about the philosophy, to help people make new friends. Many things, really.

INTERVIEWER: Can you explain the difference between 'vegetarian' and 'vegan'?

TONY: Yes, vegetarians don't eat meat but will drink milk, eat eggs and so on. A vegan is more strict and won't eat or wear or use anything that comes from an animal. Vegans want to avoid as far as possible all cruelty to animals for food, and for clothing or any other purpose. So I don't wear leather, I don't buy animal-tested products … all that.

INTERVIEWER: What about your diet? What do you eat?

TONY: The same things as everyone else eats. Really normal food you know – pizza and chips, Indian curries, sausages . . . But I just eat vegan versions of these, often using soya alternatives.

INTERVIEWER: Is it healthy?

TONY: It depends what you eat. Veganism is not always healthy. I think many of us eat too much processed food with too much sugar, salt and processed fats. And then you combine that with a stressful lifestyle. All I can say is that I try to eat healthily and I take multi-vitamin tablets every day to help.

INTERVIEWER: What about the future? Is veganism the lifestyle of the future?

TONY: Well, it's interesting. The number of vegans is growing in the UK – it's about 250,000 now. But it's also international. There are vegan societies from Australia and New Zealand to Sweden, Italy, Spain and Austria. It's global. And it's not only that people want to be kinder to animals. It's also a movement about how we feed the world population efficiently and healthily. If you want to know more, join our celebrations on World Vegan Day on 1st November.

INTERVIEWER: So do you enjoy your job?

TONY: Absolutely. And I enjoy it fundamentally because I'm doing something which I believe in morally. For me, a job must be about more than just making money. So, I'm helping to protect people, animals and the environment – it's the whole picture and one solution for a range of dilemmas that excites me. I'm also helping people to learn, which I enjoy. And for me too, it's an interesting job to work with the media. I learn a lot every day, and that's also important. For me, a job should help you to learn and develop as a person, every day, every minute. A job should be a process of continuous learning.

Track 30.2 tapescript ▶▶|

INTERVIEWER: So do you enjoy your job?

TONY: Absolutely. And I enjoy it fundamentally because I'm doing something which I believe in morally. For me, a job must be about more than just making money. So, I'm helping to protect people, animals and the environment – it's the whole picture and one solution for a range of dilemmas that excites me. I'm also helping people to learn, which I enjoy. And for me too, it's an interesting job to work with the media. I learn a lot every day, and that's also important. For me, a job should help you to learn and develop as a person, every day, every minute. A job should be a process of continuous learning.

What do you think?

Is there anything else that is important for students in their jobs?

The words you need ... for continuous learning

- Read the rubric and ask students:
  How many words do you think you know?
  How many words have you learnt during the course?
  What techniques do you use for learning vocabulary?
- Tell them what techniques you use for the languages you have learnt or are learning. It might also help to stress that learning vocabulary is not only about remembering the word, but also using it accurately in the correct context.
- Explain that you are going to review techniques for learning vocabulary.
- Ask students to do the exercises and ask them which of the techniques they use.

It's time to talk

- Ask students to work in pairs. Can they add their own ideas to the list? Quite detailed reporting back will be useful here because students can broaden their own range of learning strategies by listening to other people's.
- Try to convince students of the importance of studying little and often: even five minutes a day will bring benefits over time. Also stress the importance of reviewing what they study. Revision and consolidation of new language is essential. Suggest that when students study a new language item, they look at it again the next day, then the next week and then the next month. This should ensure that it becomes fixed in their long-term memory.
- You may want to use the Extra classroom activity here (see pages 84 and 114).

Saying goodbye

Track 30.3 tapescript ▶▶|

Getting away

A: Right, I think I should be going.

B: Already? It's only half past nine.

A: Sorry, I really must be going. I promised I'd get back early tonight.

B: It's a real pity, the party's only just starting.

A: Yes, I'd love to stay but I really have to go. I'll see you next week. Bye.

Getting away quickly

A: OK, have a nice weekend everybody.

B: Oh, can I just ask you a quick work question before you go?

A: My train goes in around 20 minutes. Can we leave it until Monday?

B: But I just need to run over the agenda for Tuesday morning.

A: Sorry. Can you ask Olivia? I really have to go. Bye.

Give me a call

A: I have to go to a meeting now.

B: OK, but there are a couple more points to discuss.

A: Well, call me next week. We can talk over some more details then.

B: I will. I'll give you a call on Monday morning.

A: Fine. Talk to you then. Bye.

Until the next time

A: I've just come to say goodbye. I'm leaving now. My train's at five-thirty.

B: OK, well it was really good to see you again.

A: Same here. It was great working with you, as always.

B: Yeah, I enjoyed it too. And, hopefully, see you next year.

A: Yes, until then, take care. Bye.

What did we do today?

Check the Remember section quickly and remind students of the objectives of this lesson.

Follow up

Encourage students to:

1 write down their action plan for their future learning of English

2 review their vocabulary learning book

3 to have as much contact with English as possible. If they don't, they may well forget what they have learnt!

Revision 2 Units 16–30

ANSWERS

Grammar

1 1 some / a few   2 a few / some   3 some / many / most
4 any   5 no   6 a little / some   7 much   8 each
9 much

2 1 11 billion bananas are eaten by Americans every year.
2 20 billion hot dogs are consumed by Americans every year.
3 Six billion Oreos are produced by Nabisco every year.
4 100 billion M&Ms are manufactured by the Mars M&M factory in Hackettstown, New Jersey every year.
5 Mars's first candy was sold in 1911 by Frank and Ethel Mars.

3 *Possible answers*
1 If I take early retirement, I'll move to a smaller house.
2 If I had more money, I'd buy a new car.
3 If I could have dinner with anyone in the world, I'd choose Zac Goldsmith.
4 If I could work in another country, I'd try to learn the language first.
5 When I next go on holiday, I'll take lots of books with me.
6 If I said that to my boss, I'd lose my job.

Pronunciation

1 1 A: Did you say 51 88 57 83 / five one, double eight, five seven, eight three?
   B: No, it's 51 88 97 83 / double oh four seven, five one, double eight, <u>nine</u> seven, eight three.
2 A: Is that M–A–R–K–U–S?
   B: No, it's a <u>C</u>. M–A–R–<u>C</u>–U–S.
3 A: One hundred and thirty-five?
   B: No, not thirty-five. It's one hundred and <u>forty</u>-five.
4 A: The second?
   B: No, the <u>twenty</u>-second.

Track R2.1 tapescript ▶▶I

1 A: What's her number?
   B: It's 0047 51 88 97 83.
   A: Did you say 51 88 57 83?
   B: No, it's 0047 51 88 97 83.
2 A: What's his email address?
   B: It's marcus.ritter@zurich.ch.
   A: Is that M–A–R–K–U–S?
   B: No, it's a C. M–A–R–C–U–S.
3 A: Where do they live?
   B: It's 145 Queen Street.
   A: One hundred and thirty-five?
   B: No, not thirty-five. It's one hundred and forty-five.
4 A: When's the next meeting?
   B: It's on the 22nd of September.
   A: The second?
   B: No, the <u>twenty</u>-second.

2

1 Shall we go and get some lunch?
   →

2 Can I have a cup of coffee?
   →   →   →

3 I'm afraid I'm a bit too busy.
   →   →

4 I've been working here for over a year.
   →   →

5 Maybe I should take that job after all.
   →   →   →

6 How about trying that new Indian restaurant?
   → →   →

Business vocabulary

1 appraisal   2 pension   3 recruit   4 trade union
5 workforce   6 downsizing

Business communication

1 1 Shall we get started?
2 Does everyone have a copy of the agenda?
3 Our objective today is to review all our projects.
4 What do you think?
5 If I understand you correctly, you think it's a good idea.
6 Sorry, can you let him finish?
7 Can we fix a date for the next meeting?
8 Are there any further points?
9 I think we can finish there.

2 1 details   2 flight   3 flight number   4 arrange
5 pick me up   6 take a train   7 return flight
8 hotel reservation

Social phrases

1 f   2 b   3 a   4 h   5 g   6 d   7 e   8 c

General vocabulary

1 rise   2 poached   3 rich   4 Subtitles   5 violence
6 thriller   7 memory   8 reduction   9 situation   10 poverty

4 Extra classroom activities

Teacher's notes

Introduction

There are 30 photocopiable activities designed to supplement each of the 30 units in the Student's Book in this section. Each activity is supported by some Teacher's notes. There are various possibilities as to when to do them:

- instead of the *It's time to talk* section of the unit
- in addition to and following *It's time to talk* – especially if your lessons are more than 90 minutes long
- as consolidation in the following lesson
- as consolidation later on in the course: you may want to use one if or when a natural break arises in a subsequent lesson.

However, do bear in mind that, unlike the Better learning activities, there is a direct link between the 30 Extra classroom activities and the 30 units in the Student's Book. Each Extra classroom activity should be used to reinforce and consolidate learning which has already been initiated and your lesson planning should take this into account.

Procedure
Most of the activities involve pair or groupwork of some kind, so before you do any of these activities, you should read, in particular, the notes on:
- pair and groupwork on page 13, and
- feedback and correction on page 14.

Timing
We have not indicated timings for individual activities because this will finally depend on you, your class and the time available. Do note, however, that:
- some of them are essentially supplementary exercises which will only take 10 to 15 minutes to do in normal circumstances; others are quite developed communicative activities which could take considerably longer
- you should assess how much time you think an activity will take, and how much you want it to take, at the planning stage. You may wish to spend as much if not more time on the feedback as on the activity itself.

What to do
See the Teacher's notes for each activity.

1 Jobs and current projects

- You may want to present the idea of handling first meetings as an important skill within the international workplace, where it is important for individuals to represent themselves and their organisations professionally, especially to visitors and counterparts, rather than simply get to know someone at a purely personal social level.

- Allow students time to write down que... areas such as job, company, current pr... could be done as homework, or as a 'tes... ...s prior to the activity. You can divide the class into two teams to create a fun competitive atmosphere. Or you could elicit the questions and write them on the whiteboard for reference during the role-play.

- During feedback on their questions, consolidate their understanding of the present simple and present continuous, as students are likely to overuse the latter.

- You could model the activity before they start, to show how important it is to have positive body language and voice projection in first meetings, as well as grammatically correct questions.

- After the activity, encourage students to give feedback to each other on how effectively their partner 'managed' the conversation – asking questions, maintaining positive body language, etc.

2 The organisation quiz

- This activity is a quiz mostly about business and companies but also about international organisations. It is quite challenging and students may actually learn something while they test their general knowledge.

- Divide the class into teams – ideally about three to six students in each team. You need to have an even number of teams. So if you have a class of 12, four teams of three would be best so that teams can pair up as Team A and Team B.

- Initially teams work alone to find out their score on their test. Check each team's answers quietly, ensuring the other teams don't hear the answers.

- Each team then asks their partner team the same questions. There are 12 questions in each test, with a total of 15 points. A competitive spirit should emerge.

- As an option, students can continue the quiz by making up their own questions, but this will need planning time and possibly research as well.

Answers

Team A quiz
1 B 2 C 3 A 4 A 5 C 6 A 7 B 8 False (It is Nokia) 9 C
10 False (It is South Korean) 11 B 12 1 C 2 D 3 A 4 B
Team B quiz
1 C 2 B 3 A 4 B 5 B 6 C 7 False (It is General Motors)
8 A 9 C 10 False (It is Finnish) 11 B 12 1 D 2 A 3 B 4 C

[yo]ur way round

- [We woul]d start this activity by brainstorming with
  [stud]ents what practical information they try to find out
  [a]bout a place they don't know before they visit it. Things
  like size of the city, public transport, left luggage, tourist
  information, currency rate and exchange should come up.
- Elicit the questions before students start the activity.
- If your students are from Bangkok or Hong Kong – or if
  your students prefer – you can also adopt a framework
  approach to the activity, that is, you ask students to think
  of cities they know (but which their partners don't) and
  then ask them to prepare questions and answers under
  the headings given: currency, transport, etc.
- In either case, encourage students to use their
  imaginations to ask other questions and to provide more
  details. But stress that the emphasis should be on
  providing *practical* information for finding one's way
  around a place one doesn't know.

4 Telling a story

- Students should complete the sentences individually. Go
  round the class checking and help the weaker students. Be
  careful not to correct all the answers and allow students
  to start the reading aloud phase of the activity with one
  or two mistakes. Encourage students to listen carefully to
  each other's answers as they read aloud.
- Monitor students in pairs reading the sentences to each
  other and provide correct answers where students are
  unable to do so themselves.
- After the activity, go through the answers with the class
  (ask pairs of students to read their answers aloud) in order
  to clarify fully the uses of the past simple and continuous.
- You could set a homework activity for students to write
  short stories about their own business travel or holiday
  adventures using the target grammar. These could be
  corrected and then read out in class at a later date.

Answers

Dinner at eight!
Last night the phone rang at six o'clock. I didn't answer
because I was having a bath. When I checked who the caller
was, I found out that it was a friend who I was going to meet
that night for dinner at eight at his house. I called back but
nobody answered. I thought my friend was cooking the dinner
so I decided not to call again.

When I was ready, I caught a bus to his house. When I arrived
at eight I could see through the window that he was working. I
knocked but he didn't hear me so I decided to climb up to the
window to attract his attention. The wall was very slippery
because it was raining and I fell into his garden.

When my friend heard the noise he came to the window and
asked me what I was doing. He started laughing when I
explained that I was trying to get his attention. When I asked
him why he wasn't preparing dinner for us he looked
surprised. He told me that he called earlier to say he was
preparing an important presentation and so couldn't see me
that evening.

A terrible business trip to the USA
The flight
I dropped my mobile phone while I was checking in. I got
soaked when I was boarding because I didn't have an
umbrella. When the flight attendant was serving me coffee,
she spilt it all over my laptop. I fell down the aircraft steps as
I was getting off.
The hotel
The room was very noisy because the hotel was on a main
road. I felt exhausted when I woke up. While I was having a
shower the hot water stopped, so I had a cold shower!
The meeting
Someone took the last parking space just as I was arriving
at the company. I had to park two blocks away. I was dressed
casually but everyone else was wearing formal clothes. The
meeting was a total waste of time because most of the key
people didn't attend. They were celebrating the CEO's
birthday at a special party next door.

5 Swapping jobs

- Students should discuss the first question before you give
  each pair two of the job advertisements. Some of the jobs
  may be more suitable for some students than others. Help
  them with language in the advertisements as appropriate.
- Explain that each student in the pair should choose one of
  the jobs for a job swap. You may need to check that they
  don't both choose the same job. They should complete the
  information in the table on their own before they ask
  their partner about the job he/she has chosen.
- Make sure they discuss their answers to all the questions,
  and tell each other what they think about their choice of
  job.
- You could follow this up by asking pairs or groups to write
  the specifications of their ideal job for a one-week job
  swap. You could encourage them to be imaginative and
  then have a class vote on which is the most appealing job.

6 How are you feeling?

- Prepare for this activity by photocopying the page and
  cutting the input into ten strips (or as many as you need),
  one for each of the different conditions. You can give each
  student a copy of the Objective, Introduction and What to
  do sections; or simply give the information orally. Put the
  useful phrases on the board.
- Explain the activity and do an example dialogue with a
  student. Then distribute the strips. Depending on
  numbers, you may wish to give more than one strip to
  each student and you may wish to give out the same
  situation to more than one student, so that, for example,
  there are two students who discover that they both ran in
  the same marathon. Give some forethought to which
  strips you give to which students to avoid potential
  embarrassment in certain situations.
- Manage the activity as a serial pairwork activity (see page
  13) although you or they may wish to have groups of three
  as well as pairs. Keep them circulating.
- Listen in and note useful language while students are
  talking for you to use in your feedback.
- Ask for feedback on content (what was each of them
  suffering from?) as well as on language.

7 How do things compare?

- Ask students to add their own ideas to the lists of adjectives, adverbs, people and things. Give examples of some words that they might add. You could set a time limit of two minutes to keep this phase fun and snappy.
- Explain how in pairs, students should make each other generate comparative sentences. The best way is to model the activity by asking a student to give you an adjective and the names of two people. You then make a correct comparative sentence. The student then tells you if your sentence was grammatically correct and also comments briefly on whether he/she agrees with the content of your statement. The comment will make the activity more fun and non-technical. You could repeat this modelling several times in order to show how to build sentences with both adverbs and adjectives and encourage the opinion-giving phase.
- Monitor the students as they do the activity in pairs or small groups.
- For homework, students could write six comparative sentences – three with adjectives and three with adverbs – which they read out in the next lesson.

8 To move or not to move

- Divide the class into groups – ideally about three to six students in each group. You need to have an even number of groups. So if you have a class of 12, four groups of three would be best, so groups can pair up as Group A and Group B.
- Make sure students understand all the background information.
- The groups should start by discussing among themselves the arguments they have and who should make which points.
- In the main discussion, it may be possible for a compromise decision to be agreed between the partner groups.
- Following this activity, students may want to discuss real situations where businesses have relocated jobs.

9 Happy headlines

- This can be quite light-hearted and creative, especially if students can come up with their own ideas and opinions for the headlines given and also ideas for other feel-good headlines.
- To give them a flavour of what you expect, it could be a good idea to run through one news item with you providing the news to one of the students. Embellish the story liberally, especially to give the reactions of different parties concerned in each case, and to give your own opinion.

10 It's my turn

- For this game, you will need to make one photocopy of the page for each group rather than for each student, although you might prefer them to have one each. You will need a die for each group and enough counters for each student.

- Your main role will be to monitor the groups and referee when there is a dispute about whether an answer is correct.
- As groups finish, encourage the students to review the squares which have not been landed on and check that they can make correct sentences.
- For homework, students could write sentences about themselves using specific squares as a cue.

11 That's really rich!

- This is an extension of the game in the Student's Book but with a variation. Students play it in the same way in pairs, but here with each choice the players get to hear how much their investment is; the amounts vary, so they may choose between a small risk or a bigger one.
- As a follow-up, students may like to make up their own choices.

12 Environmental case study

- If you have fewer than seven students, you can give more than one role card to one or more of them (as long as the opinions on them don't conflict: the chair and role 2 are generally pro-driver, the others are against). Check understanding of *fed up* and *jams*.
- Make sure that the chair (who should be linguistically one of your stronger students) understands that he/she must manage the meeting and end with a summary of points which he/she promises to report back to the city council.
- Give students a little time to prepare their roles. Encourage them to think of other arguments to strengthen their case. Give appropriate help with the language on the role cards, for example *park and ride services* and *fares*, although don't pre-teach to the whole class. Encourage students instead to explain any such terms to the others if need be.
- Decide in advance how long you want the meeting to last (20 minutes?) and tell the chair to keep to this time. Allow time for feedback at the end of the meeting.

13 The future

- There is a competitive element in this activity to encourage students to practise the different forms of the future. Give each group the pieces of paper and make sure they understand what to do in order to play the game.
- Remind them that in order to gain a point they have to use *will*, *going to* or the present continuous correctly in their reply. The other members of the group therefore have to check the replies carefully, but you will need to act as referee.
- In some cases, different answers are possible depending on the context in which the sentence or question is spoken. You will have to adjudicate accordingly.
- Once they have finished the game, give feedback about the grammar in each situation.
- For homework, students could write similar short dialogues from their own workplace context.

1 Your colleague says: I can't open the email you sent me!
   You say: I'll resend it (now / immediately / this afternoon / later).

2 Your colleague says: Do you have any plans for tonight?
   You say: I'm eating (out with friends). / I'm going to eat (in a restaurant with friends).

3 Your colleague says: (*on the phone*) I can't talk just now. I'm in a meeting!
   You say: I'll call you back (this afternoon / later / tomorrow).

4 Your colleague says: When are you leaving?
   You say: I'm flying at ten o'clock tomorrow morning.

5 Your colleague says: What are you doing tonight?
   You say: I'm going to meet (a friend). / I'm meeting (a friend).

6 Your colleague says: You forgot to send the attachment with your email.
   You say: I'll fax (it to you now / the document to you immediately).

7 Your colleague says: When are you going to speak to Caterina?
   You say: I'm going to talk / I'm talking (to her / Caterina / later / tomorrow).

8 Your colleague says: When are you meeting Jean-Pierre?
   You say: I'm seeing (him / Jean-Pierre later today / tomorrow / next week).
   We assume the person answering has made an appointment with Jean-Pierre. If not, the going to form is possible as the person answering is only reporting an intention.

9 Your colleague says: When are you going to Germany?
   You say: I'm flying (to Germany next Saturday).
   We assume the person answering has booked a flight and the arrangement is fixed.

10 Your colleague says: When are you going to finish (the report)?
    You say: I'll do it this afternoon.

14 Can you help?

- Explain that each member of the group works for the customer services department in a different organisation. Give the group members their letters of complaint.
- Make sure they understand exactly what the problem is and remind them that they need to decide how they are going to deal with the problem before they start telling their partners about it.
- Monitor their discussions and encourage them to use appropriate language. Remind them to use the language they practised for the future in Unit 13.
- To finish off the activity, you could ask the groups to feedback on how well their partners dealt with the problems and whether the customers would be satisfied.

15 Home improvements

- The student playing the home-owner role should first use the space on the activity sheet to draw a rough plan of each floor of his/her home and then suggest some ideas for extensions or improvements. The ideas in the box are intended to stimulate students' own thinking.

- The group as a whole can exchange ideas about both improvements and costs during the feedback process.

16 Promoting your organisation

This activity may take some time to complete as the task is creative and requires use of grammar which many students find difficult. You can set it up as a classroom activity as an alternative to *It's time to talk* or as a project.

Classroom activity

- Divide students into groups. Explain that it is a workshop activity to produce a web page which will attract graduates to their organisation, and that it is important for its future success. Encourage students to invest energy in the task itself as real work usage of the target grammar.
- Go round the class monitoring and correcting the sentences produced by the groups. You may need to prompt students with ideas at certain points, so prepare yourself accordingly.
- When they have finished, the groups should read their sentences out and you can have a class vote on which web page will be most effective.

Project

- As with the classroom activity, students work in groups to produce web pages, from which the class will select ideas to build a final web page. You could encourage students to use Powerpoint, web editing software or a sheet of A3 paper to produce an appealing piece of visual work which can be presented in class in a future lesson.
- Students should submit the sentences to you before they finalise their work so that you can check the grammar.
- Each group should present their work to the class and the class should then choose the best sentences to produce the final web page.

17 What can it be?

- While students are thinking of their individual products you may need to give some help with vocabulary. Make sure that you are the only person to see what each student's product is.
- Make sure students understand the rules before you start the activity.
- The questions asked are likely to be in two categories, as shown on the page: yes/no questions and more open questions relating to dimensions, colour, etc.
- You should occasionally interrupt the activity and ask individual students to recap. This is useful as students will have to repeat what they have understood from the questions and answers. The summary description provided by the student in the hot seat before departing also gives an opportunity for more detailed description.

18 Can I help you?

- Go through the procedure for the activity with the students and ask them to read through the example dialogue: you could ask two of them to read it aloud.
- Then emphasise the fact that the mini-dialogues don't need to be more than two or three turns long. The feedback and the exchange of sample language which

they've collected will be just as important as doing the dialogues.

- Monitor the pairs and be ready to provide appropriate language as required.
- Ask pairs of students to act out different situations after they've completed the pairwork phase.
- During feedback, write sample language on the board and encourage students to make notes of expressions which appeal to them.

19 Solving problems

- Ask students to complete the gapped telephone conversation in pairs. Then one pair should read out the dialogue so you can check the answers. You can also ask students to stand up and read through the dialogue in different pairs while you monitor pronunciation.
- Explain that the pairs are going to plan and perform a short, realistic work telephone conversation which integrates four examples of *if* and *when* in first conditional sentences in one of the situations. Monitor the pairs during the planning process.
- The pairs perform their dialogues for the class. The rest of the class should listen and note down the examples of *if* and *when* sentences. They must then check whether the sentences were grammatically correct.

Answers

1 Will it be OK if
2 If we run
3 If two more people do
4 when you have
5 If I have time
6 When we know

20 Launching a new product

- First check that students understand what they have to do and all the vocabulary in the input. The magazine in the activity is for the European market. The European references can be changed to another part of the world if that is more appropriate.
- This is a very open activity and may generate some disagreement: the intention is to generate discussion and there are no right and wrong answers. Nevertheless, here is an assessment that might help after the activity. Point out that other assessments are possible.
- The discussion may be extended when groups compare their solutions, and students may have their own ideas and experience to draw on.

Assessment

The better ideas are probably 1, 2, 3, 7 and 8. However, the total cost would be €235,000 so one of these methods has to be left out.
4 is not necessary if 7 is chosen.
5 is an expensive way to find out what perhaps the company can do without using a market research company.
6 is expensive and too general.
9 is too expensive.
10, 11 and 12 are all too general and therefore waste money.

21 Film classics

- You could begin by brainstorming useful vocabulary for talking about films (as always, encouraging students to suggest not just single words but useful collocations) and write their ideas on the board. Headings for these could be: reasons to like a film (story, camerawork, special effects, etc.); jobs in the movies; types of film; and so on.
- During feedback, you can also ask them how many of these films they know; which ones they do and do not like; and whether they would have preferred other choices.

22 Responsibilities, rules and advice

- Students work in pairs to complete the matching activity. Explain that they will have to distinguish between past, present and future job responsibilities. Clarify the distinction between *rule* and *advice* with a quick translation if you can, or simply by asking students for examples of a work rule and some advice about work.
- As an alternative to teacher-centred feedback, you could ask one pair to act as the teacher and check everyone's answers. Make it fun by telling the pair acting as teacher to give positive feedback, saying 'Good' or Well done' if the answers are correct.
- For the second part of the activity, ask students to work with a different partner. It may be useful to elicit a few examples of the kinds of question you want and write them on the board. For example:

	Job responsibilities	Rules at work	Tips for success
Questions	Do you think you will have to use English more in your job in the future?	Can you smoke in your office?	Can you give me any tips about …?

- After writing their questions, students should form small groups and ask and answer the questions.

Answers

1 Past job responsibilities
   I had to learn a lot about IT in my first job.
   I didn't have to travel so much in my last job.
2 Future job responsibilities
   I will have to speak a lot more English.
   In future I won't have to be in the office every day. I can work from home more.
3 Current job responsibilities
   I don't have to start work until 8.30 am.
   I have to work at weekends sometimes.
4 Rules at work
   You mustn't use the management car park except in case of emergency.
   You mustn't drink any alcohol.
5 Advice about work
   You must slow down. You're working too hard.
   You need to buy a new suit!

23 An appraisal interview

- Make sure students understand their roles and what they have to do. Allow them time to prepare their questions and answers. Encourage them to expand on the information they have.

- If there is time after the role-play, they may change roles and repeat the activity. This time, instead of using identical information, they can simply use the framework provided but make up different responses. Before doing this, suggest they look again at the Student's Book to remind them of some of the target language.

24 A serious problem

You can apply the same principle to dealing with other social issues if you can provide a short introductory text and some suggestions about how the issue should be dealt with.

25 What would you do if … ?

- Ask students to complete the questionnaire on their own. Then create small groups for students to predict the other group members' choices and compare their answers. Encourage students to take turns asking the questions in their groups. Make sure they ask each other the complete second conditional questions and that they reply with full sentences. Encourage follow-up questions such as 'Why?' It may be best to model this group process with one of the groups in front of the class before asking all the groups to work independently.
- When all the questions have been asked, groups prepare their own second conditional questions for another group. Note that groups do not have to prepare the answers, simply the questions. When each group has prepared three or four questions, these can be asked of an individual within a different group or all the members of a group.

26 There's a problem, I'm afraid

- Tell students they will practise key telephoning language. They should read through their information first and think about what to say, even though they won't understand the whole situation until the end of the conversation.
- Ensure that Student B is the first to speak. Students should respond as indicated.
- A more challenging extension to the activity is to try to repeat a similar conversation without role cards. Let the students prepare for such a conversation simply by agreeing on a service problem for one of them to call the other about. They can reverse the roles so that this time Student A is the person called and B is the caller. This can be repeated a second time, reversing the roles, and based on a new service problem.

27 Guess who's coming to dinner

- After the main activity, pairs can present their menus and recipes to the class and, with luck, some useful recipe swapping will take place. This activity is also compulsory for the teacher!
- The title for this activity comes from the 1967 Stanley Kramer film starring Katherine Hepburn, Spencer Tracey (his last film), Katherine Houghton and Sidney Poitier.

28 Useless facts

- Ask students to prepare their questions in pairs or small groups. Encourage them to predict the answers to their questions to inject a fun element. Alternatively, you can divide the class into two groups and run the activity as a competition with points awarded on the basis of the answers: 3 points for a close answer, 2 points for a moderately close answer and 1 point for a possible answer, with the teacher acting as arbiter.
- Remind students to say whether the sentences which they are asked are grammatically correct <u>before</u> answering the questions.
- For homework, students could research three similar questions to ask each other in the next lesson.

Possible questions

Student A
1 How many glasses of milk are produced in the lifetime of the average cow?
2 How many kilos of lipstick are consumed in the lifetime of the average woman?
3 When was Diet Coke created?
4 How many cigarettes are smoked per person each year in China on average?
5 When were women first given the vote in the USA?
6 Where is the largest taxi fleet in the world located?

Student B
1 When was the toothbrush invented in China?
2 How many people were injured in the Great Fire of London in 1666?
3 When was the first police force established?
4 How many fan letters were received by Mickey Mouse in 1933?
5 Who was the largest painting on earth painted by?
6 How many kilos of rubbish are produced by everyone each day?

29 The way things are

- Students should first answer the questions individually and then exchange information with their partners, noting down the answers. The questions raised should certainly generate some discussion.
- When they come to writing their own questions, they may need prompting. Possible questions: *Would you like to have a life coach? Do you think your 5 year target is realistic? How could you improve your work–life balance?*
- You could end by asking students to volunteer anything interesting they learned about their partner.

30 Saying goodbye

- Since this is the last activity in this book that students are likely to do, you may feel it appropriate to call upon their acting as well as their linguistic talents on this occasion.
- Cut the activity page up into strips and distribute the situations to pairs of students.
- While each pair is performing, make notes of useful language for leave-taking – or delegate this task to other members of the group – and get feedback on language as well as dramatic effect after each dialogue.
- The class should identify the pair most likely to receive Oscar nominations at some stage in their future careers.

1 Jobs and current projects

Objective
To practise asking and answering questions with the present simple and present continuous tenses when meeting people.

Introduction
In this activity, you are going to talk about yourself, playing the role of a project manager. Some of the information includes general facts about your work and personal life (present simple). Other information will focus more on what you are doing now or what is happening at the moment in your job and business (present continuous).

What to do
You are a project manager attending a conference in Paris about international project management. You meet someone (your partner) in a coffee break between talks at the conference.

1 Read the information in 'Your profile', and prepare to answer questions about yourself.
2 Write questions to get information about your partner's job, company, current project, etc.
3 Talk to your partner. Ask and answer questions and note down your partner's answers. Begin your conversation with 'Hello, are you enjoying the conference?' End the conversation with 'Anyway, I must go to the next talk. Nice meeting you.'

Input

Student A

Your profile

General

Job	IT specialist
Company	Datatech, a German company based in Stuttgart
Company activity	Software solutions for small companies
Your office	Marseilles, France
Main responsibility	Technical support for all staff
Home	Just outside Marseilles

Now

Current project	A project to develop new support software
Current work location	Stuttgart for three months
Paris hotel	Hotel George VI , near Notre Dame
Current state of business	Business is good; a lot of business in Russia, especially St Petersburg
Other	Conference is very useful

Input

Student B

Your profile

General

Job	HR Manager
Company	GoSports, a London-based company
Company activity	Producer of sports clothing
Your office	Vienna, Austria
Main responsibility	Training and recruitment
Home	50 km north of Vienna in small village

Now

Current project	Management development programme
Current work location	50% in London, 50% in Vienna
Paris hotel	La Residence, near Bastille
Current state of business	Business is excellent; enormous expansion of activity in China
Other	Conference is very enjoyable

2 The organisation quiz

Objective
To ask and answer questions about companies and organisations.

Introduction
In this activity, you will do a quiz about international companies and organisations.

What to do
1 Work in two teams, A and B. In your team, look at the questions and decide on the right answers.
2 Check the answers with your teacher. What is your group score (out of 15)?
3 Then ask the other team the same questions. What is their score?

Input

Team A

1 Which country's national airline is Avianca? ☐
   A Mexico   B Colombia   C Pakistan
2 Where is Microsoft based? ☐
   A San Francisco   B Pittsburgh   C Seattle
3 What does Unicef stand for? ☐
   A United Nations Children's Fund
   B United Nations International Children's Education Fund
   C United International Centre for Equality Funding
4 Which well-known company uses a tick as its logo? ☐
   A Nike   B Vodafone   C Jeep
5 What is the country of origin of the Fujitsu Corporation? ☐
   A Finland   B South Korea   C Japan
6 Where is the headquarters of the Hong Kong and Shanghai Banking Corporation? ☐
   A London   B Hong Kong   C Tokyo
7 Wal*Mart – the world's biggest retailer – reported a turnover of $247bn in January 2002. How many people does the company employ worldwide? ☐
   A 850,000   B 1.4m   C 600,000
8 Motorola is the worldwide market leader in mobile phones.
   True (T) or False (F)? ☐
9 Who is the market leader in the manufacture of computer mice? ☐
   A Hitachi B Hewlett Packard C Logitech
10 Daewo is a Chinese automotive company.
   True (T) or False (F)? ☐
11 How many countries were members of the World Trade Organisation in 2004? ☐
   A 200   B 146   C 106
12 Match these companies to the sector they operate in (*4 points*):
   1 Novartis   ☐   A engineering
   2 Willy Betz ☐   B automobiles
   3 Siemens   ☐   C pharmaceuticals
   4 Kia   ☐   D transportation / road transport

Input

Team B

1 Which country's national airline is Qantas? ☐
   A Canada   B Philippines   C Australia
2 What does WHO stand for? ☐
   A Welfare Holistic Options
   B World Health Organisation
   C World Homes Organisation
3 Which well-known brand uses four linked circles as its logo? ☐
   A Audi   B The Olympic Games   C Chrysler
4 What is the country of origin of the pharmaceuticals giant GlaxoSmithKline? ☐
   A USA   B UK   C Switzerland
5 Where is the World Bank located? ☐
   A Seattle   B Washington   C New York
6 How many employees does Nokia have worldwide? ☐
   A 28,000   B 40,000   C 55,000
7 Volkswagen is the world's biggest car company.
   True (T) or False (F)? ☐
8 Microsoft had a global turnover in 2003 of approximately how much? ☐
   A $3.2bn   B $8.5bn   C $13bn
9 Europe's biggest selling car in history is what? ☐
   A VW Beetle   B Austin Mini   C VW Golf
10 Nokia is Swedish.
   True (T) or False (F)? ☐
11 One of these is not a partnership. Which one? ☐
   A Chrysler and Mercedes Benz
   B Fiat and Volkswagen
   C Renault and Nissan
12 Match these companies to the sector they operate in (*4 points*):
   1 Taco Bell   ☐   A telecommunications
   2 Mannesman   ☐   B petroleum engineering / oil
   3 AGIP   ☐   C shipping / container transportation
   4 Maersk   ☐   D fast food

3 Finding your way round

Objective
To practise asking and answering questions about how to find your way round a town or city you don't know.

Introduction
In this activity, you will ask and answer questions about getting round a major city.

What to do
1 Read through your input and make notes of the questions you want to ask.
2 Decide with your partner which of you will ask questions first.
3 Ask or answer questions about the city in question. Add any details you can.
4 Change roles and repeat the exercise.
5 Report back to the class on useful information you learnt.

Input

Student A
You are going to give your partner practical travel information about finding your way around Bangkok and he/she is going to give you information about Hong Kong.
Ask about:
• the currency
• transport from the airport: how? how much?
• transport round the city: how? how much?
• accommodation: where? how much?
• security: is it safe?
• visa requirements: do you need a visa?

FINDING YOUR WAY ROUND BANGKOK
Currency
The baht (THB50 = €1 approx.)
From the airport
Take a taxi from the International Airport. It shouldn't be more than 300 baht. Only take a taxi in the official taxi queue. Limousines are more expensive.
Round the city
Do take the Skytrain.
Don't take a motorbike taxi ('motorci') – definitely dangerous and bad for your health, especially your knees.
Hotels
Recommend the Pan Pacific Bangkok. Five star. Great views from the 27th floor. Rooms from US$126. Near the railway station.
Security
Fairly safe.
Visa requirements
Not usually required for visit of less than 30 days.
When to visit
October and November are best.

Input

Student B
You are going to give your partner practical travel information about finding your way around Hong Kong and he/she is going to give you information about Bangkok.
Ask about:
• the currency
• transport from the airport: how? how much?
• transport round the city: how? how much?
• accommodation: where? how much?
• security: is it safe?
• visa requirements: do you need a visa?

FINDING YOUR WAY ROUND HONG KONG
Currency
The Hong Kong dollar (HK$10 = €1 approx.)
From the airport
Take the Airport Express (train). HK$70. Fast and comfortable.
Round the city
Taxis: Easy to find and cheap. Starting at HK$15 per trip.
Underground (the MRT): fast and cheap. Buy a travel card for a week's stay. Use your card at the end of each journey.
Walk: Hong Kong is so small that it's often quicker to go on foot.
Ferry: An amazing experience. From HK$2.
Tram: Also an amazing experience. From HK$2.
Hotels
Recommend the Novotel Century Hong Kong. On the island. Rooms from HK$880.
Security
Watch out for pickpockets.
Visa requirements
Not usually required for visit of less than three months.
When to visit
September to December are best, though watch out for typhoons.

4 Telling a story

Objective
To practise telling a story.

Introduction
In this activity, you are going to tell a story using the past simple and past continuous tenses.

What to do
1 Complete the sentences to make a story using the past simple or past continuous of the verbs in brackets.
2 Read your story to your partner.
3 Then swap your stories and check that your partner used the tenses correctly.

Input

Student A

Dinner at eight!
Last night the phone .... (ring) at six o'clock. I didn't answer because I .... (have) a bath. When I checked who the caller was, I .... (find out) that it was a friend who I was going to meet that night for dinner at eight at his house. I called back but nobody answered. I thought my friend .... (cook) the dinner so I .... (decide) not to call again.

When I was ready, I caught a bus to his house. When I .... (arrive) at eight I could see through the window that he .... (work). I knocked but he didn't hear me so I decided to climb up to the window to attract his attention. The wall was very slippery because it .... (rain) and I .... (fall) into his garden.

When my friend heard the noise he .... (come) to the window and asked me what I .... (do). He .... (start) laughing when I explained that I .... (try) to get his attention. When I asked him why he .... (not / prepare) dinner for us he .... (look) surprised. He .... (tell) me that he called earlier to say he .... (prepare) an important presentation and so couldn't see me that evening.

Input

Student B

A terrible business trip to the USA
The flight
I .... (drop) my mobile phone while I .... (check in). I got soaked when I .... (board) because I .... (not / have) an umbrella. When the flight attendant .... (serve) me coffee, she .... (spill) it all over my laptop. I .... (fall) down the aircraft steps as I .... (get off).

The hotel
The room .... (be) very noisy because the hotel was on a main road. I .... (feel) exhausted when I .... (wake up). While I .... (have) a shower, the hot water .... (stop) so I .... (have) a cold shower!

The meeting
Someone took the last parking space just as I .... (arrive) at the company. I .... (have) to park two blocks away. I was dressed casually but everyone else .... (wear) formal clothes. The meeting was a total waste of time because most of the key people .... (not / attend). They .... (celebrate) the CEO's birthday at a special party next door.

5 Swapping jobs

Objective
To practise talking about jobs and employment skills.

Introduction
In this activity, you will discuss different jobs for a job swap.

What to do
1 Work in pairs. Discuss this question with your partner:
   If you could swap jobs for a week, what job would you most like to do?
2 Your teacher will give you two job advertisements. Quickly read the two advertisements. Then choose which job you would each like to do for a week.
3 Complete the information in the table about the job you have chosen.

	You	Your partner
Name of job		
Main responsibilities		
Where the job is based		
Things I would like about this job		
Skills I have that would help me with this job		
What I would learn from this job		

4 Now ask your partner questions about the job he/she has chosen and complete the table.

Input

Regional Arts Project Manager
Are you interested in the arts?
Do you speak two or more languages?

Pavilion – a Regional Arts Organisation – requires a Project Manager responsible for planning and setting up international art exhibitions (painting, drawing, film, sculpture, ceramic and glass works).

The successful candidate will have or will develop:

* Excellent communication skills
* IT competence including Photoshop or similar
* Planning experience
* Ability to work in and manage teams

The position is based in London but involves extensive European travel.

Telephone 44-0800-454545 for details and application form.

Greenham Whitley Associates

Regional Sales Officer

Manager of Telesales office
Responsible for a team of 200 telesales operators
Based in Edinburgh

The successful candidate will have:

* Experience of managing a large sales team
* Excellent interpersonal skills
* Negotiation skills
* Ability to manage customers
* Good telephone manner

Request further details by email:
applicants@fordemployment.org.uk

NATURE CONSERVATION TRUST
FIELD WORKER REQUIRED

Survey work on Scottish west coast recording populations of seabirds
Three month summer placement (June–August) to record bird life on remote Scottish island – no electricity
ESSENTIAL: Good eyesight, ability to live alone, survival skills in difficult landscape
Telephone Thomas on 07770 987500 for an application form.

Editor required for a **leading business and finance newspaper**
The successful candidate will have:
* Good interpersonal skills
* Good numeracy and literacy skills
* Interest in business and finance
* Excellent IT skills and word processing
* Ability to persuade journalists to meet deadlines
* Good organisational abilities
Based in London and Paris
Apply to jobsunlimited@jobs.co.uk

Objective
To practise talking about health and health problems.

Introduction
In this activity, you are going to talk about different kinds of physical feelings – tiredness, stress, etc.

What to do
1 Your teacher will give you one or more strips of paper, each describing a different situation.
2 Imagine you are at an office party: you know all the other guests (the other students). Circulate and talk to several different people one after another in pairs or threes.
3 Tell each of them how you are feeling and find out how they are feeling too. Maybe they can offer you some advice.
4 These phrases will be useful:
   Hello, how are you?
   How are you feeling today?
   Maybe you should … ?
   Have you thought about … –ing?

Input

You are suffering from insomnia. You can't sleep because …

You played tennis / football / another sport yesterday for the first time in five years.

You went to a new restaurant last night. You thought at the time that the fish tasted a bit strange …

You went to a party last night. You went to bed at 4 in the morning.

You desperately need to see your dentist. Unfortunately she can't see you until the end of the week.

You slipped going down some stairs this morning. Now you can't stand up straight.

You've just come from the airport after an 18-hour plane journey.

You have / your wife or partner has recently had a baby. This is your first day back at work.

You ran your first half-marathon (21 kilometres) at the weekend.

You went for a walk in the sunshine at the weekend without a coat. Then it started to rain very heavily.

7 How do things compare?

Objective
To practise comparing.

Introduction
In this activity, you are going to ask your partner to compare people and things in a number of different ways.

What to do
1 Read through the lists below.
2 Write down some more adjectives and adverbs.
3 Write down some of your own ideas under 'People' and 'Things'.
4 Point to an adjective or adverb and one of the ideas under 'People' or 'Things' and ask your partner to make a comparison. For example, if you point to 'difficult' and 'Languages', your partner can say: *Russian grammar is much more difficult than English grammar.*
5 Take it in turns. Say if the grammar of your partner's sentence is correct and how far you agree with what he/she says.

Input

Adjectives
expensive
interesting
good
difficult
safe
clever
....
....
....

Adverbs
easily
efficiently
quickly
dangerously
well
often
....
....
....

People
You and your boss	Colleagues	Politicians
Sportspeople	Musicians	Artists
....	....	....
....	....	....

Things
Companies	Cities	Cars
Languages	Clothes	Food
Countries	Shops	Television
....	....	....
....	....	....

8 To move or not to move

Objective
To discuss a current problem that relates to globalisation.

Introduction
In this activity, you will discuss whether a business should move most of its jobs to another country where labour costs less.

What to do
You are directors of J-Craft, a European jewellery business that employs 250 people. Last year you made profits of €5m. An internal report says the following:

- Relocation outside Europe and employing local craftspeople can reduce labour costs by 70%.
- Profits would rise in the first year to €6m and in the second year to €8 m. In the third year profits would increase to €10m, and would continue to rise (see graph).
- Competition in European and world markets is increasing.

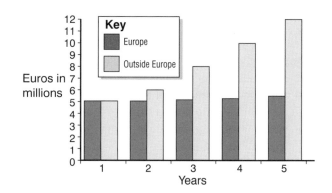

1 Work in two groups, A and B. Read the input your teacher gives you. Note that you all work for the same business but the two groups disagree about its future.
2 In groups, discuss whether to move or to stay in Europe, and try to reach agreement.

Input

GROUP A

Let's move

We'd have more money! Current profits aren't enough

The world market is very competitive – we have to move

We'd have more profits to invest in new markets

Impossible to be sure profits will continue at around €5m per year – the market is more competitive

European production and (especially) labour costs are rising

Opportunity to internationalise will open up to global markets

Recommendation
Keep sales and marketing operation in Europe, but move all production outside Europe

Input

GROUP B

Let's stay here

Not acceptable to make nearly 250 employees redundant

The sales projections may be completely wrong

Existing customers will not like it

Quality may be worse

The cost of relocation will be higher than the report indicates

Possible to enter global markets from Europe too

Recommendation
Better to open a subsidiary outside Europe but retain the European base

9 Happy headlines

Objective
To practise talking about the news.

Introduction
'No news is good news' is an English saying, and people often complain about how negative the news on TV and radio is. In this activity, you will discuss and react to some different news items.

What to do
1 In pairs, take it in turns to tell your partner the news that you have heard.
2 For each news item:
   • A tells B the news
   • B reacts and ask for more information
   • A gives more details based on the information following each headline. Feel free to invent as much extra information of your own as you can. And give your own views.
3 Now change partners and interview two or three other people in your class. If you have time, add your own headlines and invent your own stories.
4 Report back to the whole class on the best news stories that you have heard.

Input

Student A

Two weeks' extra holiday for all
• *'People working too hard,' says minister*
• *'Government buying popularity,' say other parties*
• *Union boss says two more weeks is not enough*
• *Employers' organisation asks: Who will pay?*

Road deaths down 30%
• *'Traffic calming measures in cities having big impact,' says government*
• *Spokesman for taxi drivers says: We hate traffic calming*
• *Greens support slower traffic*
• *Drivers' lobby says no connection between speed and road deaths*

Smoking banned everywhere
• *New law bans smoking in all public and private buildings*
• *Opinion polls show majority support new law*
• *'Cigarettes will be illegal in five years,' says anti-smoking expert*
• *Smokers say: We are not criminals*

Extra-terrestrials make contact
• *Spaceship lands in park in centre of capital*
• *Small green men say: Take us to your leader*
• *Message of peace and love from another galaxy in perfect English*
• *President says: We want exclusive trade contract – they came here first*

Input

Student B

10% growth forecast for next five years
• *We understand the secret of permanent growth, say economists*
• *No more poverty*
• *Everyone will be 30% better off than today*
• *'We will not raise taxes,' says government*

New pollution-free car launched
• *Italian reveals new invention: I built it in my garage at weekends*
• *New car runs on solar power – achieves speeds of 150 km per hour*
• *Share prices of big car companies collapse*
• *Major football star orders a dozen; says supporting the environment is important*

National team wins fifteenth game in a row to win the big Cup
• *Longest unbeaten run in national team's history*
• *Swedish coach has managed a miracle*
• *Fans dance in streets all day and all night – work stops*
• *Players ask for more money*

First humans land on Mars
• *Historic pictures of first footprints on red planet*
• *More water discovered – is there life on Mars?*
• *Strange noises trouble astronauts*
• *McDonald's announces restaurant plans*

10 It's my turn

Objective

To practise using the past simple, present perfect simple and present perfect continuous tenses.

Introduction

In this activity, you are going to play a game which tests your ability to use the past simple and the present perfect simple and continuous.

What to do

Work in groups of three or four. Take it in turns to roll a die, move the number of spaces on the board and complete the task on each square. If a person makes a mistake with the task, they do not move forward and remain in the original position. If a person throws a six, they do NOT move and they miss their next turn.

There are different types of task on the squares.

1 Make a sentence. This means you have to make a sentence including the target word.
2 Make a question. This means you have to make a question which will generate the answer in the square.
3 Correct the grammar mistake. This means you have to correct the grammar mistake in the sentence.
4 Rebuild this sentence. This means you have to make a new sentence which has the same meaning but uses the key word stated.
5 Sometimes you just follow the instructions on the board telling you to move forward or back.

Input

START				
Make a sentence about yourself which includes 'since'.	Make a question for this answer: 'I met some friends.'	Make a sentence about yourself which includes 'ago'.	**Go back two squares.**	Correct the grammar mistake: 'I am here since three days.'
Correct the grammar mistake: 'I have done it last night.'	Make a question for this answer: 'No, I haven't. I've been to Lisbon but not to Porto.'	**Go back to the beginning.**	Make a question for this answer: 'I have worked here for the last ten years.'	Rebuild this sentence using *for* instead of *since*: 'I've been living here for the last ten years.'
Nominate one player to go back four squares.	Make a question for this answer: 'I worked there for two years.	**Go forward two squares.**	Make a question for this answer: 'No, I haven't. But I would love to go there.'	Correct the grammar mistake: 'When have you arrived?'
FINISH	**Go back seven squares.**	Make a question for this answer: 'Not yet. I plan to finish it tonight.'	Rebuild this sentence using *since* instead of *for*: 'I've worked here since 2001.'	Make a sentence about yourself which includes *last night*.

11 THAT'S REALLY *Rich!*

Objective
To talk about investments.

Introduction
In this activity, you will continue the game THAT'S REALLY RICH! You have an extra $50,000 to invest. At the end of the game, see who has the most money.

What to do
1 Work in pairs. Student A should ask Student B to choose a number from 5, 6 or 7. Then Student B should ask Student A to choose a number from 8, 9 or 10.
2 You should each read the investment choice to your partner, who makes his/her choice. Tell him/her the result of the investment.
3 After doing all the choices, the winner is the student who has the most money. You may combine this with the result from the first game in the Student's Book.

Input

STUDENT A
Each player starts with $50,000.

5 THAT'S REALLY RICH!
Bet $10,000 on the result of a football match. If the result is 3–0, you will collect $100,000.
OR
Lend $15,000 to your cousin who is setting up a business in Moscow.
Result:
Football bet: Your team is winning 3–0, but lets in a goal in the last minute of the game. The result is 3–1, you lose your money.
Your cousin's business: The business does well. Your cousin returns the loan after two years. No profit for you, but you are happy.

6 THAT'S REALLY RICH!
Invest $25,000 in a high technology business in Toulouse.
OR
Invest $20,000 in yourself – you plan to become a horse trainer.
Result:
Hi-tech business: The business is taken over by a competitor and closed down. You get $20,000 back, but you lose $5,000 of your investment.
Horse training: Your new career goes well and you recover the $20,000, but you make no profit from your investment.

7 THAT'S REALLY RICH!
Spend $30,000 as a share in a remote Scottish island. You plan to turn it into a theme park and holiday camp.
OR
Invest $25,000 as a share in a flat for a relative who is going to work in Paris for three years.
Result:
Scottish island: You did not do your research. The island is a site of special scientific interest and no development is allowed. You lose $20,000 of your investment.
Paris flat: An excellent investment. You later sell the flat and make $25,000 profit.

Input

STUDENT B
Each player starts with $50,000.

8 THAT'S REALLY RICH!
Spend $5,000 on lottery tickets.
OR
Spend $5,000 on an all-expenses paid luxury trip to the Prix de L'Arc de Triomphe horse race in Paris. If all your bets go well, you will win $10,000.
Result:
Lottery: You were warned! You lose all your money.
Paris horse race: You have a great trip and your bets are successful. You win $10,000.

9 THAT'S REALLY RICH!
A friend of yours is an art critic for a national newspaper. On a visit to New York, you go with her to an exhibition in a Manhattan gallery. On her advice, you buy a painting for $5,000.
OR
Invest $10,000 in shares in a group of companies in the Asia Pacific region.
Result:
Painting: You later decide you don't really like the painting and you sell it at auction in Paris. Your friend was right about the painter. You make $5,000 profit.
Shares: The region experiences good growth and the companies do very well. You sell the shares and make $10,000 profit.

10 THAT'S REALLY RICH!
Buy a Louis XVI table and six chairs at an auction near your home. They cost you $15,000.
OR
Buy an antique, supposedly original, manuscript of a Grieg piano sonata at a local charity event. You do not know if it is genuine. You pay $1,000.
Result:
The furniture: Sadly, the furniture is destroyed in a fire. You forgot to check your insurance. They pay you $5,000.
The manuscript: You take it to Sotheby's in London. It is genuine. You sell it for $20,000.

Objective

To discuss a major environmental problem – increasing traffic.

Introduction

In this activity, you will take part in a meeting to discuss how to deal with increasing traffic volumes in the city where you live.

Input

What to do

You live in a city with traffic problems. You receive this notice.

1 Read the notice.
2 Read the role card your teacher gives you. Plan how to make your points, and think of extra ideas.
3 At the meeting, ensure that the chair takes note of what you have to say.

FED UP WITH TRAFFIC PROBLEMS?

Fed up with never finding anywhere to park?
Fed up with the high cost of city parking? Fed up with constant jams and the time it takes you to get to work?

Come to a
PUBLIC MEETING
next Thursday at 7.30 pm in the city hall and share your views.
The meeting will be chaired by a senior city council representative.
YOUR CHANCE TO TELL THE COUNCIL WHAT YOU THINK

ROLE CARD 1
You are the **chair of the meeting**. Your job is to:
• control the meeting
• identify what you think are the most important recommendations at the end.
You may wish to tell the participants at some stage that your city has been given some money to help with new transport solutions.

ROLE CARD 2
Your main concern is **the local economy**. You are the owner of a shop in the city centre. Make sure the chair takes note of your opinions:
• you want it to be easier and quicker for drivers to get in to the city centre
• you want more (and cheaper) car parks in the city centre
• you want to encourage drivers to come to the city centre so they can go shopping easily.

ROLE CARD 3
Your main concern is **the environment**. Make sure the chair takes note of your opinions:
• you want a complete ban on cars in the city centre
• traffic noise is very high
• pollution is damaging historic buildings.

ROLE CARD 4
Your main concern is **safety**. Make sure the chair takes note of your opinions:
• you think cars drive too fast – there are too many accidents
• the speed limit should be reduced to 30 km per hour on all main roads in the city and to 20 km per hour in the city centre
• drivers who break the speed limit should pay instant fines.

ROLE CARD 5
Your main concern is **health**. Make sure the chair takes note of your opinions:
• asthma is increasing, especially among children – you think this is caused by traffic fumes
• you want a complete ban on cars in the city centre – this will reduce the level of fumes
• you think people should walk and cycle more
• the council should provide free cycles and create more cycle lanes on roads.

ROLE CARD 6
Your main concern is **public transport**. Make sure the chair takes note of your opinions:
• you think that public transport services should be much more efficient and fares should be less expensive – this would encourage people to use public transport
• you think the council should construct a light railway or super tramway through the city
• the council should provide more park and ride services.

ROLE CARD 7
Your main concern is **money**. Make sure the chair takes note of your opinions:
• you think drivers should pay a charge to enter the city centre – this already happens in some major cities
• drivers should pay more to park in the city centre – car parking charges should be doubled.

13 The future

Objective
To practise talking about the future.

Introduction
In this activity, you will talk about future actions which we decide to do at the moment of speaking (using *will*), decisions and plans we have already made (using *going to*) and fixed future arrangements, especially in relation to personal travel and meetings (using the present continuous).

What to do
Work in groups.

1 Your teacher will give you some pieces of paper. Each piece of paper has a sentence or question that you will have to reply to. Put the pieces of paper in a pile face down.
2 Turn over the first piece of paper. If you think you can answer the question, pick the paper up before someone else in the group does. You have five seconds to answer the question. Your reply <u>must</u> contain the verb in brackets and the correct form of *will*, *going to* or the present continuous. Sometimes more than one answer is possible.
3 If the other people in your group think your answer is grammatically correct then you score one point. The game continues until all the questions have been answered correctly. The winner is the person with most points.

Input

✂ -

1
Your colleague says: I can't open the email you sent me!
You say: (resend) ....

2
Your colleague says: Do you have any plans for tonight?
You say: (eat) ....

3
Your colleague says: (on the phone) I can't talk just now. I'm in a meeting!
You say: (call back) ....

4
Your colleague says: (leave) .... ?
You say: I'm flying at ten o'clock tomorrow morning.

5
Your colleague says: What are you doing tonight?
You say: (meet) ....

6
Your colleague says: You forgot to send the attachment with your email.
You say: (fax) ....

7
Your colleague says: When are you going to speak to Caterina?
You say: (talk) ....

8
Your colleague says: When are you meeting Jean-Pierre?
You say: (see) ....

9
Your colleague says: When are you going to Germany?
You say: (fly) ....

10
Your colleague says: (finish) .... ?
You say: I'll do it this afternoon.

14 Can you help?

Objective
To practise talking about customer service problems.

Introduction
In this activity, you are going to solve some customer service problems.

What to do
1 Work in groups of three. Imagine that you each work for the customer services department in a different organisation. Your teacher will give you a letter of complaint you have recently received.
2 Decide what you will do to solve the problem in your letter of complaint.
3 Take it in turns to explain to the other members of the group:
   • who you work for
   • what the problem is
   • what you are going to do to help the customer.
Do your partners think you would work well in customer services?

> **Useful language**
> I work for ...
> My job is to deal with ...
> The customer is complaining that ...
> The customer's complaint is that ...
> I'm going to write a letter of apology ...
> I'm sending the customer £100 as compensation for ...
> I'll phone the customer to explain ...

Input

Student A
You work for the customer services department in a bank. You have received this letter:

On May 23, I discovered there had been three incorrect payments totalling £1,635 from my current account using my credit card. One was for a phone bill, one was to a shop and one was a payment to a store card. They were all for well over £500.

I phoned you and reported the incorrect payments that day but I have had no reply from you. It is a huge sum of money for me to lose - I was going to use this money to pay for a new car.

Can you help?

Input

Student B
You work for the customer services department in a computer company. You have received this letter:

I'm writing to complain about the PC I recently bought. I have tried connecting the PC to the internet but have been unable to do so after several attempts. I have spent over ten hours now on the telephone to your technical support staff who have also been unable to connect me to the web. The last person I spoke to was very unhelpful and in the end claimed that it wasn't your company's problem and that they could do nothing else to help me.

I work from home and need internet access to be able to do my job properly. I now calculate that I have lost at least three days' work because of this.

What are you going to do about it?

Input

Student C
You work for the customer services department in an electricity company. You have received this letter:

I recently received a letter from your company threatening me with legal action over an unpaid electricity bill of £149 dating from January last year. I had never previously received any letters about this bill and was very surprised as I had paid the bill in February. I immediately contacted you about this and was told that it was a mistake and that I would hear nothing else about it.

Imagine my surprise this morning when I received another letter from you saying that you would be cutting off my electricity supply on Friday!

Please check your records and ensure my electricity supply is not cut off. You have already admitted your mistake and I now want a satisfactory explanation from you and some compensation for the time I have wasted. I am seriously considering changing my supplier.

15 Home improvements

Objective
To practise talking about the different parts of your home.

Introduction
In this activity, you will talk about your own home and how you would like to change it.

What to do
You have inherited some money (about €50,000!) and want to extend your home. You have arranged a meeting with an architect who will listen to your ideas and who may make some suggestions of his/her own.

1 Decide with your partner which role you should take first.
2 Draw a rough plan of each floor of your home and think about how you would spend the money to improve your home.

3 Describe the place where you live to the architect (your partner).
4 Describe what you want to do with the money and listen to his/her advice.
5 Now reverse roles.

Example dialogue

A: On the ground floor there's a kitchen, living room and dining room. The kitchen is quite old and I'd like to have a fitted kitchen.

B: A fitted kitchen can be very expensive. It depends how big your kitchen is of course, and what you'd like to have in it. How much would you like to spend?

A: My budget is €10,000. What can you recommend?

Input

For a house or an apartment, you could think about:

	Prices from
a sauna	€2,500
a fitted kitchen	€10,000
a new bathroom with Jacuzzi	€10,000
an indoor gymnasium	€20,000

For a house, you could also think about:

	Prices from
a garage	€5,000
an outdoor tennis court	€10,000
a conservatory	€12,000
a loft conversion	€20,000

Ground floor plan

First floor plan

Second floor plan

16 Promoting your organisation

Objective
To practise using quantifiers.

Introduction
In this activity, you are going to talk about how to attract people to work in your organisation.

What to do
You are working on a special project with the objective of attracting the best young graduates to your organisation. You have to write a new page for your website which sells the benefits of working for your organisation.
Work in groups.
1 Write sentences using as many of the quantifiers as you can, as in the examples.
2 Read out your sentences to the class.
3 Discuss which sentences for the web page will be the most effective in attracting the best graduates.

Input

all	All employees will receive the training they need to develop in this organisation.
every	
each	
most	
much	Look carefully at our offer. The competition doesn't give you much in comparison.
many	
a few	
a lot of	
no	
any	If you have any friends who you think might want to apply, tell them. We'll give you a bonus if we recruit them.
some	

17 What can it be?

Objective
To practise talking about and describing products.

Introduction
In this activity, you will practise:
- describing a product
- asking and answering questions about it
- summarising information about it.

What to do
1 You should think of a product that you use at least once a week, then tell your teacher so no one else hears what the product is. Don't tell anyone else. Write down what the product is but show it to no one except your teacher.
2 Each student gets a turn in the 'hot seat' to answer questions about their product. The rest of the class tries to work out what the product is.

Input
....

Rules
- Each individual student should only ask a maximum of FIVE questions, and no more than TWO at any one time.
- After two questions, another student should ask a question.
- Occasionally stop the questioning so one student can recap what you have found out about the product.
- When the product has been identified correctly, the student in the hot seat should describe the product in as much detail as he/she can.
- The student who correctly identified the product has the next turn in the hot seat.

Example questions
Is it something you use every day?
Is it something you carry around?
Is it a mechanical product?
Is it electronic?
Is it made of plastic?
Is it made of plastic and metal?
Do you use it at home?
Do you use it mainly for work?

Where was it made?
What colour is it?
How long is it?
How much does it weigh?
How high is it?

18 Can I help you?

Objective

To think about and practise using expressions for helping people in everyday situations.

Introduction

In this activity, you will offer help to people in everyday situations and think about what you say when you do this.

What to do

Work with a partner. You are both helpful people.

1 Look at the situations (1–8).
2 For each situation, you are going to act out a mini-dialogue. Take it in turns to start.
3 After each dialogue, write down phrases you have used which you think can be useful when offering help to people.
4 Share your phrases with the rest of the class when you have finished.

Useful language
Can I help you?
Shall I call the police?
Would you like me to ... ?
Sorry to bother you ...
That's very kind of you.
It's nothing at all. Anyone would do the same.
Thank you so much again. It was extremely kind of you.

Example dialogue for input 3
A: Excuse me. Sorry to bother you but I think you dropped this.
B: Oh, it's my wallet! It's got all my money and cards in! That's very kind of you. How lucky! Thank you very much.
A: No, it's nothing at all. Anyone would do the same. Well, I'm glad you found it. Goodbye.
B: Goodbye. And thank you so much again. It was extremely kind of you!

Input

1 A colleague is having problems with his/her computer. You offer to help.

2 A colleague is very overworked and says he/she will have to stay at work until 8 o'clock this evening to finish things off. It's 6 o'clock and you want to go home, but you know it's your colleague's partner's birthday and that they have something planned.

3 You find a wallet in the street. You think that a woman about 10 metres ahead of you dropped it but you're not sure.

4 An old lady is standing at the side of a very busy road. She looks as if she may want to cross to the other side.

5 A visitor to your organisation wants to make some photocopies.

6 A colleague calls to tell you that her car has broken down about 10 kilometres from the office.

7 A visitor offers to take you to lunch but at the end of the meal he discovers his wallet is at home and he has no money with him.

8 A colleague thinks his/her mobile phone has been stolen.

19 Solving problems

Objective
To practise using *if* and *when* with the present simple and *will*, *can* and *may*.

Introduction
In this activity, you are going to talk about problems.

What to do
1 Complete the telephone conversation using the phrases in the box.
2 In pairs, prepare a role-play of a real or possible work-based telephone conversation using one of the following scenarios. Do NOT write down the conversation. You should discuss the situation and plan what each person will say. You can practise the telephone call together (speaking quietly) before you perform the role-play for the class.

> **Telephone scenarios**
> Solving a problem   Leaving a message
> Arranging a meeting

When you plan what to say during your phone conversation, you must include four first conditional sentences: two sentences with *if*, and two sentences with *when*, using the present simple and *will* form of the future.
Examples:
Solving a problem If you check the intranet, you will find a troubleshooting guide for laptops.
Leaving a message When she gets back into the office, I'll give her the message.
Arranging a meeting If you let me have your arrival details, I'll arrange for a taxi to pick you up.

3 Perform your conversation for the class. The other students should listen for the *if* and *when* sentences which you use and note them down. When you have finished the role-play, they should tell you if the sentences were grammatically correct or not.

Input

if I have time	when we know	will it be OK if
when you have	if we run	if two more people do

Telephone conversation

HANS: Hans Schmidt speaking.
DANIELA: Hi, Hans. It's Daniela. I've got a problem.
HANS: What's wrong?
DANIELA: I only have two participants registered for the sales training course next week and registration closes at four tomorrow afternoon. (1) .... we run the course?
HANS: No, we'll have problems. (2) .... the course, the HR manager will be very unhappy. She always says we need at least six participants to make courses cost-effective.
DANIELA: I know. I suppose a few more people may register today or tomorrow. (3) .... , do you think we can run the course?
HANS: Yes, it's possible. I think we can make a decision (4) .... the final numbers at four tomorrow. Could you call me back tomorrow afternoon?
DANIELA: OK. (5) .... , I'll call a few people and try to persuade them to register.
HANS: Good idea. (6) .... the final numbers, we can talk again.
DANIELA: OK. Bye.

20 Launching a new product

Objective
To practise speaking about marketing.

Introduction
In this activity, you are going to talk about and compare some different marketing ideas.

What to do
Work in teams of three or four. You and your team have €200,000 to spend on marketing a new monthly magazine, called *Europa*, for young professionals. Look at the ideas below.
1 Decide which ideas are good and which ideas are not.
2 Choose a set of good ideas that will not cost more than €200,000.
3 Compare your opinions with another group. How similar are their ideas to yours?

Input

		Cost
1	Advertise in up-market newspapers in major European countries.	€50,000
2	Advertise in in-flight magazines for leading European airlines.	€25,000
3	Employ agents on a commission to secure subscriptions.	€25,000
4	Cold call offices of businesses in major cities in Europe.	€20,000
5	Employ a market research company to identify target readers.	€50,000
6	Use direct mailing to businesses in European capital cities.	€75,000
7	Do a free copy promotion to businesses after cold calling.	€75,000
8	Pay for airport, station and street advertising in main cities.	€60,000
9	Organise a campaign of TV advertising on satellite news channels.	€100,000
10	Deliver sample copies to homes in up-market residential areas.	€70,000
11	Run promotions offering free copies with luxury foods.	€20,000
12	Hand out free copies in the street to young people.	€40,000

21 Film classics

Objective
To practise talking about films and the cinema.

Introduction
In this activity, you will discuss different films and choose a film you would like to see.

What to do
You are on a business trip to a town where the cinema near your hotel is running a festival of classic films. You have a free evening with your colleagues.

1 Work in groups of three or four. The other students are your colleagues on your business trip.
2 Tell the other members of the group which of the films showing tonight you would like to see. If you know a film and your partners do not, give more information about it. Try to convince your colleagues to see your film.
3 Agree with your colleagues which film you will all go to see.

Input

Tonight's classic films are:

Film	Country	Year	Director	Starring	The story
The Sound of Music	USA	1965	Robert Wise	Julie Andrews Christopher Plummer Eleanor Parker	Based on the true story of the von Trapp family in pre-war Austria. Winner of five Academy Awards.
Metropolis	Germany	1927	Fritz Lang	Brigitte Helm Gustav Froehlich Alfred Abel	A magnificent futuristic city is maintained by workers enslaved underground. The first science-fiction movie.
Shrek	USA	2001	Andrew Jackson Vicky Jenson Scott Marshall	Mike Myers Eddie Murphy Cameron Diaz	Already a classic. Computer-animated comedy starring a princess, an ogre and a donkey!
Amélie	France	2001	Jean-Pierre Jenet		Watch Amélie find love in this wonderful romantic comedy.
The Good, The Bad and the Ugly	Italy/Spain	1966	Sergio Leone	Clint Eastwood Lee Van Cleef Luigi Pistilli	One of the greatest Westerns of all time by a master of the genre. Unforgettable music!

22 Responsibilities, rules and advice

Objective
To practise using *must*, *have to* and *need to*.

Introduction
In this activity, you are going to talk about work.

What to do
1 Match the sentences below to the correct heading (1–5). Compare your answers with a partner.
2 Write some questions to find out the following from your partner:
   • his/her job responsibilities (past, present and future)
   • rules he/she follows at work
   • tips he/she has for success at work.
3 Ask and answer questions with your partner. When you answer the questions, try to use *must*, *have to* and *need to* in your answers.

Input

> Example question and alternative answers
> Q: Do you have to work more than 40 hours a week?
> A: I think everyone has to work more than 40 hours a week sometimes.
> A: No. I don't need to work more than 37 hours according to my contract.
> A: I don't think I have to but I must ask my boss. I think she expects it.

Headings
1 Past job responsibilities
2 Future job responsibilities
3 Current job responsibilities
4 Rules at work
5 Advice about work

☐ You mustn't use the management car park except in case of emergency.
☐ You must slow down. You're working too hard.
☐ I had to learn a lot about IT in my first job.
☐ I don't have to start work until 8.30 am.
☐ You need to buy a new suit!
☐ I didn't have to travel so much in my last job.
☐ I will have to speak a lot more English.
☐ You mustn't drink any alcohol.
☐ In future I won't have to be in the office every day. I can work from home more.
☐ I have to work at weekends sometimes.

Your questions

....
....
....
....
....
....
....
....
....

23 An appraisal interview

Objective
To practise speaking about human resources issues.

What to do
Student A

Conduct an appraisal interview with your partner. You are the human resources manager at PGA Associates, a marketing consultancy company.

1 Use the form to ask the employee (your partner) questions, and note down his/her answers.
2 Give him/her recommendations, suggestions and positive news.

Note: You know that your company is growing and recruiting more staff and also that it plans to introduce a staff development programme, including opportunities for training in communications skills, foreign languages and IT skills. Not all the staff know this.

Introduction
In this activity, you are going to do a role-play based on an appraisal interview.

What to do
Student B

Conduct an appraisal interview with your partner. You are an employee at PGA Associates, a marketing consultancy company. Your partner is the human resources manager.

1 Use the notes on the form to help you answer the questions in the interview.
2 Raise the four problems listed under issues. Note down any recommendations your HR manager suggests.

Input

Student A

Name	Paul/Paula Lemont
Current position	Administrator
Best things about the company	....
Best things about the job	....
Things he/she doesn't like about the job	....
Target this year	....
Issues	....
	....
	....
	....
Recommendations	Tell PL about the company's plans. You think that PL should not wait for the company to start the training courses; he/she should study at evening classes and the company would pay.
Notes	....
	....

Input

Student B

Name	Paul/Paula Lemont
Current position	Administrator
Best things about the company	Working environment, good communication among staff
Best things about the job	Friends and colleagues
Things you don't like about the job	Routine, repetition, same thing every day
Target this year	More responsibility
Issues	You want: foreign language classes; IT skills training, especially database and Excel; more contact with customers; more responsibility
Recommendations	PGA should provide training opportunities; suggest a PGA newsletter – to tell employees about company plans and achievements
Notes	....
	....

24 A serious problem

Objective
To discuss a social issue and ideas for dealing with it.

Introduction
In this activity, you will make recommendations about how to deal with a serious social problem – in some countries at least: football hooliganism.

What to do
1 Read the article and look at some suggestions for dealing with the problem.
2 Discuss these questions with your partner:
   • How far is this a problem in your country?
   • Why is it a problem in Britain?
   • What can be done to reduce the size of the problem?
3 Report back to the class with your recommendations.

> Useful language
> I think ...
> The problem is ...
> The reason for ...
> It would be a good idea to ...
> It would help if ...
> Do you agree?
> What do you suggest?
> What happens in your country?

Input

BAD YEAR FOR FOOTBALL

Last year there was an increase in violence connected with football. Football-related arrests in England and Wales increased by 19% from the previous year and reached a new high of 4,793, according to a government report. The report highlighted the fact that younger men are becoming football hooligans and that 79% of arrests took place outside stadiums. Police are currently looking into ways to stop this rising problem but opinion is currently divided about how best to achieve this.

Suggestions
Provide more money for policing to:
· police the grounds
· police the route from the stadium to the town centre and railway station
· take action against racist chanting
Ban alcohol inside football grounds
Re-introduce military service in the UK for 18–20 year olds
Place banning orders on fans preventing them from attending matches
Build all-seater stadiums
Send more football hooligans to prison
Take passports away from known hooligans to stop them travelling to matches in other countries
Improve controls on ticket sales at international matches
Introduce closed circuit TV cameras inside and outside all football grounds
Make all football fans buy tickets for matches in advance
Take away points from clubs whose fans behave badly

YOUR OWN IDEAS:
....
....
....

By how much do you think your recommendations will reduce the level of football hooliganism?
....
....

25 What would you do if ... ?

Objective
To practise using the second conditional tense.

Introduction
In this activity, you are going to talk about what you would do in some hypothetical situations.

What to do
1 Answer the questions on your own.
2 Work in groups. For each question, choose a person in your group and predict what he/she chose as the answer to the question. Check with the person whether the group's prediction was correct.
3 Ask follow-up questions to make the group members explain the reason for their choices.
4 Write some similar *What would you do if ...?* questions of your own to ask another group.

Input

What would you do if ...

1 **your organisation offered you a one-year position in Australia with three times the salary?**
   a Accept immediately ☐
   b Refuse immediately ☐
   c Take some time to think about it ☐
   d Your own answer ☐ ....

2 **your organisation reduced your annual holiday by one week to save money?**
   a Leave the organisation ☐
   b Accept the decision ☐
   c Negotiate a smaller reduction with your manager ☐
   d Your own answer ☐ ....

3 **a member of your project team seemed very unmotivated?**
   a Talk to them privately ☐
   b Report the situation to the project leader ☐
   c Do nothing because it's the job of the project leader ☐
   d Your own answer ☐ ....

4 **your boss told you that you had to give a 30-minute presentation of your organisation in English to a group of important overseas visitors?**
   a Take an intensive English course to prepare ☐
   b Find a colleague who was willing to do it instead of you ☐
   c Stay at home sick on the day of the visit ☐
   d Your own answer ☐ ....

5 **you won a holiday competition – a week anywhere in the world as long as you go next week?**
   a Travel to a place you have always wanted to visit ☐
   b Refuse the holiday because you are too busy ☐
   c Donate the value of the holiday to a local charity ☐
   d Your own answer ☐ ....

6 **you found a briefcase with €5,000 in cash under a train seat on your way to work?**
   a Take it to the police immediately ☐
   b Do nothing and leave the briefcase on the train ☐
   c Keep the money and buy a new car ☐
   d Your own answer ☐ ....

7 **a colleague used one of your ideas to suggest a cost-saving change in your organisation and received a large bonus payment?**
   a Ask your colleague for 50% of the bonus payment ☐
   b Do nothing but decide not to share ideas at work with this colleague ☐
   c Complain to your boss about your colleague's behaviour
   d Your own answer ☐ ....

8 **a colleague asked you to speak only English at work together as a way for you both to improve your English?**
   a Say it is a good idea and do it ☐
   b Agree to speak English together but only during lunch ☐
   c Refuse ☐
   d Your own answer ☐ ....

9 **your bank credited your account with €5,000 in error?**
   a Report the mistake to the bank immediately ☐
   b Do nothing and wait for the bank to correct the mistake
   c Spend the money immediately ☐
   d Your own answer ☐ ....

10 **your organisation offered you a six-month career break on half pay to re-energise yourself?**
   a Accept the offer and travel round the world ☐
   b Refuse because you suspect the company wants you to leave ☐
   c Ask for time to think about it ☐
   d Your own answer ☐ ....

26 There's a problem, I'm afraid

Objective
To consolidate key phrases used in telephoning, especially for handling complaints and problems.

Introduction
In this activity, you will practise making a telephone call with a partner.

What to do
1. Read through the information about your telephone call and think about what you will say.
2. Work with a partner. Student A telephones Student B, and Student B speaks first.

Input

Student A
You are the caller.

- STUDENT B STARTS THE PHONE CALL.

- Introduce yourself. Tell Customer Services that you have received a contract in the post. There are some problems with the contract.

- Give the number (33288G).

- You are not happy. Ask to speak to the Customer Services Manager.

- Complain that you are not happy with this quality of service.

- Say there are a number of mistakes – it's not what you had agreed

- Agree and give a telephone number.

- Confirm as correct or correct any mistake.

- Reply. Say you look forward to hearing from Sophie Kessler. Ask for an email to confirm that she will call.

- Give your email address.

- End the call.

Input

Student B
You answer the phone.

- YOU START THE PHONE CALL.

- Say: Customer Services, how may I help you?

- Ask for the reference number for the contract.

- Confirm the number. Explain that the person responsible for this contract is away today.

- Explain that the Customer Services Manager is not available today (at a conference).

- Apologise and ask what exactly the problem with the contract is.

- Apologise and offer to ask the Customer Services Manager, Sophie Kessler, to telephone the caller on Monday.

- Check the telephone number.

- Apologise again for any problem with the contract.

- Agree and ask for the caller's email address.

- Confirm and end the call.

27 Guess who's coming to dinner

Objective
To practise talking about food and favourite dishes.

Introduction
In this activity, you will plan a menu containing some of your favourite foods.

What to do
You and your partner work in the same organisation. Two important foreign guests are coming to visit your organisation. You want to welcome them with a show of hospitality and have therefore decided to invite them to a meal which you will cook together.

1 Decide your menu together.
2 Describe how to prepare each course.
3 Show your menu to other students in the class and decide which menu would be the best dinner.

Input

MENU

Starter

Main course

Dessert

28 Useless facts

Objective

To practise using the present simple passive and past simple passive.

Introduction

In this activity, you are going to talk about strange and interesting facts about our world.

Useless facts is a website dedicated to interesting pieces of information that you don't really need to know.

What to do

1 Look at Useless factfile 1. Write questions using the present simple passive and past simple passive to get the missing information in the sentences, as in the example. Then work with a partner. Ask the questions and note down your partner's answers.

2 Use Useless factfile 2 to answer your partner's questions. Before you answer, tell your partner if the grammar of his/her question is correct.

Input

Student A

Useless factfile 1

1 Nearly .... (number) glasses of milk are produced in the lifetime of the average cow.
How many glasses of milk are produced in the lifetime of the average cow?

2 Almost .... (number) kilos of lipstick are consumed in the lifetime of the average woman.

3 Diet Coke was created in .... (year).

4 An average of .... (number) cigarettes are smoked per person each year in China.

5 Women were first given the vote in the USA in .... (year).

6 The largest taxi fleet in the world is located in .... (city) – a fleet of over 60,000 taxis.

Useless factfile 2

1 The toothbrush was invented in 1498 in China.

2 In the Great Fire of London in 1666, half of London was burnt down but only six people were injured.

3 The first police force was established in 1667 in Paris.

4 In 1933, 800,000 fan letters were received by Mickey Mouse.

5 The largest painting on earth was painted by Robert Wyland. It is a 35,356 m² mural of a whale.

6 About two kilos of rubbish are produced by everyone each day. Most of it is paper.

Input

Student B

Useless factfile 1

1 The toothbrush was invented in .... (year) in China.
When was the toothbrush invented in China?

2 In the Great Fire of London in 1666, half of London was burnt down but only .... (number) people were injured.

3 The first police force was established in .... (year).

4 In 1933, ... (number) fan letters were received by Mickey Mouse.

5 The largest painting on earth was painted by .... (person). It is a 35,356 m² mural of a whale.

6 About .... (number) kilos of rubbish are produced by everyone each day. Most of it is paper.

Useless factfile 2

1 Nearly 200,000 glasses of milk are produced in the lifetime of the average cow.

2 Almost three kilos of lipstick are consumed in the lifetime of the average woman.

3 Diet Coke was created in 1982.

4 An average of 1,800 cigarettes are smoked per person each year in China.

5 Women were first given the vote in the USA in 1869 in the state of Wyoming.

6 The largest taxi fleet in the world is located in Mexico City – a fleet of over 60,000 taxis.

29 The way things are

Objective
To practise talking about your current job and how you hope your career will progress.

Introduction
In this activity, you will answer questions about your career and discuss your plans with a partner.

What to do
1 Answer the questions on your own.
2 Ask your partner the questions and note down his/her answers.
3 Think of two more questions to ask your partner and write them down.

Input

	You	Your partner
Current job title		
Company/organisation		
Length of time in current job		
5 year target: What would you like to be doing?		
10 year target: What would you like to be doing?		
Would you like to learn new skills or study something new? If so, what?		
What is your idea of the perfect job/career?		
Do you think you have a good work–life balance?		
If you could change ONE thing about your current job, what would it be?		
What is the best thing about your current job?		
Your question:		
Your question:		

30 Saying goodbye

Objective
To practise saying goodbye.

Introduction
In this activity, you will perform short role-plays of people saying goodbye in different situations and focus on useful language for doing this.

What to do
1 Your teacher will give you a situation to act out with your partner. Each pair will be given a different situation.
2 Practise the situation with your partner.
3 Now each pair should perform their role-play in front of the rest of the group. The others must say what the situation is at the end of each role-play.

Input

A parent saying goodbye to his/her child on its first day at school.

A husband saying goodbye to his wife at the airport. She is leaving for a three-month business trip.

A conductor saying goodbye to the orchestra he/she has worked with for a long time after their last concert together. The leader of the orchestra responds with a speech of thanks.

A senior manager saying goodbye on behalf of the company to an employee who is retiring after 30 years' service. The employee responds.

An employee saying goodbye to another who is leaving. The employee is in love with the one who is leaving but has never said so.

An employee saying goodbye, on behalf of the other employees in the department, to a rather unpopular department head who is leaving after three or four years in the job.

A dinner guest saying goodbye to his/her host and hostess at the end of an evening spent in their home.

A student saying goodbye to a teacher at the end of a year's English course.

----

5 Better learning activities

Teacher's notes

Introduction

As well as the 30 photocopiable Extra classroom activities, each one linked to one of the units in the Student's Book, there are ten learning-to-learn activities which can be done in parallel with the main course. There is a certain amount of overlap between activities but this should not be a barrier to doing them all since it should serve to emphasise some of the key points. They do not necessarily take up a lot of time but can be critical in encouraging students to think about how they learn and therefore to learn better. Indeed, if any of them question the usefulness of such activities, you might invite other students to reflect on what proportion of the course might usefully be given over to this.

The aims of some of these activities are quite sophisticated and the language resources of your students may well be limited. However, as we have said elsewhere, we strongly believe that both students and teachers can say a great deal if they **make the most** of the limited language resources at their mutual disposal.

Since there are ten such activities in the Teacher's Book, you might think about doing one activity every third lesson or so. Learner training enthusiasts will certainly argue that it is valid to spend 5% to 10% of your time (effectively 5 or 10 minutes of a 90-minute lesson) on this if it leads to higher motivation, retention and effectiveness thereafter.

Procedure

Most of the activities themselves are self-explanatory. They are all designed as pairwork activities and so can be managed in the same way as for any others: see the notes on pairwork in the Introduction (page 13). The big difference will lie, however, in the amount of attention you pay to language use and accuracy. As you monitor pairwork communication, your focus should be very much on content rather than form, for here you have the opportunity to learn not only about your students' learning styles but also about the language learning process in general.

Timing

The length of time that it will take to do one of these activities will vary a great deal from class to class. As you get to know each class you teach, you will learn to judge how long you can and should spend on them. Some of the questions are very open-ended and you may wish to delete them from the activity to speed things up: go ahead and do so. Or you may wish to break up activities so that you look at just one or two questions at a time. This is fine too. Sometimes, however, the time you spend on feedback from pairs to the group may be longer than for normal language-focused activities. Learners will learn better if you can help

them to extend their repertoire of learning strategies. By encouraging students to share their ideas, you are helping them all to widen this range.

Which language?
If you have a monolingual group, you may find it appropriate to discuss some of these questions in the students' native language. The only thing to be conscious of is how far the sponsor (the organisation paying for the course) and the students themselves will tolerate this. Hopefully, the organisation will also see the longer-term benefits of improving the learning strategies of its employees.

What to do
- Regardless of the instruction in the *What to do* section of each activity, you can decide whether it is more useful for any given activity for students to report back to the class about themselves or about the person they were working with.
- You can sometimes provide copies of activities for homework so that students are ready to talk about their answers during the following lesson.

1 Why do you want to learn English?
- This activity is best done early in the course because it will provide you with important needs analysis information and also because it will help to focus students' attention on how they use English and what their objectives are.
- Explain, if necessary, that *profile* is another way of saying *describe* or *focus on*.

2 Defining general targets
- This is the second of the three activities which are best done earlier rather than later in the course because they will provide you with further information about the needs and expectations of your students. Since there is the possibility of overlap – especially between Better learning activities 2 and 3 – you may choose to do one of them in depth to the exclusion of the others or alternatively do all three but spend less time on each. However, all three are designed to help you as well as the students themselves to gain insights into their profiles and needs, so you should make decisions about which to use and for how long, based on your views of their interest and tolerance.
- The ideas for this activity are drawn from section 3.6 'Encouraging student self-reliance' in Sylvie Donna's excellent *Teach Business English* (Cambridge University Press 2000, pages 56–7). This book is thoroughly recommended not just in relation to ideas about developing student motivation and autonomy but to anyone who wishes to improve their skills as a teacher of professional English.

3 Fixing targets and making plans

- This activity is also best done early in the course.
- Discuss with your students how successful learning of any kind needs a plan and also how they manage their time so that an action plan for learning English can be incorporated into an overall time management scheme. This activity is designed to encourage students to focus on more specific targets – long-, medium- and short-term – and to review these regularly.
- Once students have fixed short-term targets for this week, you can encourage them to do this on a weekly basis hereafter and to start a diary (see also Better learning activity 9) or notebook in which they can note their weekly resolutions. This will not only encourage you in turn to ask them about their weekly targets but also encourage you to articulate clearly – if you are doing a weekly class with them – what yours are for them so that they can take account of these in their own plans.

4 What kind of learner are you?

- For more information about Howard Gardner's theories of intelligence and for further reading on this subject and ideas for classroom applications provided by James Chamberlain of the Fachhochschule Bonn-Rhein-Sieg and the Berlin-Brandenburg English Language Teachers' Association, go to the *English365* website: www.cambridge.org/elt/english365.
- The answers to input 2 below are guidelines only. Many if not all of these, of course, engage more than one intelligence. You – and your students – may well have different ideas which you can contribute to the discussion. If students need prompting for their own ideas, suggest things like: lectures, mime, role-play, writing stories, group brainstorming, etc.

Answers

1 1 d 2 f 3 a 4 g 5 c 6 h 7 e 8 b
2 Storytelling: 2, 6
  Memorising written lists of vocabulary: 2
  Listening to audio CDs: 3
  Learning the words of pop songs: 3
  Doing logic puzzles: 1
  Taking part in group discussions: 6
  Keeping a diary: 7
  Reading books: 2
  Reading cartoon books: 4
  Singing in English: 3
  Going on visits: 4, 5, 6
  Taking part in problem-solving activities: 1
  Watching films: 4

5 Learning grammar

- Ask the students to read through the questions on their own first of all and check understanding, in particular the meanings of *fluency* and *accuracy*.
- Be ready to explain to the uninitiated what a grammar practice book is, for example *English Grammar in Use* by Raymond Murphy, published by Cambridge University Press.
- Ask students if they have memorised any examples of grammar rules which have personal significance to them.
- You could finish this activity with the important maxim: 'Always learn examples as well as rules.'

6 Language learning resources

- Students should not have too much trouble brainstorming possible resources but if they need prompting or structure, you could suggest that they think in terms of
  - Place: multimedia lab, language lab, resources room, library, etc.
  - People: librarian, learning facilitator, IT technician, etc.
  - Visual: TV, video, etc.
  - Audio: CDs, radio, etc.
  - PC: internet, intranet, CD ROM, etc.
  - Text: dictionaries, readers, grammar reference books, grammar and vocabulary practice books, magazines, newspapers, etc.
- Useful discussion will hopefully be forthcoming at the reporting back stage and some learners at least will learn that it's not necessarily the most expensive solutions which are the best.

7 I can't find the word

Other ideas could be:
- I say the word in my own language.
- I say the word in another language which the listeners might recognise.
- I use my hands to show what I mean.
- I quickly ask myself if I need the word at all or whether I can do without it.
- I stop talking and search my mind for the missing word.
- I try to find another word with more or less the same meaning.
- I try to explain what I want to say in more general terms.
- I stop talking and signal that I can't go on.
- I use an all-purpose word like 'thing' instead.

8 Your vocabulary notebook

- For this activity, it will help if you can ask students in advance to bring their vocabulary notebooks (or, if feasible, their laptops if any of them keep a vocabulary database on PC) to the lesson.
- You can ask students to do the matching exercise and then discuss the issues. Alternatively you can ask students to do the matching for homework or deal with the two sections on two separate occasions.

Answers

1 l 2 h 3 i 4 k 5 a 6 b 7 j 8 c 9 f 10 d 11 g 12 e

9 Keeping a diary

- Do this activity at the end of one of your lessons, so allow 10 to 15 minutes for it. Explain that many learners find keeping a diary of their learning experiences (in the classroom and in self-study) helpful in monitoring and consolidating progress. Discuss with them how far they think this could be useful. Explain that it's one more possible learning tool which may not suit all learners but which works very well for some.

- Having overcome the possible scepticism of some class members, ask students to read the diary extract and then ask them to write a diary for this lesson. This could also be a homework task although it's good for them to do it while the lesson is still fresh in their minds.

- The questions in the activity are one possible framework but not one that students have to follow. If they prefer to write a free paragraph or two, encourage them to do so.

- One issue here will be the language the diary entries are written in. If you can read the student's native language, then they may well prefer to write in their own language and you should not discourage this. If students want or have to write in English, then focus on content rather than on form: encourage them to express their feelings about the lessons and their learning rather than use the writing as an opportunity for correction (although they may ask for this as well).

10 Metaphors for language learning

If you are by now sensitive to the different learning styles of your students (and serious congratulations if you are!), then you will be able to estimate in advance how many of them will find this activity appealing and how many not. It does tend to enthuse some learners and leave others cold (see Better learning activity 4). But on the other hand, nearly all teachers use metaphors to describe the learning process at some time or other; and many students find some at least of the images genuinely helpful. If students go away with even one image which they find helpful, then the activity will have paid off.

Answers

1 d   2 e   3 f   4 a   5 c   6 b

1 Why do you want to learn English?

Objective
To profile your English learning past and present.

Introduction
In this activity, you are going to think about the background to your English learning and your reasons for wanting to learn more.

What to do
1 Answer the questions in 1 to 5 below.
2 Talk about your answers with a partner.

Name ....

Input

1 **What is the background to your English learning?**

When did you last study English?   ....

Is this your first adult course in English?   ....

Did you study English at school?   ....

Were you good at English at school? Why? Why not?   ....

Did you like English at school?   ....

Do you like English now?   ....

2 **When do you use English?**
Write in the figures for you:
I use English for:
Work ☐ %   Travel ☐ %   Pleasure ☐ %

3 **Why do you need English?**
Write in the figures for you:
I need English for:
Work ☐ %   Travel ☐ %   Pleasure ☐ %

4 **How important is English to you?**
Use this scale to answer both questions:
3 = very important   2 = quite important   1 = not very important   0 = not at all important
How important is English to you?
• in your personal life ☐
• in your professional life ☐

5 **Which are the most important areas of English for you to work on?**
Speaking ☐   Listening ☐   Reading ☐   Writing ☐
Pronunciation ☐   Vocabulary ☐   Grammar ☐

2 Defining general targets

Objective
To think about where you are at the moment in English, where you want to be, and how you can get to where you want to be.

Introduction
In this activity, you are going to think about:
* your current level in English
* your aims for your English
* how you are going to improve your learning.

What to do
1 Complete the sentences below.
2 Talk about your reasons with a partner.

Input

Name ....

1 My English is now good enough to . . .

Professional life
For example:
* introduce myself
* answer the phone
* write a simple email

Your ideas:
* ....
* ....
* ....
* ....

Private life
For example:
* order a meal in a restaurant
* buy tickets
* book a hotel room

Your ideas:
* ....
* ....
* ....
* ....

2 I want my English to be good enough to . . .

Professional life
For example:
* make a simple presentation
* take part in a meeting
* discuss basic human resources questions

Your ideas:
* ....
* ....
* ....
* ....

Private life
For example:
* talk about the news and current affairs
* talk about sport
* explain a menu

Your ideas:
* ....
* ....
* ....
* ....

3 I am going to improve my rate of progress on this course by . . .
For example:
* participating actively in the class
* asking and answering more questions in the class
* reading more English outside class

Your ideas:
* ....
* ....
* ....
* ....

3 Fixing targets and making plans

Objective
To think about your target level in English and to make a plan for learning English.

Name ....

Introduction
In this activity, you will think about your level and how to plan your learning. The questions in the activity will help you decide on your plan.

What to do
Work with a partner to answer these questions, then report back to the class.

1 What is your general level in English now?
2 Which general level would you like to have in English?
3 Which level do you need for your job?
4 How long do you think it will take for you to reach this level?

Levels of English

0 I do not speak English.
1 I have a few words of English.
2 I can only do very simple things in English.
3 I can communicate in English only if people speak very slowly and clearly.
4 I can communicate in English but I make a lot of mistakes and I often have to ask people to speak more slowly.
5 I can work in English but I often have problems understanding and sometimes people have problems understanding me.
6 I can work quite well in English but I know I sometimes make mistakes.
7 I don't have any big problems in English but I sometimes make small mistakes.
8 I speak English as well as a lot of native speakers.

Input

Time
I plan to give .... minutes to my English every day.

Long-term
My current level is ☐
My target level is ☐

My long-term targets are to be able to:
1 ....
2 ....
3 ....
in English.

My reward to myself for reaching these targets will be:

....

Medium-term
My medium-term targets are to be able (by the end of this course) to:
1 ....
2 ....
3 ....
in English.

My reward to myself for reaching these targets will be:

....

Short-term
My short-term targets are to be able (by the end of this week) to:
1 ....
2 ....
3 ....
in English.

My reward to myself for reaching these targets will be:

....

4 What kind of learner are you?

Objective

To show how understanding of the idea of multiple intelligences can help improve learning.

Introduction

Howard Gardner is a Harvard psychologist who writes about intelligence. He thinks that there are eight different kinds. In this activity, you will use these ideas to learn more about your own learning style.

Name ....

What to do

1 Cover up the list of definitions (a–h) and look at the list of intelligences (1–8). Talk with your partner about what you think each one of them means. For each type, describe someone who has a developed form of that kind of intelligence.

2 Uncover the definitions (a–h) and, on your own or with a partner, match one idea with each kind of intelligence (1–8).

3 Discuss with your partner which you think is your strongest intelligence and which is your weakest. Rank the other types in between and discuss your ranking with your partner.

4 Now look at the different activities in input 2. With a partner, decide which of them you associate with each of Gardner's eight intelligences. You may want to match some of them with more than one intelligence. And you may disagree with your partner – there is not necessarily a single set of right answers for this.

Input

1 Different kinds of intelligence

1 Logical-mathematical $\dfrac{X-4y^3}{3KX\sqrt{2}\,(1-K)}$

2 Linguistic

3 Musical

4 Visual-spatial

5 Bodily-kinaesthetic

6 Interpersonal

7 Intrapersonal

8 Naturalist

Definitions

a Loves sounds and rhythm
b Loves animals, plants, wildlife, the environment
c Loves dancing, sport, touching
d Loves number, logic, systems
e Loves being alone, meditation, the inner life, self-analysis
f Loves words, verbal expressions, reading
g Loves images, pictures, designs, doodles
h Loves people, communication

2 Different kinds of activity

Storytelling
Memorising written lists of vocabulary
Listening to audio CDs
Learning the words of pop songs
Doing logic puzzles
Taking part in group discussions
Keeping a diary
Reading books
Reading cartoon books
Singing in English
Going on visits
Taking part in problem-solving activities
Watching films

Can you add other activities to this list and say which intelligences they appeal to?

5 Learning grammar

Objective
To think about the role and importance of grammar in language learning.

Name ....

Introduction
In this activity, you are going to do a class survey to find out what other students think about grammar.

What to do
1 To do the survey, first think about your own answers to the questions.
2 Then talk to as many members of your class as you can.
3 Prepare a summary of your findings. What did you learn?
4 Report back to your class and to your teacher.

Input

Class questionnaire

Part 1: Grammar survey

1 How much do you like grammar?
   A lot ☐   Quite a lot ☐   Neither like nor dislike ☐
   Not much ☐   Not at all ☐

2 How much do you know about the grammar of your own language?
   A lot ☐   Quite a lot ☐   An average amount ☐
   Not much ☐   Nothing at all ☐

3 Is learning grammar more important than learning vocabulary?
   A lot more ☐   More ☐   Equally important ☐
   Less ☐   A lot less ☐

4 Is fluency more important than accuracy*?
   A lot more ☐   More ☐   Equally important ☐
   Less ☐   A lot less ☐

5 What percentage of your learning time do you think you should spend on learning grammar?
   75% or more ☐   50–75% ☐   25–50% ☐
   Less than 25% ☐

6 Do you have a grammar notebook?
   Yes ☐   No ☐

7 Do you have a grammar practice book?
   Yes ☐   No ☐

8 If you have a grammar practice book, how often do you use it?
   Very often ☐   Often ☐   Not very often ☐
   Rarely ☐   Never ☐

Part 2: Open questions

9 How do you learn grammar? Do you have any hot tips for learning grammar? ....
   ....

10 How do you stop making mistakes? ....
   ....

> * *Fluency* means being able to talk without hesitating too much; talking easily; feeling confident about talking (even if you make mistakes).
> *Accuracy* means not making mistakes.

6 Language learning resources

Objective
To think about the different tools available to people who want to learn a language.

Introduction
In this activity, you will decide what are the most useful language learning resources for you for learning English.

What to do
Your organisation has given you €200 to spend on your English outside your class.

1 With a partner, brainstorm the different resources you could buy and add to the list below.
2 Decide first which are high (H), medium (M) and low (L) priority for you. Explain your choices to your partner.
3 Now decide how you want to spend your €200 and tell your partner.
4 Report back to your class and to your teacher.

Name ....

Input

Item	Priority	My choice	Cost
For example:			
DVD films	☐	☐	....
Audio cassettes	☐	☐	....
Grammar practice books	☐	☐	....
Graded readers	☐	☐	....
Your own ideas:			
....	☐	☐.	....
....	☐	☐	....
....	☐	☐	....
....	☐	☐	....
....	☐	☐	....
....	☐	☐	....

Total cost

....

7 I can't find the word

Objective
To think about what you can do when you are speaking English and can't find the right word.

Introduction
In this activity, you will think about and discuss what it is best to do when you forget words or don't know the right word in English.

What to do
1 Read the situation in input 1 and the examples. Write down your own ideas.
2 Discuss with your partner:
 • which of these things you usually do
 • which of these things it would be good to do
 • which of these things it would not be good to do, and why.
3 Now look at input 2. Does anything change?

Name ....

Input

What do you do when you can't find the word?

1 You know this situation. You are with a group of people speaking English, for example, in your English class. You are talking about something and everyone is interested. Suddenly you lose the word you need. What do you do?

For example:
• I start the sentence again, hoping that this time it will be OK.
• I look it up in my dictionary.
• I ask someone who speaks my language for a translation.
• I mime the missing word.

Can you think of any other techniques you can use when you can't remember a word?

Your ideas:

....

....

....

....

2 Now imagine you are making a presentation in English and the same thing happens. Would you do the same as in the informal group?

Your ideas:

....

....

....

....

8 Your vocabulary notebook

Objective
To think about how a vocabulary notebook can help you learn vocabulary, and about different ways of organising it.

Introduction
In this activity, you will focus on different ways of organising a vocabulary notebook.

Name ....

What to do

1 If you have a vocabulary notebook or if you have a vocabulary database on your laptop computer, show it to your partner. Tell him/her about:
   • how long you've been keeping it
   • the different sections – how it's organised
   • how you use it.
2 Read through the list of ways that different people use to organise their notebooks (1–12) and match them with the examples (a–l).

3 Tick the ways you already use and discuss with your partner the techniques you use and others which you can add to the list. Which ways do you like best?
4 Try writing your own examples for some of these ideas.
5 Decide on two or three new ways that you want to try in the future.
6 Report back to the class and your teacher.

Input

1 ☐ I write new words and their translations in the order I meet them. ☐
2 ☐ I organise new words and their translations alphabetically. ☐
3 ☐ I organise new words grammatically – nouns, verbs, adjectives, etc. ☐
4 ☐ I write words + phonetic script. ☐
5 ☐ I write words + parts of speech. ☐
6 ☐ I write groups of words with the same root. ☐
7 ☐ I write my own definitions of words in English. ☐
8 ☐ I write my own examples of words in English. ☐
9 ☐ I group words into themes like sport, cinema, finance, etc. ☐
10 ☐ I draw pictures of words. ☐
11 ☐ I draw mind maps of words. ☐
12 ☐ I write words and their opposites. ☐

a turnover (noun), turn over (verb)

b analyse, analyst, analysis, analytical

c Market: I went to the market to buy some fresh fish.

d Mask:

e sensitive – insensitive
  late – early (or on time)
  legal – illegal

f Football: to take a corner, to win a penalty, to score a goal, a substitute, on the bench

g problem ——— FINANCIAL ——— difficulties
  situation   Times   adviser

h toll – péage
  town hall – mairie
  turnover – chiffre d'affaires

i Adjectives:
  seasonal
  scary
  shy
  stressful

j Market (general, not business): a place where people go to buy and sell things, e.g. a fish market, a fruit and vegetable market

k advertisement – / ədˈvɜːtɪsmənt /

l 13 November: gutter – caniveau
  14 November: smile – sourire
               worried – inquiet

9 Keeping a diary

Objective
To develop a habit which can help you think about what you are learning and so help you to learn better.

Introduction
In this activity, you will practise writing a diary entry for the lesson you did today.

What to do
1 Write one or two sentences about today's lesson under each question.
2 Discuss what you wrote with your partner.
3 Discuss whether you think keeping a diary could help you improve your learning.

Name ....

Input

What were the main objectives of this lesson?
1 To learn marketing vocabulary
2 To practise leaving telephone messages

What did I enjoy?
· The listening
· Practising leaving messages on the answerphone. Difficult but useful for me in my job.

What didn't I enjoy?
· The revision at the start of the lesson was a bit boring – it was too easy.
· The vocabulary exercises: I enjoyed the vocabulary less than the phone work.
  Some of it could be useful but this is not my job and I'm not so interested in marketing.

What were the main objectives of this lesson?

What did I enjoy?

What didn't I enjoy?

How did I feel during the lesson?

What did I learn?

What will I revise?

What will I remember?

10 Metaphors for language learning

Objective
To use metaphors to think about the way you learn a language.

Introduction
Some people find some metaphors helpful in thinking about how we learn a new language. In this activity, you are going to look at a number of metaphors used to talk about language learning, and their meanings; and think about how useful they are to you.

Name ....

> **metaphor** *noun* a way of describing something by comparing it with something else which has some of the same qualities *(Cambridge Learner's Dictionary)*

What to do
1 Cover up the list of ideas (1–6) and look at the images (a–f). Talk with your partner about how each of them could be used to talk about language learning.
2 Uncover the ideas (1–6) and match one idea to each image (a–f).

3 Rank the ideas from 1 to 6: 1 is the one you like most or find most useful, 6 is the one you like least or find least useful. Discuss your ranking with your partner.
4 Discuss with your partner these and any other useful metaphors for language learning that you can think of.

Input

The images

a

The wine glass: half full or half empty?

b

The golf swing

c

The wall

d

The jigsaw puzzle

e

The plateau

f

The computer programmer

The ideas
1 The more vocabulary and grammar you have, the better you can see the big picture and the easier it is to fit new pieces into it.
2 You don't always make steady and regular progress when you are learning a language. Sometimes it seems as if you have been at the same level for a long time.
3 If you want to change your mental programme, you need to think about what you're doing and adopt a logical approach to the problem.
4 Be positive about what you can do, not negative about what you can't do.
5 When you can't remember a word or a phrase, you have to find another solution.
6 When you try to unlearn something that you've been doing for a long time (like a typical mistake in English), your performance can become temporarily worse than it was before.

> **plateau** *noun* 1 a large area of high, flat land; 2 a period when the level of something stays the same *(Cambridge Learner's Dictionary)*

Teacher's diary

Date	Class

Unit objectives

How do I rate the lesson?

1 Terrible ☐   2 Not very good ☐   3 Satisfactory ☐   4 Good ☐   5 Excellent ☐

What went well?

What went less well?

Did I try anything new?

What should I think about for next time?

Anything memorable?